BRAVE AT HEART

A CHRISTIAN COACH'S JOURNEY THROUGH LIFE & CANCER.

BY BLAKE SEBRING

Cover photos by Judd Johnson, Leverage Photography

Edited by Melody Foreman
Cover and interior design by Angel North

DEDICATION

*Dedicated to Marc's wife, Lisa,
and their seven children.*

May you hear his voice every time you pick up this book.

AUTHOR'S NOTE

Discussions with Marc and Lisa were conducted over the last seven weeks of Marc's life and are delivered in present tense. The individual memories submitted by others were mostly written after his passing on May 9, 2022, and are usually delivered in the past tense.

BRAVE AT HEART

VERSES

Some of Marc and Lisa's favorites:

"Whatever you do, do your work heartily, as for the Lord and not for people." **Colossians 3:23**

"Have I not commanded you? Be strong and courageous. Do not be afraid; do not be discouraged, for the Lord your God will be with you wherever you go." **Joshua 1:9**

"So we fix our eyes not on what is seen, but on what is unseen, since what is seen is temporary, but what is unseen is eternal." **2 Corinthians 4:18**

"As for us, we cannot help speaking about what we have seen and heard." **Acts 4:20**

"Therefore, my dear brothers and sisters, stand firm. Let nothing move you. Always give yourselves fully to the work of the Lord, because you know that your labor in the Lord is not in vain." **1 Corinthians 15:58**

"We also glory in our sufferings, because we know that suffering produces perseverance; perseverance, character; and character, hope. And hope does not put us to shame, because God's love has been poured out into our hearts through the Holy Spirit, who has been given to us." **Romans 5:3-5**

"Whoever wants to be my disciple must deny themselves and take up their cross and follow me. For whoever wants to save their life will lose it, but whoever loses their life for me and for the gospel will save it." **Mark 8:34-35**

PREFACE

In March 2022, Blake Sebring wrote an article about Marc for the Fort Wayne Journal-Gazette. He kept so many of Marc's quotes that talked boldly about Jesus being his strength and hope, it was clear Blake wanted to share Marc's message with as many people as possible. He told us, "We have to write a book," and started visiting most weekday mornings, asking Marc and I questions about our life.

What a gift those mornings were! I am forever grateful for the time we were given to share these precious memories. Our faith was renewed and strengthened as we told Blake stories of how God had been so faithful to us. We could see His sovereign, faithful hand throughout our lives and marriage.

The Lord gave Marc strength to keep sharing up until a few days before He brought Marc Home. May 5 was the last day Blake came to our home, yet there was so much more of our story to tell, details that only Marc and I know. And so I have felt the weight of not knowing how to finish the book without him. How can I possibly come close to mentioning all of the people who have meant so much to us over the 49 years the Lord gave Marc? Since we graduated high school, Marc played on seven teams and coached six. In the almost 27 years of marriage that the Lord blessed us with, we have lived in two countries, four states and 17 cities. Every place God brought us has been full of people who mean so much to us, but this book only mentions a comparative handful. It's hard for me knowing there are many important people and places in our life we never got to speak about.

Although there is still so much to say, my heart is at peace, knowing it is time to share a fraction of what the Lord has done in and through and for Marc, and so this book is just the beginning of our testimony. To GOD be the glory, great things HE has done! May you taste and see that the Lord is so good!

Lisa Davidson • October 6, 2023

"But blessed is the one who trusts in the LORD, whose confidence is in Him. They will be like a tree planted by the water that sends out its roots by the stream. It does not fear when heat comes; its leaves are always green. It has no worries in a year of drought and never fails to bear fruit." **Jeremiah 17:7-8**

Homecoming 2022 family pic

Witnessing the largest shutout win in Chicago Cubs history 21-0 vs Pittsburgh · April 23, 2022

Celebrating after Marc's Strongman competition, two weeks before finding out the cancer had spread · August 2021

FOREWORD

Narrator: *Mitch Kruse was not just a trusted friend and mentor to Marc Davidson; he was a brother. Months before he died, Marc asked Mitch to prepare and deliver his eulogy. He knew Mitch would understand and deliver the message Marc wanted, trusting it would also be what God wanted. As you'll read, Marc's trust was fulfilled. Kruse is the author of "Restoration Road," "Street Smarts from Proverbs" and "Wisdom for the Road." Mitch produced 500 television episodes of "The Restoration Road with Mitch Kruse," which aired internationally.*

After his imposing shadow had darkened the doorway, when I met the large man who entered the boardroom, I felt an instant connection.

Like me, he was task oriented. Since elementary school, he would make a list of his daily assignments, placing a checkmark beside each one after completion. Lakewood Park Christian School had big shoes to fill in its position of basketball coach and athletic director, and it was obvious this candidate was a slam dunk. I was immediately drawn to his overflowing passion for Christ. Still, I had no idea how God would use him to impact my life.

Several years later during the winter of 2021, my friend Marc Davidson texted me that he wanted to get together the next morning before he started his teaching and coaching day at Blackhawk Christian School. Marc had experienced lingering fatigue from his bout with COVID-19, which led to further testing that revealed a tumor on his kidney. In a matter of weeks, surgeons removed the entire organ, and as a follow-up to the surgery, radiologists scanned Marc's body.

When that same imposing world Strongman champion entered my door, he sat down, thanked me for meeting as he sipped the coffee my wife, Susan, had made for him and uttered the words that reverberated in my soul. "My scans came back, and it ain't good. A rare form of cancer that takes most people before they have symptoms has spread with tumors into my lungs. Doctors have given me three months to a year unless God heals me," Marc said.

"I wanted to ask you today, should I be real, or should I be strong?" Coach did not want to burden his family with the pain he would suffer.

I believe the Holy Spirit took over my words when I replied, "If you aren't real, then there is no need to be strong."

I encouraged Marc to document his journey with God for his family and to speak to as many groups as he could to communicate the Gospel. Because his life's passion had been dying to win everyone to Christ, Marc agreed to do both. We prayed for healing, wisdom and God's will. As he left, with his sense of humor still intact, Marc embraced me and said, "I used to think COVID-19 saved my life. Now, I see it just bought me a little extra time."

During the next 16 months, we would witness Marc dying to win.

Jesus's dominant theme was the kingdom of heaven—God's divine reign, rule and order in the hearts and lives of people on this earth now and in the future.

"Then he called the crowd to him along with his disciples and said: 'Whoever wants to be my disciple must deny themselves and take up their cross and follow me. For whoever wants to save their life will lose it, but whoever loses their life for me and for the gospel will save it. What good is it for someone to gain the whole world, yet forfeit their soul?'" (Mark 8:34-36).

These three verses that dominated the Messiah's teaching paint the portrait of Marc Davidson's life: dying to win.

God pulls toward those who are separated from Him by breathing life into their souls so that they may turn to Him and experience reconciled relationships. Hebrew scholars describe God breathing life into the clay (Genesis 2:7) as a continual inhaling and exhaling, rather than a one-time breath. In fact, rabbinical tradition is that God's proper name YHWH is the sound of inhaling on the first syllable and exhaling on the second. Consequently, from our first breath until our last, each of us continually repeats the name of God.

We must inhale the breath of life from God and exhale His breath of life to others, dying to win people to Christ. Marc's life gave us at least three characteristics that each of us can implement for the rest of our lives on this side.

The first characteristic of inhaling and exhaling the breath of life evidenced in Marc was worship. Deny themselves communicated an act of worship, shifting from being lord of one's own life to fully surrendering to Christ as Savior and Lord, the Breath of Life. We were created to worship. That was the posture of Marc's heart.

Marc surrendered his life to Christ at 5 years old, when he prayed with his dad. Although he began to grow in college at the University of Illinois, he recognized that basketball had become an idol. Being socially introverted, Marc was discovering his identity in his basketball performance. "When the crowd cheered for me, it felt good. When my name was in the newspaper, it felt good."

He later reflected about his unhealthy approach to basketball, "It was a huge castle made of sand that God washed all away, which was exactly what I needed."

"My level of commitment was insane. When it was not working out, I could not see it as anything but a very big deal. God was still dealing with that flesh. It drove me even more to succeed and not fail. I felt like I had hit rock bottom. I recall I would wake up, and I could literally feel my heart drop down into my gut. I hardly ate, I hardly slept, I fell into depression. I had to hit bottom to see that basketball was never going to satisfy me."

Working a camp in the summer of 1993, Marc became overwhelmed with God's unconditional, non-performance-oriented love. "I didn't have to perform a certain way. Mitch, like you once said to me, 'I could stop clenching my fist, and now hold it with an open hand.' I rediscovered my love for basketball and learned that it was a tool to advance the Gospel of Jesus." Marc would now worship God through basketball. He began to search for schools with a seminary to honor God's calling on his life, choosing Trinity International in Deerfield, Illinois, where Marc was All-American.

Fast forward 30 years, Marc took this again to God as an act of worship when he prayed, "God, show me my heart." Those five words led to the Holy Spirit revealing two lies from the enemy: You can't really trust God, and you deserve better. Marc shared, "My next prayer came from a place of righteous indignation deep in my soul, and it was simply this: By the power of the risen Savior Jesus Christ—to hell with you, Satan—to hell with you and your lies! My soul screamed this! Hallelujah, thank you Jesus for victory (1 Corinthians 15:56-58)!"

Marc typed these words to his family: "The Holy Spirit exposed something else deep in my heart, and it was this: I BLAMED HIM for what I went through in college. And at that time, I thought it was His job to fix it. I've since come to realize we are never promised that. His heart toward me is ALWAYS good! That is His nature! Through my depression in college, He was with me, and His heart toward me was good—every single moment. ... And yet, I had never truly dealt with the fact that I BLAMED HIM. I began to weep like I've never wept before. I've repented countless times, but never quite like this. I wailed over my sin, and the Spirit proceeded to restore me as only He can do! HE reminded me that I am His child (Romans 8:16), my sins are forgiven (Psalm 103:12), my heart is sealed with His Spirit (Ephesians 1:13), He has given me an inheritance (Ephesians 1:11-17), He is my Eternal Hope! (Romans 15:13)."

Marc concluded, "As He restored me, the Spirit spoke this to my heart: 'You've been praying for healing for nearly a full year. I am healing your SOUL!' Hallelujah, thank you, Jesus! Our Great God is all about restoration. It's what He does!"

Marc inhaled the breath of God through worship. He exhaled that worship through his encounters with those of us who were blessed to know him. Marc knew our first step to reconciling the banished is not toward them, but toward God. When we worship God, we exhale the breath of life to others who will be drawn to Him (1 Corinthians 14:24).

Jesus lived a life of worship, perfectly modeling a fully surrendered heart to the Father.

The second characteristic of inhaling and exhaling the breath of life portrayed in Marc was the Word. Take up their cross meant wholehearted trust in Jesus's strength, not one's own. It connoted a one-way path, sacrificial, regardless of the cost, especially the temptations of this world. When we take up our cross, we embrace our weakness because in our weakness, He is strong (2 Corinthians 12:10). We do this best through reading, studying, memorizing and meditating on the teachings of the Bible.

Marc inhaled the Word each day, so he was able to exhale the Word to those he encountered, drawing them to Christ, whether at home, in the huddle, during practice, in a game, in the classroom or even at a restaurant. Marc knew that the more we get into the Word, the more the Word gets into us, including in our prayers. Prayer is being online with God, who shapes our desires to be like His. In that connection, we upload our requests, and He downloads His presence.

In the last months of his life on earth, Marc shared with his family and me, "God continues to teach me about prayer. If I'm being honest, I would say that through much of my life, I've tended to view prayer as a means to an end, rather than as an end in itself. God is showing me that while prayer can be a means to an end, it ought always to be viewed primarily as an end in itself. It is certainly appropriate to call upon God in our time of need—we see examples of this all throughout the Scriptures. But that should not be the only time we call upon Him. Prayer is ultimately about connecting with your Creator God—we can do this by pouring our hearts to Him (Psalm 62:8), declaring His glory (Psalm 96:3), repenting of our sin (1 John 1:9), dying to our flesh (Galatians 5:16), drawing near to Him (James 4:8), resting in His presence (Matthew 11:28-30), declaring His victory (1 Corinthians 15:57) and practicing His presence every moment of every day (Galatians 2:20). Prayer is not about getting what we want from God, it is about becoming someone HE desperately wants to make us (Romans 8:29-30)."

Jesus is the Word of God (John 1:1), the ultimate expression of the Father, the Giver of the breath of life. Each of us makes a choice to either trust in our gifts or the Giver. The Word transforms our perspective to trust in the Giver. Marc wrote, "Think about your life for a moment—think about the area in which you feel the most confident, the most secure, the most comfortable. It could be precisely the area in which God will do His pruning work. Why? Judges 7 tells us—so that we arrive at the all-important realization that it's all about HIS strength and not our own. Apart from Him, we can do nothing (John 15:5)! And yet in Him, we can do all things (Philippians 4:13)."

The third characteristic of inhaling and exhaling the breath of life in Marc's life was work out. Follow me meant "to work out, or live out," one's salvation because it is God who works in us to fulfill His purpose (Philippians 2:12-13). This is relationship, not religion.

Marc worked out each day as he inhaled the breath of God, curling a 110-pound dumbbell with each arm. Marc also exhaled the breath of God with his daily life, especially with his family, focusing on becoming a rapid Holy Spirit-responder. Marc met Lisa in elementary school. Seven years later, he asked her out. (That's when he knew he needed to work on that rapid Holy Spirit-responder thing.) Marc and Lisa married after college. He played professionally in France, where they were blessed with five sons in eight years, Marc's own basketball team.

Many years later, at a Steven Curtis Chapman concert in 2008, Marc cried when he heard "When Love Takes You In," a song about adoption. Shortly after the concert, Marc's grandmother passed away, leaving them an inheritance. Marc remembered saying, "Okay, Lord, if we are ever going to adopt, it's now." Marc and Lisa met with friends, Phil and Shari Chapman and Matt and Amy Swartz, who had adopted children from Ethiopia, so they decided to work through the same agency.

Everyone was surprised when the process unfolded abnormally quickly. Marc and Lisa received a picture of the twins before traveling to meet them and staying four days. The new bond made it difficult for them to return to the United States. When the legal process was completed, Marc and Lisa traveled to pick up their twins and bring them home. Marc recalled, "When the van pulls in that drive, the kids in the orphanage peer outside to see who is in it. Even at 2 years old, the twins saw us and knew we were coming for them. The twins had nothing. To me, that was a beautiful picture of salvation. We come to Jesus with nothing."

On December 6, 2012, Marc and Lisa adopted Jaela and Isaiah, and life for all of them would never be the same. Marc transparently shared with me, "Some of my hardest prayers have been about them. They have been through enough. Their mom died (after) childbirth. Their dad died (before) they were born." Coach paused to take a deep breath and then added, "Man, having a daughter has changed everything."

In a devotional composed during his bout with cancer, Marc penned: "The really hard part about all of this is family. The thought of leaving you all behind brings a pain to my heart like nothing I've ever felt. Lisa, aka My Queenie, you are the best person I know—I want to grow old with you. All you kids are amazing. You kids are my greatest contribution to this world by far. ... I love you all more than anything in the world. You all make me so proud. My desire to experience these things is a normal and good thing, and my trust in God's sovereign plan is obviously also a good thing. He's teaching me to rest in the tension. I am ready to spend eternity with Jesus—I know that heaven is going to be beyond anything I can possibly imagine. And yet—I also want to continue serving Him here on earth as a husband, father, grandpa, friend, teacher and coach. ... Not my will, but His will be done!"

Those are the words of a man who would daily work out his relationship with God, following Him, inhaling and exhaling His breath of life, dying to win others to Christ. Near the end of his life, I asked Marc, "What's the closest you have felt to Jesus?" He said, "The last three months. I am so close to Jesus. Prayer comes easily. He keeps reminding me of who I am and who He is."

Jesus worked out—or lived out—God's design for each of us, providing us a portrait of how to live, dying to win others to the transformational life in Christ, inhaling and exhaling the breath of God by the power of the Holy Spirit at work within us.

You see, it wasn't merely Marc Davidson we were drawn to; it was Christ in Marc.

Mitch Kruse • June 2022

INTRODUCTION

For the last 19 months of his life, Marc Davidson knew he was dying from terminal cancer. But during every minute of those days, he taught everyone around him how to live a Godly life, how to lean into adversity to present an example, and how to encourage growth in his own faith by sharing it with others.

During his postgame mid-court huddles, Marc's passion to speak about Jesus probably affected thousands over that time, including all those sitting in the stands leaning forward who were wondering what was so interesting that coach might be telling all those kids. It was an opportunity not seen before, even in Indiana, the capital of high school basketball.

While plenty of individuals have inspired overwhelming noise, no one before had ever quieted high school basketball gyms in this state like that. What was he saying? And by golly, why? What could possibly be so important when he could be concentrating on his own situation?

Marc understood perfectly:

"I feel like since the beginning, the Lord is saying, 'I'm going to open doors to you through cancer that otherwise never would have been opened. What I want you to do is testify and make My name great.' Lord, as long as there is breath in these lungs, I'll shout it from the mountaintops.

"When people understand you are terminally sick, they'll say, 'Let's at least hear the man out.' If cancer opens that door, we'll use every opportunity that we have."

Cancer may have scraped away his body, but the experience only strengthened Marc Davidson's soul. The more he shared, the stronger his message became. As the pounds continued melting off, why was this man who was obviously dying taking from his limited time praying to share with so many people he didn't even know?

Well, Marc prayed plenty, and this is what he believed Jesus asked him to do. To Marc, there was nothing more important than taking

BRAVE AT HEART

this opportunity to witness to and hopefully help others. That's where the urgency came; he knew he was dying and there was nothing anyone but God could do about it, and He was asking him to do this. Marc had limited time to get the word out, and after all, hadn't this been his true life's calling anyway? This wasn't anything new to Marc, just another, more public opportunity with the clock running down.

And he always thrived in those situations.

Maybe he could still make a difference, maybe even a big one, in somebody's life. And really, wouldn't that be the greatest reward possible, the most humbling, awe-inspiring answer from God, knowing he was doing exactly, precisely what the Lord wanted him to do? Despite the pain, the diminishing time, the deficit of humanity, he was standing up for what he believed in the most in this world, the hope of grace and mercy provided by Christ for everyone.

If his message saved even one or two people and made them reconsider and study a little bit further, that would be worthy of his last breath if that's what it took. He was serving his God no matter what—literally. And it was all worth it, every last sip of air used to say "Amen" so many times with so many people.

The ironic thing is those same people strengthened him, too. As much as he was giving out to them, he was getting much more in return with prayers and best wishes and people willing to help spread his message. Marc Davidson passed away May 9, 2022, but not before helping others and gaining strength from fulfilling God's will.

Can you imagine the thrill that must have been?

Well, actually, yes—you can.

That's what Marc's message and his testimony were really all about. It wasn't to bring attention to his struggle or to ask for prayers for himself. Marc knew those would come, but they would mean so much more if people listened to what he was saying and opened their hearts to Jesus so they could actually feel that same strength and peace he was experiencing. By giving them the hint, the inspiration to understand and share in what he was saying, everyone could feel this strength—even during horrible, inexplicable stress like what he was going through—if they just gave a chance to what he was telling them. They could reconsider and be activated by his message. They could become believers.

They really could.

And that's why he took this time, gambled his last breaths, because he believed so much in that possibility that he just had to share it with others. What a waste it would have been if he had just stayed home, curled up and died, as maybe most people would have—giving up, pulling inward, hiding away until it was over.

Marc Davidson didn't know how to do that. He'd been sharing his faith publicly since he was in school, and it was part of why he coached and worked at private schools all his life. He needed that opportunity to share, to provide the chance to make the difference in someone's life that makes an eternal difference. It's a large part of who he was.

He just thought he'd have quite a few years left to share it with more people. God had other plans and put the urgency on his heart. The timing and opportunity of Marc's last few months allowed him to reach out to many more people than maybe he would have if he'd lived a longer life. He never questioned that, and like any coach giving a fantastic pregame speech, Marc said, "Let's do this!" and charged out of the locker room ready to take this last chance and share it all with whomever would listen.

Cancer wasn't adversity for Marc Davidson, it was opportunity, the ultimate chance to fulfill God's will. It was the perfect way to reach out to those around him and ask them to join him, not in his upcoming death, but in his upcoming eternal life with Christ.

That is what this book is about. Marc's time on earth may be over, but his story will continue in those he inspired.

Blake Sebring • June 2022

BRAVE AT HEART

Marc on the bench with one of his primary students during the JV game vs Wayne · January 2022

Marc using his Strongman skills to share his faith at a Fellowship of Christian Athletes summer camp

Marc sharing his faith with kids at his basketball camp at Aurora Christian · June 2008

CHAPTER 1

Narrator: *During the fall of 2020, Marc Davidson started feeling ill. As the assistant athletic director, a physical education teacher and the basketball coach at Fort Wayne's (Indiana) Blackhawk Christian High School, he was coming off a state championship and the Masters Heavyweight Division title at the Strongman National Championships in Las Vegas. There's no way he should have been so tired, he told himself. Figuring it was leftover COVID-19, which he'd battled in July, he put off going to the doctor, though his wife, Lisa, was trying to steer him that way.*

Marc: As a physical education teacher, I had to teach outdoors in August because of social distancing protocols. You're already exhausted getting back into the swing of things, and then I was post-COVID-19 and working all day outdoors, but we stuck with it and held out through August. I felt like I was just dealing with all that and then adjusting to getting back to school, which is always a bit of a drain.

Lisa: He would be miserable. He'd come in and see me in my classroom, and he was just miserably exhausted. He was lifting still, and he'd still get the adrenaline rush from that because he always feels better when he works out. But he'd come home and be asleep in his chair by 8 p.m. He would come home and sit there and couldn't keep his eyes open.

Marc: I had a break for my lunch of about 44 minutes. My appetite was dwindling, so I would snarf down a little bit of food, plop down for a nap and set my alarm.

Initially, I thought COVID-19 was just kicking my butt. I was sweating profusely at night, so much that I was losing weight involuntarily. I think I lost about 30 pounds. My appetite was dwindling, which if I'm not eating right, you know something is wrong. I was 315 pounds at the peak of my competing in Strongman.

In September, I experienced a level of fatigue I'd never felt, but I was trying to tough it out. I never had energy. I couldn't understand it, because I was exhausted but I didn't get any relief from sleeping. I'd wake up just as exhausted. You expect to feel refreshed, but there's never any relief.

Finally, I got to a point where I knew I needed to do something. Lisa gave me a little nudge and said we have to call somebody. I finally broke down and called my friend who is a doctor, Dr. Mark Pierce, which I think was the first time I ever called a doctor in Indiana. I don't get sick, and I hate going to the doctor, I don't like hospitals. It'll be fine.

Lisa: Marc had talked to Dr. Pierce, a father of several Blackhawk students, many times while attending volleyball matches over the years and had established a friendship with him. That was who Marc reached out to and asked if his fatigue and other issues could still be lingering COVID-19 symptoms. Marc had been the epitome of health, so he hadn't needed to be seen for any issues while we were living in Indiana. Other than the occasional sports injuries, and maybe needing stitches, he never needed anything.

Dr. Pierce started running tests, which led him to diagnose Davidson as being anemic. His blood numbers were erratic, so there was no doubt something was wrong.

Lisa: You get to the point where you just want some kind of an answer because something is not right. Dr. Pierce ordered tests, trying to get to the bottom of Marc's anemia. He had so many different things measuring out of normal range in his blood work. They had ordered a colonoscopy and CT scan to try to get to the bottom of why he was so anemic.

Marc: One day, I was at Blackhawk in the auxiliary gym covering lunch when the doctor called and asked if I was sitting down. That's how they told me they found the tumor.

Lisa: They found a large tumor on his right kidney. I am an open book, and I share things with people, so we had friends and family who we were asking to pray. They, too, were looking for answers as to why Marc was having all these symptoms. After news of the tumor, people started reaching out to us and letting us know that they or a loved one had a tumor that was found on their kidney and was removed and later found to be benign and that they lived full, healthy lives. That brought us some peace to know it wasn't super uncommon.

The next step was to have an appointment October 23 with a urologist to discuss how to move forward. Because of COVID-19 protocols, Marc had to go to the appointment by himself, and I FaceTimed into the meeting.

The urologist in Fort Wayne was pretty laid-back about it and suggested we just wait for Marc to have surgery over Christmas break. That was more than six weeks away. Marc's brother Matt is good friends with a urologist in Illinois. We overnighted Marc's scans to him to get his second opinion. He reached out to one of his colleagues, one of the best surgeons in the country, who got Marc in for surgery right away. We are forever grateful for this door that the Lord opened.

Four days later, on Oct. 27, Davidson had surgery in Naperville, Illinois, to remove a kidney and 13 lymph nodes, which were sent to the Mayo Clinic for a pathology report. The diagnosis came back as renal epithelioid angiomyolipoma (EAML), a rare but vicious cancer.

Marc: Mayo said, "We know very little about this stuff. What we do know is it's super aggressive." What's the plan? "Pray it doesn't come back." We didn't start on any kind of pills at that time, just planned to continue scans every three months to make sure the cancer hadn't spread.

Lisa: They could identify what it was, but they couldn't really prescribe anything. In studies, chemo and radiation had proven ineffective treating EAML. The team of doctors at Mayo seemed relaxed and nonchalant, which surprised me, so we just hoped and prayed the surgeon got it all out of there. The team of doctors at Mayo told us they believed Marc was more likely to die of a heart attack than he was of his cancer.

Marc: I was relieved. Yes, give me a coronary in 20 years. I'll take it. They were pretty laid back.

The Mayo Clinic reported only one of the 13 lymph nodes came back as being positive for cancer, but there was hope that surgery had removed everything. Then a scan in February showed cancer had spread to Marc's lungs. A recommended kidney specialist at the University of Chicago told the Davidsons he might see three cases of this disease in five years. As an experiment, he started Marc on a chemotherapy pill with minimal side effects, and Marc started feeling stronger and even competed in a Strongman event in April. The next scan in May showed a little bit of shrinkage of the tumors found in his lungs, so the news was better. Throughout the summer, Marc felt good. Encouraged, he continued lifting and finished second in a Strongman competition on Aug. 14, 2021.

Marc: On Aug. 31, we go to the University of Chicago for a routine scan, and they do lab work first and then the scan, and we meet with the doctor. He's like, "I'm not a radiologist, but let me look at this real quick." He was looking more at the lungs because that's where everything had been spreading and said everything looked great and he'll see us in three months. Lisa and I were beyond excited. We went out and had a nice meal in Chicago to celebrate a good report, and we were about to get on the interstate when I get a call from the doctor, who apologized and said the radiologist looked at the scan and found a large tumor just above my bladder and another spot on the bone.

It was actually growing and spreading when we felt it was shrinking.

Lisa: Since surgery in October, Marc had been getting stronger, and he hadn't experienced any side effects with the chemo pill. So we were completely shocked with the news that a new, large mass had been found. It was almost immediately after we got the word about the new tumor that he started feeling bad again.

CHAPTER 2

Narrator: *When he was first diagnosed, while praying for God's healing, Marc also prayed for opportunities to use this situation to point people toward God. Blackhawk Christian High School already had a tradition of praying with opponents after home games when Bluffton Coach Karl Grau suggested he'd like to pray for Davidson after their 2021 Bluffton Sectional game.*

Marc: I feel like Lisa and I just prayed every night that God would open doors to share our faith. And we just agreed in prayer and said because I felt like the Lord was speaking to my heart, saying, "I am going to give you a platform through your sickness, and I want you to testify to make My name great." I think we were just so united in praying for that.

My dad used to do testimonies at halftime, and I got to watch that stuff all the time. They would not start the 10-minute clock, and a player would come out and share his favorite verse and what it meant to him. Then we would go to the locker room and start the clock. In all those years, there was only one school that refused to stay out and listen.

When my dad started this, it was at halftime of home games, and the coaches were not a part of the actual testimonies. The seniors got the first chance, and I thought it was pretty cool. When I came back from France and started coaching, I think we started praying together in Georgia after games. Sometimes I would share a very brief "You guys are well-coached, best of luck the rest of the season," and then I might say something like, "We love basketball, but for us, basketball is not the end-all and be-all of our existence. We need to keep our eyes on our eternal perspective." Then I'd say a quick prayer.

When I got sick, I just really felt that prompting of the Holy Spirit, and from the beginning, we just prayed, "Jesus, we want for Your name to be exalted." That's at the point where I started sharing a little more detail about my story at home games. In 2021, at the sectional with the Bluffton game, Karl Grau took the initiative, and we talked about this before the game. He said, "Coach, I'm a believer. I would love to pray for you after the game." I said I would love that and let's do it. I didn't know him, but (Marc's assistant) Mike Lindsey had known Karl for years and always had great things to say about him.

That's kind of how it springboarded.

Lisa: I'll never forget the 2021 semistate game against Blackford with Luke Brown when we walked into the gym at Elkhart Memorial, and on the back of their shooting shirts, they had "#Davidson Strong, Even in Indiana some things are bigger than basketball."

Marc: That was super cool. There were a lot of things like that from people that you don't know are in the fight with you, which is pretty cool. There were times where I prayed for them and times when they prayed for me. It was just a sweet time of fellowship.

At the state finals in 2021, Parke Heritage had done the same thing. Their principal, Dwight Ashley, reached out to me via email that week and said, "We want to pray for you after the game." A lot of people don't know that, because I think the TV cameras cut away, but they prayed over me. That was meaningful.

Late in the 2022 season, as part of his message, Marc chose to lean into Matthew 7:24-27 and Jesus's parable about the people building houses on sand and those building on rock.

Marc: Jesus said the foolish man builds his house on the sand, and when the storms come and the wind blows, that house comes crashing down. But he said the wise man builds his house on the rock, and when the storms come and the wind blows, that house will stand. I tell them that storms are coming for all of us at some point and time in this life. I'm in a storm right now, but my house is standing because I have a solid foundation in my relationship with Christ.

I just talk about how everything else, when you get a diagnosis like mine, you come to realize the things that really matter and ultimately the things that really don't. My faith in Christ is obviously the most important thing. My message is pretty brief.

I just kind of tell them where I'm at and what my diagnosis is and how Jesus is carrying me through that.

Lisa: One of my favorite things that Marc has said when he's sharing how his cancer has spread is, "Unless the Lord heals me, I've got terminal cancer. But the fact is, we are all terminal." This was so shocking to me the first time that I heard him say that, but it is so true to live in this reality. We are all dying. The sooner we realize that we're not promised tomorrow and we need to deal with the fact that we need to be prepared to die. What's after death?

Big or small, private or public school, the teams convened at center court following their game. During the two minutes or so that Marc spoke, the gyms were incredibly silent, most people in the stands leaning forward trying to hear what he was saying. After the 2022 Bluffton Sectional title game against Adams Central, most of the court was filled with fans from both teams coming out of the stands to listen and pray with him, a remarkable display of community and compassion.

Marc: Sometimes that can be hard, especially in the postseason when you are talking to kids whose high school careers just ended. But I just feel like the Lord has given me a message that I have to share. I kind of feel like Peter when he told the Sanhedrin (Acts 4:20) he couldn't help but talk about the things he'd seen and heard. I just feel like I can't help talking about it.

My message is whatever God puts on my heart. The centrality of it is always about Jesus, but sometimes I might share a different Bible verse.

I'm walking out of the gym that night, and a young gal from Adams Central said she appreciated my testimony and was praying for me. I don't know these people, but to know they are praying for me ... I feel that. That's how the early church was described. They love each other before they know each other. I felt that in so many different ways; it's been pretty unbelievable.

The Lord continues to give me strength that I can't even explain. There are so many times when I'll be sitting there before a game or before a speaking event, and I'm talking to Lisa about how I'm not sure I can do this right now. I feel so physically weak, but when I step up there, the Lord fills me with strength, and He's done that time after time. I'm not overflowing with energy, but I have enough to get the job done.

It's like when He says to Paul, "My grace is sufficient for you because My power is made perfect in your weakness (2 Corinthians 12:9)." I'm living there. Physically, I feel so weak that I'm crawling, and spiritually I feel like I'm in a full-on sprint toward the finish line.

I feel like since the beginning, the Lord has been saying, "I'm going to open doors for you through cancer that otherwise never would have been opened. What I want you to do is testify and make My name great." Lord, as long as there is breath in these lungs, I'll shout it from the mountaintops.

When people understand you are terminally sick, they'll say, "Let's at least hear the man out." If cancer opens that door, we'll use every opportunity that we have.

Marc sharing his faith in a post-game huddle with Bishop Luers • January 2022

CHAPTER 3

Narrator: *Though there's no official position, Judd Johnson is the photographer for Blackhawk Christian basketball—and a ton of other sports, too, through his Leverage Photography organization, which is such a blessing to so many. Judd donates the proceeds to help families who are trying to adopt. What an amazing calling! His God-given gifts and servant heart have allowed him closer access to Marc's testimonies than anyone else who is not actually part of the teams involved.*

I've had the great fortune of photographing Blackhawk Christian boys basketball over 70 times since 2013. During this time, I've gotten to know the Davidson clan. If you have ever been behind a camera, you understand that the images you see and capture are written on your heart in a way that is hard to explain. My goal when taking photos is to block out the distractions and focus on the game action. The combination of visually seeing the action through a lens and then freezing the action burns those images in my soul. This process deeply connects me with the subjects because I'm the only one who saw that action at that angle at that moment. So at times, it is hard not to get emotionally involved with the game, the players and/or the schools I serve.

This connection evolved with the Davidson family over the years. It started with watching Wes and Will play and seeing Coach on the sidelines. Then it was Frankie's turn, then Marcus and, most recently, Jimmy. As I showed up to more and more games, there were more opportunities to get to know Coach and his family. The photography coupled with conversations have "Marc'd" me for the rest of my life.

Here are a few things I'll remember about Coach.

Clothes never fit him well. He was a giant of a man, and no suit could contain his physique. If you ever stood beside him, his presence was just BIG. As the 2021-22 season progressed, Coach's weight loss gave him a different challenge. The home-game suit fit a bit loose; the more casual away attire seemed to be more comfortable but still couldn't hide his changing body.

But Coach wasn't about the clothes he wore.

Coach loved to eat. When training for his Strongman competitions, he would consume massive amounts of calories. We had a connection with food. I love to cook for people, and he loved to eat. In the brief moments we would interact, he would ask what meat I would be smoking next. That was his not-so-subtle way of wondering if any of that would find its way to the Davidsons. And on a few occasions, it did. But Coach also wasn't about the food he enjoyed.

What Coach was about was his unwavering faith and love of Christ. I'm not sure there was ever a conversation he had where he didn't use a Scripture reference. It was his way of saying, "This is my roadmap to life." He never apologized for his faith and led with his faith in all areas of his life. When I was just getting to know him, I wondered, is this guy real?

As I was getting to know Coach and Lisa, it was obvious their family was special. I sensed we had other things in common besides ill-fitting clothes, food and the love of sports. Adoption was another way for me to connect with the Davidsons. Coach and Lisa adopted Jaela and Isaiah from Ethiopia. Even with five boys, they had room and love for two more kids. I wanted to know more of their story, so I brought lunch over and got to hear Coach share their adoption story. Coach quoted Ephesians 1:5, "God adopted us into his family through Jesus Christ, and it gave Him great pleasure." For the Davidsons, it was as simple as this: God adopted us, and we are called to adopt. For them, it was a simple act of obedience. But as many of you know, adoption is far from simple.

Coach lived his life. It didn't matter what the challenge was, you obey God's teaching and leading. A simplistic yet profound way we should all live. It was around this time that Lisa and I spent time in the vestibule of a local gym during a Senior Night presentation. We shared stories of growing up. I came from a large family; she was an only child. Her biggest concern was if her kids would care for each other as they grow. With the vast age differences and her never being part of a big family, it was hard for her to imagine. I reassured her that from what I had observed, their family was doing great. So over the years, I would send her photos catching her boys loving and supporting their siblings. Strong families don't just happen. It takes hard work, and with the Davidsons, the evidence shows they did the work with God leading the way.

One of the traditions Blackhawk basketball is known for is after a home game, the players ask the opposing team to stay and circle up for a word of prayer. Most every team accepted this invitation. I think over the years, different people may have talked and even prayed, but these last few years, Coach was on a mission.

Coach would talk for about three minutes. He shared his story and related it back to Scripture and Jesus. As we have established, Coach has a big presence. Leading with, "As some of you may have heard, I've been diagnosed with Stage 4 cancer. And the doctors tell me that I'm terminal," really captures everyone's attention.

In these three minutes, it wasn't about the game that was just played; it was about souls that may be lost. I'm sure some were shocked by his boldness, just as some were probably shocked by his calmness. But like all great coaches, he instructed clearly and put the responsibility of execution on those who heard his words.

Coach knew he could design the best game plan, but if poorly executed, the game would be challenging. The game plan works when the players embrace the plan. I heard him say this countless times as praise to his players for embracing and executing the game plan. So again, in these three minutes, Coach was drawing up a life game plan for anyone who could hear. Coach knew that he couldn't give someone else salvation. Each person must ask for it—execute the game plan. Coach's hope and prayer was that someone at some time heard his words and turned their life over to Christ, then that was the greatest win of all.

I recorded one of his postgame talks. This is the transcript of what Coach wanted everyone to hear.

"Coach (Jeremy Rauch of Snider), thank you for letting me talk to your team. You guys are really good, and we'd love to see you make a deep run in March. Real quick, some of you may have heard, I've been diagnosed with Stage 4 cancer. And doctors tell me that I'm terminal. I'll tell you guys, when you get a diagnosis like that, what it really does is help you realize what's important in life. A lot of time, we can spend our time and energy on things that ultimately don't matter. But I'll tell you guys, my faith and my family are things I'm leaning to. And the other stuff honestly like ... when I think about the Scripture in Matthew which says, 'What does it profit a man if he gains everything in the world and yet he forfeits his soul?' Because one day, we are all going to stand before our Creator, and we're going to have to give an account of how we lived our life. And on that day, fellas, I'm telling you, it's not going to matter your scoring average or it's not going to matter the trophies you've won or the banners you've put in the gym. That stuff will be absolutely meaningless. And all that matters on that day is, did you receive Jesus Christ as your Savior?

"And I tell you guys, that is the greatest decision you ever can make. He offers a free gift of salvation to each and every one of you. And I would encourage you, if you've never made that decision, I would encourage you to do so. When I was your age, I'll tell you, basketball meant everything to me. My identity was based on what I did out here [on the basketball court]. And God did work in my heart and helped me understand this game is temporary. And He fulfills my life in a way that basketball never did, never could. So I want to encourage you with that. Let me pray for you real quick. 'God, I just thank you for tonight, Lord. I thank you for Snider. And I wish them the best the rest of the season, Lord. And I pray for these young men that if any of these guys have not surrendered their heart to you, I pray Lord they make that decision. If they don't know what I'm talking about, I pray they will take the initiative and find someone to talk to who can explain to them what it means to follow Jesus. 'Cause that is the greatest decision they ever could make. I pray it in Christ's name. Amen.' Hey, good luck the rest of the way."

April 3, 2021, Blackhawk had just won its second state championship in three years. Coach Davidson gets back to the locker room after his required press appearance. He sits down, and the first thing he says is, "I'm so proud of you guys." In fact, he says that a few times in the few minutes he talks basketball. His tone isn't that of a coach but as a dad telling his kids how proud he is of them. But even after winning the state title, Coach is still coaching his team. It isn't about the X's and O's on the court. It is about the game of life. He uses the same Matthew Scripture to tell his team even that [pointing to the state trophy] will fade, and all that matters is that you live for Jesus.

The website JohnHarrell.net shows Coach's record as 227-70. Marc would be the first to tell you that no one will remember that in years. Those records will fade. What Marc's focus was all those years on the court—how Marc would love to have his success measured—is to see the players, the students, the opposing players, the opposing coaches, the teachers, his kids, his friends—ALL—surrender their life to Christ and live fully for Him. In the end, that is the only "win" Marc ever wanted.

Judd with Marc and the boys • February 2021

CHAPTER 4

Narrator: *As Marc said many times, he was born in the middle of the cornfields of Minooka, Illinois. The date was March 1, 1973, something he repeated a million times every time he entered a hospital during his last year of life.*

His parents, Don and Stephanie, met while attending Minooka High School. He was a sophomore, and she was a freshman. He became the first person from his family to attend college, at Illinois Wesleyan, while she went to Illinois State University. They married straight out of college, and Don Davidson became a teacher and coach in Yorkville, Illinois. He was coaching baseball and basketball, and Stephanie was a home economics teacher. In 1975, Paul House started a new school, Aurora Christian.

Marc: Every time my dad would go to pray, the Lord would put Aurora Christian on his heart. That was strange because they didn't even have a sports program at the time. The Lord kept prodding his heart, so he went ahead and took a job there, making a third of what he made at Yorkville. He was a six-year varsity coach who went to a school with no sports.

Sometimes, the call of God is on a collision course with common sense. He was obedient and went to Aurora Christian to start the sports program.

My freshman year—my dad loves to tell this story—I had found out I had made the varsity team, and I came to him and said, "Dad, I have a goal. Over the next four years, I want our teams to win 100 games." Dad thought, well OK, we'll see how that goes for you. We ended up winning 104 and lost 16. I knew my niche was rebounding. We had a lot of guys who could score, and dad said if you want to play, rebound the dag-on ball. As a freshman, I averaged 18.5 rebounds per game. I was an obsessive-compulsive rebounder. That was my only job.

My sophomore year was our first year as an official member of the Illinois High School Association. We had quite a bit of success in basketball that first year. We kind of snuck up on people because

I don't think they were expecting much from us. We won the regional tournament, which comes before the sectional in Illinois. We won the first game of the sectional, and then we played in the final against Luther South. They were ranked No. 1 all year, and nobody gave us a chance. They were huge and quick and super talented. They had a few players that went on to play in college. We pulled off the upset and beat them, and that really put our sports program on the map. I had 23 points and 10 boards.

After averaging 11 points as a freshman, Marc grew two inches to 6 feet 6 inches, 215 pounds as a sophomore. Aurora Christian lost in the super-sectional his sophomore season but advanced to state his junior year. The school was ranked No. 1 during his senior year, but an ankle injury slowed Marc, and the team lost in the regional final. Marc finished with an average of 25.6 points, 13.9 rebounds and 5.9 assists. He was an all-state selection his last three seasons.

Marc: Lisa came to Aurora Christian in fifth grade, and I was in fourth grade. We probably didn't officially meet until junior high. I was scared of her, of course, because I was super introverted. She helped bring me out of my shell. She was super outgoing. We started dating as she was about to graduate at the end of my junior year. She was the first girl I dated. I didn't know how to talk to girls.

Lisa: You were also very determined and focused to give all your attention to basketball.

Marc: I was ridiculously driven in basketball, but at some point, she caught my eye, and the switch flipped. What really drew me to her was that she was so outgoing. She could maintain the conversation. If I had to keep the conversation going, that was not a good role for me at that time.

Lisa: His dad loved me and let me be a stat girl for the baseball team. I didn't know a thing about baseball, let alone taking stats.

Marc: I found my way to sit by her on the bus, and that's when the sparks started flying.

While in high school, Lisa had gone on summer mission trips to Italy and Africa, and Don Davidson had invited her to come to the Davidsons' home church, Helmar Lutheran, to share her experiences.

Marc: It was a Sunday night service. Lisa spoke that night, and my dad says to this day he walked out of that service saying, "Marc needs to marry her." This was in October 1989. He didn't say it to me at that time. He said she was the type of woman I would need and really be drawn to.

Lisa: Marc was the absolute hero of the whole school. I never thought in a million years that he would glance my way. Every girl in the school thought he was so cute, so good-looking and such a stud. We all knew he was focused on basketball and didn't think he really had any interest in dating anyone.

Marc: That's on me, though. I had tons of friends, but with the girls, I didn't say too much. I didn't know what to say.

That baseball season was very instrumental. We'd just sit and talk and get to know each other. It totally started as a friendship that I couldn't believe turned into something more.

Their friendship and attraction started so late in the school year, they went to her senior prom with different people. The romance blossomed that summer before Lisa attended North Park College.

Lisa: We saw each other a lot that summer of 1990. We loved spending time together, so it was hard to say goodbye when I went away to college. Even though it was only an hour away, we knew that being apart could change things. But instead, I think it made us realize what a special thing we had. I remember the first time Marc told me he loved me. It was December 1990.

Marc: I knew pretty early. I'm still learning what it means to truly love her. But I would have told you I loved her early on.

Lisa: I started out at North Park in nursing but then decided to switch to elementary education. I decided to transfer to the College of DuPage and then to the University of Illinois.

CHAPTER 5

Lisa's parents met while working at Northrop King Seed Company in Minneapolis, Minnesota. Her mom Kay was 30 and her father John "Jack" Bartley was 34 when Lisa was born, and she was an only child.

Lisa: My parents were both born and raised in Minnesota. Dad got a job in Bristol, Illinois, soon after they were married, which is what brought them to buy a house in North Aurora. They brought me home to it from the hospital, and it was the only house I lived in until I went away to college.

I am so grateful for the hard work and sacrifices my parents have made for me. I had no idea how my life would change when they decided to send me to Aurora Christian when I was in fifth grade. God put it on their hearts to send me there, and look at all that God had in store for me.

Marc and I had a very similar upbringings in that when the church doors were open, our families were there. We went to Sunday School and church, all the potlucks and Sunday night special services. Our parents were involved in small group Bible studies with other families, so church felt like being a part of a family. Both of our pastors preached the Gospel that salvation is only found in Jesus. Both of our churches supported and prayed for missionaries. My pastor, John Riggs, took us on a mission trip to a Native American Indian reservation in Wisconsin when I was a freshman. The Lord used him to keep urging me to go on a summer mission trip, and I signed up to go to Italy with Teen Missions International in 1988.

That's when God changed my whole life. It was the summer between my sophomore and junior year of high school, and I was just 15 years old. We started with two weeks of boot camp in Merritt Island, Florida. There were probably 50 teams of 25 kids split between two boot camps.

After the two weeks, we had a very special commissioning service as each team was called out from the big top tent meeting and got on a bus and headed to where they would be spending the next six

BRAVE AT HEART

weeks. "Italy 8811" drove all the way to JFK airport in New York City, where we flew to Paris and took a train to Reggio Calabria in the southern tip of Italy.

It was on this trip that God opened up my eyes to see that the world is a whole lot bigger than Aurora, Illinois. You see the universal language of love and kindness despite culture and language differences. We would meet with Italian Christians, and to see them worship in Italian brought tears to my eyes. It made me understand that even though the world is so big, there is such beauty in being part of the family of God, worshiping the same God.

There was an older Italian man named Salvatore who came to work with us every day, and he didn't speak any English. Even though we couldn't have a conversation, it was obvious he loved the Lord. Salvatore came to the train station when it was time for us to leave. I will never forget him running alongside our train car as we were starting to pull away and shouting something to us. We were able to figure out he was saying Joshua 1:9, "Have not I commanded you? Be strong and of good courage! Be not afraid, neither be thou dismayed for the Lord thy God is with you wherever you go!" That's when Joshua 1:9 became my favorite verse, and oh how God has encouraged me with that promise over the years.

The next summer, I signed up to go with Teen Missions again but this time to Zimbabwe, Africa. God grew my faith on these trips and opened my heart to understand that there was no better or safer place to be than in the center of God's will.

I received some of the greatest blessings of my life as my faith grew exponentially. I experienced the joy of serving, I was pushed to trust God more and more, and God kept growing my heart and gave me a love for meeting new people and experiencing new places.

Marc: Her parents giving her their blessing to do that ... you think about the impact that had on her life and so many other things.

Her dad never got rattled or worked up. He was just cool and relaxed and never got his feathers ruffled over stuff. I just loved his demeanor. He went at his pace and kind of shuffled along. He was a notoriously slow driver, but you weren't going to speed him up. My mother-in-law would always try to get him to hurry, but he was living life at his own pace. I learned so much from him about his pace. He was always so relaxed.

Lisa: I was a daddy's girl for sure. Dad took me sledding and stargazing, fishing and swimming. He was always in the stands cheering for me, no matter how far away the game was.

Marc: Dad had a memory like you wouldn't believe. He would recall vivid details from stuff like his childhood. If it was a story that could be told in two minutes, he'd tell it in 15 minutes, and you just loved it. I just remember details he would recall.

Lisa: Mom would faithfully mail me care packages on my mission trips, when I was away at college and when we were in France to keep us connected to home. She would send newspapers with articles on the Cubs or the Bears. Her love language is giving, and she has always been so thoughtful and generous.

Marc: When Wesley was born, she became the doting grandmother. The grandkids absolutely melted her heart.

Lisa: My parents have been incredibly supportive over the years. With only having one child, it is especially amazing that they didn't hold me back from anything but wanted to give me opportunities to spread my wings and fly.

Whenever we would leave for France, there were tears at the airport and it was hard to say goodbye, especially when the grandkids came, but there was never anything but support. They never held us back or gave us a guilt trip. That has helped us and led the way for us to give Will and Sarah and now Frankie and Anna our blessing and support. How can we not?

We both were blessed with the very best parents.

BRAVE AT HEART

Davidson family Christmas card • 1988

Marc and his family on the court at Aurora Christian • 1989

Marc and Lisa with her mom and dad and the kids • 2003

34

Celebrating Marc and Lisa's 20th wedding anniversary • July 16, 2015

Davidson Sealcoating family pic • 2001

Marc and Lisa with Grandma D and Uncle Billy • 1999

35

CHAPTER 6

Narrator: *Don Davidson is not only Marc's father but also his first coach, and no one talked basketball and life more with Marc. They each found their coaching success at smaller schools with their sons playing on the team. They also are tremendous men of faith who love sharing their testimonies.*

When Marc was born, he was an emergency C-section because the umbilical cord was around his neck and he was breach. So honestly, he was kind of a miracle birth.

At a young age, he displayed a "huge motor," and by that, I mean he played so hard at everything he did that his legs would ache after most days. His grandmother, Grandmom Jackie, would tell him to lie on the floor and put his legs up in the air against the wall to drain them so they wouldn't ache. It seemed to work.

My first coaching experience with Marc was when he was between 8 and 12 years old, and I was head coach of the Plattville Little League team. We had a pitching mound set up in our front yard, and both Matt (2 years older) and Marc would pitch to me. I had been a high school and college pitcher, so I could at least help them with their fundamentals.

Many times, the second son has the advantage of playing with the older brother's friends and becomes very proficient because of tougher competition. Marc was an amazing example of that.

Whatever he did, it was always full bore—"working heartily," Colossians 3:23—and he had a burning desire to be the best at whatever he did, an amazing commitment to excellence. As a 12-year-old in Little League, whenever he pitched, we would win, and for a 6-inning game, Marc would routinely strike 14 to 17 of the 18 out. When Marc didn't pitch, he'd play shortstop even though he was a left-hander.

He hurt his arm in Pony League (13-14 years old), and if it hadn't been for that, because he was left-handed, I thought he would have been at least an outstanding college pitcher.

In high school basketball, Marc was the only freshman I ever lettered as a varsity player at Yorkville High School or at Aurora Christian, covering a total of 43 years. I was hesitant about putting Marc on varsity as a freshman, but the seniors came to me and told me they needed Marc on the team. So after tryouts early in practice his freshman year, I told him he was going to be on the varsity team.

The next day, he came to talk to me. He said his team goal for his four years of high school was to have Aurora Christian win 100 games. At that point, I had coached for 20 years and had not had a team that had won 25 games in a season. That showed me how driven he was and what a commitment to team he had. At the end of his high school career, our record was 104-16, and in three of those losses, Marc didn't play because of an ankle sprain.

Marc was an outstanding inspirational leader for his teammates. He was an all-state player three seasons and the Chicago Tribune Class A "Player of the Year" in 1991. He was also one of the top 5 for the coveted Mr. Basketball of Illinois award for both Class A and AA players. Back then, there were only two classes in Illinois, and Class A teams were schools with an enrollment under 750, which covered about two-thirds of Illinois schools.

We tried to witness in various ways at Aurora Christian, and Marc would always be willing to share his testimony in chapels, going first. Players would also give their testimony at halftime, just like the Athletes in Action teams of that era. We printed Bill Bright's Four Spiritual Laws in our program, and we ran weekly summer basketball camps for underprivileged kids in Aurora's east side middle schools. That was a great outreach, and we preached Christ. We also ran basketball camps at the Aurora YMCA and Club 47 in Yorkville and used those opportunities to preach Christ, too.

My forte as a college player at Illinois Wesleyan was rebounding, and Marc took that to another level. He was a driven rebounder who still holds the IHSA career rebounding record—1,942 rebounds along with a career total of 2,300 points. Early in his high school career, his aggressiveness would sometimes get him in foul trouble, but he clearly learned how to channel that.

BRAVE AT HEART

When Marc played at the University of Illinois, Steph and I knew he struggled, but he wasn't really open with us until he decided to transfer. Then he spilled his guts to me. Part of Marc's problem at Illinois was that his freshman year, Andy Kaufman, one of their all-time leading scorers, wasn't eligible for academic reasons, and Marc played maybe more than he should have. If he didn't perform well every time, he tended to lose some confidence.

Between his freshman and sophomore years, the U of I team went to Estonia and Latvia and played around eight to ten games. After that trip, he had been the leading rebounder and second-leading scorer behind center Deon Thomas. But in the fall, Andy Kaufmann was back to finish his career, and he and Marc both played the small forward position. The coaches tended to give Kaufman the early starts, and when Marc came in, he wanted to succeed so badly, he put more pressure on himself. By the end of that sophomore year, he told me he couldn't play there and wanted to go somewhere to enjoy the game he had once loved.

At first, he decided to just get away, broke up with Lisa, felt he let everybody down and signed to go to The Master's College in California. Steph told me she needed to go with him just to see what it was going to be like. I cried my eyes out taking them to and coming home from the airport, asking the Lord, "Why?" When Marc got there, the coach that had recruited him had left, and the new coach didn't seem interested in Marc, so after two days, they both flew home.

Because Matt had a great experience at Trinity International University in Deerfield, I called Coach Al Bruehl, and he said, "Give me five minutes, and I'll call you back." He called their president, Ken Meyer, and because TIU is an NAIA school, they could give financial aid for athletics. Coach Bruehl called in five minutes and said enthusiastically, "Full ride!" and Marc accepted.

After her junior year of high school, Lisa had taken a short-term mission trip and came to our church for a program. She also had gone to Aurora Christian, she in the class of 1990 and Marc in the class of 1991. After she gave that program, I told my wife, "She would be a perfect partner for Marc," so we started to pray for that.

The rest is history.

We absolutely loved Lisa, and honestly, not many women are easygoing enough to have lived as many places as Marc and Lisa did before they settled down at Blackhawk Christian. She was a perfect helpmate for Marc.

Steph died in 2007 of cancer, and I married a widow from my church, Sigrid Ann Ostby. She is 100 percent Norwegian and had been a widow for 20 years after her husband died in a tanker truck accident. Interesting side note: Sig's dad, Bill Ostroot, had been pastor at Plattville Lutheran where Steph's family attended, including me for our 4 years of college. I'm nine years older than Sig, so when Steph and I were college students, little Sig was in the audience.

Sig also had three kids, all married, so between us we have 12 "kids" counting in-laws, with an age range of 18 years; 20 grandkids (14 on my side and 6 on her side); and as of this writing, 4 great-grandchildren.

Our family seal coating business allowed me to work with Matt and Marc for probably 20 years each; my son-in-law, Marshall, for about the same; my stepson, Justin, for three years; Matt's oldest, Luke, for four years; Matt's second son, Joey, for four years; and Marc's fourth son, Marcus, for three summers. We also included Marc's sons Wes, Will, Frankie and Jimmy, as well as Mindy's sons Wyatt and Hauk, for bigger jobs from time to time. All of this time had resulted in developing very close relationships with all of them.

I remember clearly when Marc ministered to me when his mom was dying of cancer in 2007 through Larry Crabb and his book, Shattered Dreams. I still have all of his emails, and they included a couple of quotes:

"When all this comes to pass, My Word to you is this: DO NOT LOSE HOPE, a plan is unfolding that you cannot clearly see. If you could see it as I do, you would still hurt, but you would not lose hope, you would gladly remain faithful to Me in the middle of the worst suffering. I guarantee you the power to please Me, not to have a good time. But pleasing Me will bring you great joy!"

"In the deepest part of your soul, you long more than anything else to be a part of My plan, to further My kingdom, to know Me and please Me, and enjoy Me. I will satisfy that longing. You have the power to represent Me well no matter what happens in your life! (That is a huge—Amen!) That is the hope I give you in this world. Don't lose it!"

These are absolutely beautiful words of encouragement, hope and the reason for our devotion.

I have never witnessed a man so used by the Lord who has been absolutely faithful (1 Corinthians 4:2) to his calling to honor Christ in every circumstance. Marc was given a huge platform because of his team's success on the basketball court, and I felt he lived out the Great Commission as well as anyone I've ever known.

Marc with his dad and coach, Don Davidson • 1990

CHAPTER 7

Narrator: *Growing up in Illinois, Marc was a huge University of Illinois basketball fan, and he was good enough to attract the attention of Coach Lou Henson. His squad known as "The Flyin' Illini" had gone to the NCAA Final Four in 1989, and they were recruiting Marc during his senior year in 1990-91, but there were complications.*

Marc: When I was a senior in high school, the Illini were under NCAA investigation. I had to sit and wait because there could have been some severe sanctions on the school, but they kind of got a slap on the wrist. They only had two scholarships to give my senior year of high school and two the year after that, and they weren't allowed to be in the NCAA Tournament my freshman year. All I needed to hear is that he had a scholarship for me. Lou Henson called me that night, in November 1990, and said, "We still want you." I knew I was going to Illinois.

I had been a lifelong fan. My dad had taken me to the IHSA state tournament, which was at Assembly Hall on campus, and they were always on TV locally. During the late 1980s, they were so good. Man, would I love to play for them. At that time, if you were from Illinois and you were good enough, you went to the University of Illinois. Our whole roster was from the state while I was there. I took time to visit DePaul, Iowa State, Northern Illinois and Wisconsin, but those were all basically backup plans for me. I knew if the Illinois sanctions weren't going to hurt me, I was going there.

It got us both to be in a place where we needed to be. I begged Lisa to come to Illinois with me.

As a freshman at Illinois, Marc came off the bench in 26 games, averaging 1.7 points and 1.2 rebounds as Illinois finished 13-15. Then over the summer, he went on a pair of overseas tours: one with the Illinois squad to Russia, where he averaged 16 points and 9 rebounds; and another two weeks with a Big Ten squad to Europe. He thought his hard work would prepare him for more playing time, but his sophomore averages were 10 minutes in 30 games with 1.5 points and 2.2 rebounds.

Marc: I knew I would have some opportunities. For me, the adjustment was not so much physically, but the mental adjustment was tough. Coming up through high school, I had never really dealt with adversity or failure, so that aspect was tough. I didn't play a whole lot my freshman year, but my formula was always the same, get your butt to work.

I worked like a dog between freshman and sophomore year, and I had all kinds of momentum coming back in my sophomore year. I was ridiculously driven, and I started putting this pressure on myself. I remember Andy Kaufmann came back for my sophomore year (from academic problems), and we played very similar styles. We just kind of battled it out throughout the fall, and Andy started, which I fully get and understand. He was a 20-point scorer from two years prior to that.

I started to put massive amounts of pressure on myself and really battle anxiety, which got worse and worse as the year went on. This was a different era, and nobody talked about nothing, and I'm struggling big-time, but I didn't tell anybody. You are kind of ashamed to admit you need some help, and I didn't talk to nobody. If I could go back and do it again, I would have talked to somebody. I had people all around me to talk to, and I didn't take advantage of that. I kept everything inside and sunk into a depression and ended up in a really bad place.

I'm thankful for my Savior Jesus Christ because He rescued me from a very bad place. He pulled me up out of that mess and basically recreated me and gave me a new purpose for why I live my life. Up until that point, my whole identity was basically about how I performed between those lines on a basketball court. That led to a whole lot of ups and downs. I had some really, really-high highs and some really-low lows. That's how it goes.

To me, the hard part was I was so driven, and I had invested so much. I remember during the season, I was just so full of anxiety. A lot of days, I would put a rock in the door in Huff gym, and after practice, I would go to Huff gym and shoot for hours and hours and hours. That drove me nuts because that was my formula. If you aren't producing, go to work even more. That had always worked, but now it wasn't working. It caused me to think more and put more pressure on myself. I didn't feel any external pressure from anyone, it was all from within. I would shoot at Huff for hours and I couldn't miss, and then I'd get into games and I couldn't make a shot, and it drove me nuts. The Lord showed me basketball was full of ups and downs. The constant in my life is my relationship with Jesus Christ, and I'm so thankful for that.

I was still struggling. I was so angry at myself. I felt I was so much better than I was showing. When you are mad at yourself, when you are full of anxiety, I found out it's so hard to play basketball. I started to hate myself because I wasn't performing the way I was capable of.

I was at a crossroads, because that massive anxiety turned into depression and became consuming and never went away. I hardly ate and hardly slept. I was just ashamed and so mad at myself that I didn't want to talk to anybody. You try to put on a happy face and make everybody try to think you are okay, and it ain't okay. I got to a point where I had no confidence in myself, and that was part of hating myself.

The coaches gave me every stinking opportunity, and I just couldn't perform. They knew what I could do, but I wasn't doing it even though they knew I was giving it my all. If I had it to do over, I'd have invited people in, but I kept everybody out. When you are struggling like that and dealing with shame, it's hard to talk about. I assume my teammates suspected I was dealing with stuff because they knew how I could play, and I just wasn't doing it.

All my life, I had been building my identity around what happened on the basketball court. I had really grown disillusioned with basketball, and God had to break me in order to prepare me. It was a painful process. We want to hang on to this stuff. Basketball was really hard for me to surrender because I was squeezing it. "Lord, I have worked so hard for this, and this is mine, and I thought it was my ticket to whatever I wanted." The Lord had to kind of pry my fingers off of it. He finally got me to a point where I could let it go.

I still had massive issues, and there was a lot of healing that needed to take place. I think there were times after the season that I shifted from hating myself to hating God. That legalistic mentality I had ... "Lord, c'mon here, I'm being obedient to You," and my thought was, "You owe me better than this." That's where my heart was at, and I went back and forth, hating myself, blaming God. I definitely needed a whole lot of healing to take place.

The identity piece was a big part of it. I didn't even realize how much I had built my identity around basketball. It was just always part of my life, and I had dealt with such little adversity and so little failure that I was just used to seeing my name in the paper and hearing the roar of the crowd, people talking to me going up and down the halls. That was all feeding this monster. I wasn't egotistical or braggadocious about it, but my pride had really built up. The Lord just had to break me down to nothing.

I didn't talk to nobody. My roommate was one of my best friends growing up, Corey Hanback, but I said nothing to him. I said nothing to Lisa. I had an InterVarsity accountability partner, Mark Ashton. He became what I would call a discipleship partner. We met once a week for prayer and to memorize the Bible together, we read books together, and he was a great influence. In hindsight, he would have been the perfect person to open up to about my struggle, but of course, I didn't do that.

When I was younger, I didn't always seek out counsel on major decisions. I reacted way too impulsively. I've learned the value of seeking wise counsel. I wish I could go back and do that again on some of those. Now, if I have an even semi-big decision, I'm going to talk to several people beforehand.

That summer of 1993, I went to a Bible camp in Lake Geneva, Wisconsin, with my childhood home church, and that was a turning point. That's where God really grabbed ahold of my heart and showed me how I had really been living for myself. He wanted to rebuild me, and He breaks us to restore us. It was not overnight. I was still fighting depression. It was a gradual process that He was able to pry my hands off of stuff, and I started letting go. Steve Larson was a youth pastor and was the speaker. Every night, he would talk to the kids. I kind of dragged my feet, but the Lord got me there, and it was for junior high and high school kids, and I was there as a counselor. It was something our church had been tied to for a long time, and my parents had gone for a long time. I had a group of kids that I was responsible for, and you'd have your evening speaker then go back to your cabins and have a quiet time. It was my job to follow up on what the speaker talked about.

When you get depressed, you turn inward, and everything is about you. That was a big step to realize when I started talking to other people, how I could minister to them and not wallow in my own situation. It wasn't overnight. As I was talking to those kids, I realized service to others can be a way out of this for me. I probably did a little bit with a self-serving motive, but I felt it was bringing some freedom. I had no choice. They said here is your group, go talk to them, pray with them. Minister to them.

Then we had campfire meetings late at night after that, and I remember Steve asked me to share on the last night of the camp. For me, my initial reaction was, "Please, no." I honestly don't remember what I shared that night, but I just remember it felt really good to serve, to think about, "How can I bless someone else and stop wallowing in my own situation?" Those were my baby steps initially.

I remember Steve spoke about the unconditional love of God. That was so refreshing. I had always known that, but I had always been striving to perform and to be good enough. If I did enough, God should bless me. He had to set me free from that as well. It was an understanding of His unconditional love and that we can't earn a thing. We're lucky we don't get what we deserve, because we deserve to be in hell eternally.

He loved me perfectly just as I am. He loved me so much that He didn't want to leave me like this, He wanted to transform me. That's what He has continued to do. There are times when we have to hit rock bottom, but rock bottom is a great foundation to build upon. That's what God did in my life. He rebuilt me and helped me to enjoy basketball.

When I got back from camp, that's when Lisa and I broke up. I just knew spiritually I was not in a place to lead her in a relationship. Adam had to get God before he got Eve. There was so much God was working on with me, and He had to get me to rock bottom. The basketball piece He broke, which is what I needed, and the other piece I was kind of hanging onto was Lisa, and He broke that. He was preparing me.

Lisa: I had no idea that Marc was struggling as bad as he was or that the breakup was coming. We had been together for three years, and I had hoped and prayed that he was the "one" for me. I knew even though he didn't open up with me ... you know when a relationship starts getting weird. He was closed off and different, and it wasn't so easy. I knew I was putting pressure on him to get married. My friends were getting engaged that summer. His brother and sister-in-law got married that summer. That's what I want to stress to girls now: Don't beg someone to marry you! It shouldn't be a plea.

I'm an optimistic, glass-is-half-full-type of person, so of course after games, I'm just trying to encourage him and believe in him and build him up—help him get his mind off of basketball, but also encourage him. I knew there was a wall up, and I knew it wasn't me who could fix it.

My heart was broken when Marc broke up with me, but I remember quickly getting to the place, "OK, God, if not Marc, who do You have for me then?" But the even more beautiful realization was asking God, "What do You have for me?" I realized I didn't need a husband for God to use me. I realized I needed to let Christ complete me.

I remember just being so confused, and it came out of nowhere. I thank God for it now and tell people how I praise God for it. It was the biggest heartbreak of my life, but it made me not put Marc at the center of my life. My identity was as a child of God, not as Marc Davidson's girlfriend. Even though we're one in marriage now, he still can't be what completes me.

Marc: I don't even remember how I tried to explain it to her. I probably did a horrible job. That's what shame will do to you. I didn't want to admit that I was having any struggles. Put on a happy face and make people think everything is fine.

My whole family was so ticked at me because they knew who she was, and they said, "Marc, you are out of your mind." But I knew I had to get right with God. We took about a six-month break, July to

February. I don't think either of us thought we'd get back together, either. God had to get my heart right and work in His timing.

I think God needed to do that work in both of us. We found our identity in Him and Him alone. It was painful at the time, of course.

God is always about restoration. He loves you just as you are, but way too much to leave you there. God had to do so much in me before I was even close to thinking about leading a relationship.

Marc at the University of Illinois • 1992

Marc and Lisa at the University of Illinois • 1992

47

CHAPTER 8

Narrator: *Douglas Sean O'Donnell (Ph.D., University of Aberdeen) only experienced him briefly, but Marc had a tremendous, everlasting impact on his life. He is the senior vice president of Bible publishing at Crossway. Doug has served for over twenty years in pastoral ministry and has written dozens of books to help pastors, most recently, "The Beauty and Power of Biblical Exposition." He and his wife, Emily, have five beautiful children: Sean, Lily, Evelyn, Simeon and Charlotte.*

Providence can be defined as God working in His world to bring about His purposes. The Bible is filled with stories of bitter and sweet providence: Job loses his ten children, suffers even more, and then is given ten more late in life; Joseph is sold into slavery, sent to prison for a crime he didn't commit, but ends up as a ruler in Egypt who saves many people, including his own brothers who sold him to slave traders; Ruth's husband dies in a time of famine, but the Lord later provides rich Boaz as her redeemer; Jesus is tortured and crucified and yet he rises from the grave, ascends into heaven, and now rules over heaven and earth.

In His sweet providence, God sent Marc Davidson into my life to pull me through some bitter times.

The first time I met Marc was on the basketball court. He was a sophomore in high school, and I was a junior. He played for Aurora Christian, and I played for Driscoll Catholic. At that point in the season, his team was undefeated; mine had hardly a win. You can guess who won. However, it wasn't his team's domination or his athletic prowess that stood out that night as we competed against each other at the old, small gym in Aurora. It was his testimony. At halftime, he shared something about Jesus. I don't remember what, but I do remember that I had never witnessed anything like it. The next time we met was my senior year. A scout from Northern Illinois University was in the stands to eye me and Marc. Marc scored a plethora of points and boarded a billion rebounds. I scored 15 points, but all in the second half when the game was out of reach and the scout was long gone.

That summer, I was invited to try out for the Prairie State Games, a kind of in-state Illinois Olympics. I made the team, as did a host of amazing players. On that team was the Illinois Player of the Year, Marc Davidson. Marc was strong and fast, could jump out of the gym, and shot like he was from Indiana. He was also a Christian. I knew he was a Christian by the way he talked and walked. I was the sixth (or seventh) man. Marc was the first!

What was most amazing to me about Marc was not his skill on the court but his Christian witness both on and off. I knew he was a Christian by the way he talked (and did not talk—no swear words or lewd remarks) and the fact that he had a well-worn Bible bedside in his dorm. Most of the guys on the team were typical guys. We swore a lot, talked disrespectfully and immorally about girls, and (as superstar athletes!) were full of ourselves. But Marc never swore on or off the court. He only talked and acted respectfully toward girls. He treated everyone on the team, even the water boy, with dignity and kindness. And he was humble, even though he was the best player on the team.

As important as he was, he genuinely considered others more important than himself. As strong as he was, he looked out for the weak. As fast as he was, he was quick to listen and slow to speak. As popular as he was, he was unashamed to proselytize even the unpopular claims of Christ. Marc demonstrated a knowledge of God that was pistic, ethical and agapeic. He believed in Jesus, obeyed Christ's commands, and loved others. His authentic Christianity was obvious to all. Marc knew the Lord's commandments and obeyed them. Marc was a Christian. I knew this from the openness of his conversation but also, and most importantly, by his godly behavior and good works.

I became a Christian about a year and a half after tasting the salt and seeing the light of Marc Davidson. His behavior made it clear to me, as it settled during those three months on my conscience, what it meant to follow Jesus.

Then, during my freshman year of college, I learned my girlfriend was pregnant. We dropped out of college and quit our basketball teams (we both played) and returned home to work. Soon after our son Sean was born, his mom/my girlfriend broke up with me. I was devastated! At that moment, I felt like I had lost everything I loved most—my girlfriend, my son's everyday presence, my basketball career and my education. But through God's grace and in His providence, that's when the Lord saved me. I came home from work. It was after midnight. I worked the second shift as a janitor. I dropped to my knees, wept uncontrollably over my sins and cried out for Jesus to rescue me.

Soon after that rebirth from above, I started attending the College of DuPage (a community college). I was so happy to be a Christian, but I felt very alone in my Christian walk. I needed a Christian friend. I prayed for one. I prayed specifically that God would connect me with Marc. I knew Marc was at the University of Illinois, but I had no idea how to connect with him. (This was before the days of the internet. Yes, when Marc didn't have a Facebook page, email or cell phone!)

About a day after my prayer, I was sitting next to a girl named Lisa in class. I commented on her orange Illinois sweatshirt and within five minutes learned that I was sitting next to Marc's girlfriend. Sweet providence! A few weeks later, I was down at the University of Illinois. That day, Marc gave me a tour of the campus, and we had a meal together, played one-on-one and then headed back to his dorm room. There, I told him about God's saving grace in my life. He was on the top bunk, listening. As soon as I finished my testimony, he grabbed a booklet, leaped down and started to teach me how to read the Bible. Marc gave me the booklet (a Bible study on 1-2 Timothy) and encouraged me to read the Word.

Little did I know then that I would go on to earn a Ph.D. in biblical studies, pastor for two decades, teach and preach the Bible around the world, and write over a dozen books, including six Bible commentaries and two Bible study booklets. After that visit, we stayed in touch for years, and he became a person I turned to when I needed advice. I am so grateful for his wisdom in those early years of my Christian walk. Then, nearly twenty years later, again in God's sweet providence, I would serve as an assistant basketball coach under Don Davidson at Aurora Christian, when my son Sean played sophomore and varsity basketball.

During the last months of Marc's life, we reconnected. I wrote to him: "Marc, I just wanted to write to say that I'm so grateful to God for your testimony—both now through your sufferings and long ago when you demonstrated to me and many others what it means to follow Christ. Love you, brother." He replied with an "Amen," a "Thank you so much, brother," and the always fitting (and perfect summary of his life) "To God be all glory!"

Marc's senior year at Aurora Christian • 1990/1991 season

CHAPTER 9

Narrator: *The spring when he was thinking about leaving Illinois, Marc got really lucky (or was living in God's providence?). He attended his brother Matt's graduation at Trinity International University in May 1993, and TIU Coach Al Bruehl pulled him into his office just to talk.*

Marc: I walked out of his office that day thinking, "I could play for this guy. I would love it." When you are living in despair for a while, you have to get your bearings back. That was a meaningful conversation. I just felt really comfortable with him. He was the right man at the right time to help me get out of there and rediscover why I liked to play basketball. My cousin Mike Mann was there for my first year at Trinity, as well, and that was fun.

Because Trinity was an NAIA school, Marc could transfer right away, and the Illinois staff was very gracious when he told them he wasn't coming back. In fact, he was able to maintain friendships with his teammates and some of the coaches.

Marc: I played two years at Trinity International University and had two really, really good years rediscovering my love for basketball. My cousin Mike Mann was there for my first year at Trinity, as well. We had played three years together at Aurora Christian and then another year at Trinity, so that was fun.

It was definitely a process. I never had that "ah-ha" moment where suddenly everything made sense. It took a long time. The process of me surrendering was a work that God did. Had I opened up to other people, I think we could have expedited that process, but I just wasn't ready for that.

That first season, Marc became Trinity's initial NAIA First Team All-American, the conference Player of the Year and the Great Lakes Region Player of the Year. He repeated all those accolades during his second season. He finished with 25.2 points and 13.9 rebounds for his career averages.

Marc: You are coming in with expectations from the outside, but honestly, the pressure I felt was always from within. I wanted to excel and get back to playing at a high level. It was a process. My first season at Trinity, I had some ups and downs there. I was still working through the kinks and trying to get my confidence back. That was a good year, and I just gradually, little by little, started to enjoy basketball again, playing with more freedom and with more confidence.

Then my senior year, we had basically the same team coming back except my cousin Mike. Coach Bruehl had a limited budget, so what he did was get five people and a bunch of walk-ons. We figured as long as we stayed healthy, we were going to be pretty good. We had a good year, won our conference and made it to the national tournament, which the school had not done ever.

Part of what drew me to Trinity was they have a seminary. I knew God was calling me to some kind of ministry, as a missionary or some kind of sports ministry. I needed to be involved in service. Gradually, I started being able to let go of the game of basketball. I started to think less and less and less and just play.

Lisa: I could see a difference in the way that Marc was playing at Trinity, different than I had ever seen him play before. He was so much more relaxed but so confident, and I could tell he was free. One time his senior year, he dunked the ball, and he looked over at me and winked. I had never even seen him laugh on the court before, so to see him playing with such freedom and expression, it was obvious that he was loving it in a new way.

Marc: I think I just gradually started to think less, and then less and less and less. The second half of my senior year, I was really getting it put together. Corey (Hanback) came to see me play one night, and I had 37 points and 23 rebounds. We hugged and he said, "It was so good to see you playing like you again."

While Marc was getting his basketball career back on track, there was something else he needed to fix. During the winter of his junior season, the Lord began to put Lisa back on Marc's heart. They had not talked for six months during his first season at Trinity.

Marc: February rolled around, and the Lord kind of prompted my heart about Lisa, and I started to realize what I had. I just thought,

"Shoot, I've been such an idiot, I hope she takes me back." We talked for a long time, and I said a lot that first night.

She would have been perfectly justified if she had said no, but we both knew how good we were together. We had something so special, and we knew how special it could be. We talked on the phone for hours. God was in the whole thing. I have zero doubt that He wanted Lisa and I together.

Lisa: I think I saw a genuine openness and that a burden was lifted for him. I could tell. Marc had to let go of all the expectations he had of himself to perform and live up to his dream. And he also had to let go of trying to live up to everybody else's expectations of him to perform.

I became best of friends with his sister-in-law, Julie, and his sister, Mindy, when we were dating. Mindy and I were actually signed up to be college roommates at the University of Illinois when Marc broke up with me! But that just proves how close and authentic my relationships with Mindy and Julie were aside from me being Marc's girlfriend. Mindy and I roomed together even though Marc and I had broken up, I was bringing Mindy home on weekends and popping into their house to say hi to his parents. The Lord is just so good. It was painful at the time, but He helped me keep trusting Him about my future.

The day after Marc and I broke up, his mom took a picture of a rainbow over their house and put it on the fridge. It was a reminder to trust God's promise that He is God and He's in control. She gave the picture to me on the day Marc and I got engaged and told me the story behind it. She was trusting God and His sovereign plan for our lives.

Marc: If she and I had not gotten back together, she would still be friends with my whole family today.

I just remember looking back when we got back together, we knew this was it. There was a whole new maturity and feeling that this is right, and we're both in a good place and in a good place with the Lord. Everything just kept dominoing.

I proposed on April 7, 1995.

Lisa graduated in May 1995, but because I still had my student teaching to do, we initially had planned we were going to get married in December 1995.

But that spring is when I did some workouts with an agent who said, if you want to, you're going to have the opportunity to play professional basketball. The overseas season started pretty much everywhere in August, so I went to an invitation-only camp on Memorial Day weekend at Bethel College, and from there, I signed with an agent.

Then he got me into a pre-draft workout with the Bulls, and they were putting me through speed and agility drills, and that was fun. Phil Jackson was there and so were Jerry Krause and Jim Clemmons. After the workout, I felt like I played well, and I had a sit-down with Phil Jackson and Jerry Krause, who said, "You just had a hell of a workout. We'd love to have you come to our summer league." They both really liked me, and I'm on Cloud 9. I'm fully expecting to go to their summer league.

That's when the NBA lockout happened.

I went to the Bulls on a Friday and scheduled to go to the Bucks the following Tuesday, but right in there, the NBA lockout happened and they canceled it all. So that turned the focus to Europe.

Lisa: I had already bought a dress for a December wedding, but he came home Memorial Day weekend and said, "I signed with an agent. The European season starts in August, and I don't want to go without you." Living together was not an option, so we decided to get married in six weeks on July 16, 1995, on a Sunday afternoon—me in my long-sleeved wedding dress and my bridesmaids in deep evergreen dresses for a Christmas wedding. But I couldn't wait to become Marc's wife and start our life together as husband and wife. So we threw a pretty big wedding together in a short amount of time. And the adventure began!

About a month after the wedding, Marc left for Europe, meeting and trying out with teams in Spain, France, Austria and Switzerland. The teams in Austria and Switzerland offered contracts, but Marc could not reach his agent, so he declined. The next day, his agent told him he had done the right thing because they were going to get him a better deal if he was patient.

Marc: I didn't have any place to go, so I went to stay with my French agent Georges Maymon's mother in France and worked out with this team in Saint-Étienne. I didn't speak a lick of French, and she didn't speak any English. We were just in a holding pattern, and I was kind of ticked with my American agent because he told me not to take those jobs. I was sitting there by myself for two or three weeks, and nothing was opening up. Then we flew Lisa over using some of the wedding money.

Lisa: Here we were, finally married, but then just a few weeks after we were married, Marc flew over to try out for different teams throughout Europe. We finally decided to use some of our wedding money and fly me over there to join him and at least wait together for a spot on a team to open up somewhere. And wouldn't you know it, that's when I got pregnant with Wesley.

Marc: Georges's kids would take turns taking me to practice each day. The team in Saint-Étienne had their foreign guy in place, a Canadian guy. I was working this dude in practice, but they were winning, and if the team is winning, they are not going to make a change.

Ten days later and still without a contract, the Davidsons decided to fly home so Marc could start working out with an Athletes in Action team that was traveling the country playing exhibition games against college teams. After three weeks of training camp, he ended up playing only two games on the tour.

Marc: So my agent calls, and the French team that I had practiced with, Saint-Étienne, had lost two out of three and they were getting rid of the Canadian player. They wanted me to replace him, and I said, "Let's go." I was pumped. I knew all I needed was an opportunity, to get my foot in the door.

Lisa: Marc and the AIA team had just finished playing Geneva

College (Pennsylvania) in an exhibition game. We got to the hotel after the game, and there was a message left at the front desk from Marc's agent: Saint-Étienne offered Marc a contract and had him booked on a flight in the morning flying out of Cleveland! I dropped him off at the airport in Cleveland and then drove to Illinois to pack up a suitcase and join him a couple of weeks later. He flew over on Oct. 20, and his first game playing for Club Athlétique de Saint-Étienne (CASE) was Oct. 26.

We can look back on that Memorial Day weekend even before we got married and see that God was in control and ordering our steps. How blessed we have been to start out our marriage depending on the Lord and trusting in Him and waiting for His direction! We have experienced the blessing of Proverbs 3:5 & 6, trusting in the Lord with all our hearts and not leaning on our own understanding—determined to not lean our own understanding, but in all our ways, acknowledge Him. And He has directed our path! How blessed I am to be married to a man who has led our family to trust God above feelings or common sense, and together we have determined to trust God and His sovereign plan.

Marc: We stressed to our boys growing up that after choosing to follow the Lord, who you marry is the second-biggest decision of your life. You can change jobs, you can move, all that, but who you marry affects everything. I think now because we have walked through life, our younger boys, even more, understand how important it is who they marry. They can see how God, in His timing, has blessed their older brothers with amazing wives who sincerely love the Lord and have truly become a part of our family.

Marc holding Wes and Billy after the All Star Game · 2000

CHAPTER 10

Narrator: *After Marc left Illinois, he played at Trinity International University for two years under Coach Al Bruehl, who was a young coach just starting his career. Bruehl's "recruiting advantage" was that he was already coaching Marc's brother, Matt, and also had their cousin, Mike Mann, on the roster. In fact, Marc met with Bruehl when he went to Matt's graduation ceremony.*

As Marc was losing his battle with cancer, Bruehl also was battling throat cancer.

When Marc and I met, we just sat there and talked about things, and it wasn't really about basketball that much. It was just about everything that was going on, what Matt was going to do and how life was going. I don't think we talked about basketball at all, and I know for sure we didn't talk about him coming to play basketball for us, because I never expected him to.

I think he was getting a feel for what kind of a guy I was because I don't think he wanted to make a mistake and go through anything he had been through before. I think he was feeling me out, but I didn't know that at the time. I think he was searching. He loved basketball, and I think he was so frustrated and depressed at Illinois, and he didn't want to go through that again.

Marc was a hard worker, a strong Christian kid and a great fit for our university. He just wanted to play and have fun. We didn't talk about it much because I wanted him to have a fresh start. I was only 31, and I think I was in my second year as a head coach, and I just let him go play. He was a guaranteed 25 points and 15 rebounds per game.

When he came to us, it was funny: He wouldn't sit down for the time-outs. I looked at him once, and he said, "Coach, I sat for two years at Illinois, and I'm not sitting down again."

I think he felt I was a good coach for him because I let him play basketball and have fun. I would have loved for him to post up every time, but you want to give him the freedom to be who he wants to be. He'd take threes, and we were having fun and winning, averaging around 90 points per game. We didn't run anything complicated, but our team knew who to get the ball to.

He was an intimidating player for the kids we were playing against. He throws a few dunks on your head and he's rebounding over you, and they all knew he went to Illinois. He was just way better than they were.

He was one of the reasons that we got good and I went on to coach at another school.

I had seen him play a lot in high school because I was an assistant coach when we were recruiting Matt. I think Marc led the state in rebounding. I couldn't figure out why he wasn't playing at Illinois. That probably was the biggest break I ever got in coaching, when Marc came to play for us. That made us good and made me look good. Our recruiting jumped after that.

I think what happened at Illinois really got to him, and I kind of just let him go and play. He'd take a few threes, but when he went inside, he was going to score at our level. He was just too strong. For a white kid, he was one of the best dunkers I've ever seen. At our level, he was dunking all over dudes. Our gym would be packed when he was playing because people would just come to see him play.

He was a leader just because the guys respected him. His work ethic was so strong. He was the kind of kid who would go shoot 100 free throws, go lift and then come back to the gym again. And then he'd go lead the service at chapel.

I never felt he had any pressure when he played with me. He was so good, I used to tell him, "We have to do it all with you, brother." He was easy to coach, though, because he listened. His dad was a coach. He was going to do what you said, but it wasn't real hard, because all we had to do was give him the ball and he was going to score. I went to seven NAIA Final Fours at Robert Morris (Chicago), and if I had been that coach, we might have won the national title at Trinity. I wasn't experienced, but I probably did the right thing by turning him loose and letting him play.

BRAVE AT HEART

I left two years after Marc, when Robert Morris came in and offered me a lot of money to go there.

A few years later, Marc came in as coach at Trinity and took them to nationals. He talked to me about it, and I told him it was a tough job because you don't have the budget and the scholarships. I kept hearing that they kept cutting back, and you can't win if you can't get enough scholarship money for kids to be successful. It's a great experience for a young guy to get a job, but I told him it was going to be a tough one. "I might have made it look easy, Marc, but it wasn't. Finding a guy like you isn't that easy."

Over the years I stayed in touch with Matt more, to see how he was doing. He was a great kid, and he was one of the reasons I got to be where I was at. I felt like I owed him that. I had a great career at Robert Morris, won 650 games and went to seven Final Fours. I was NAIA Coach of the Year twice, and we won 15 conference championships in my 20 years. We had some good players, but I'll be honest, I never had anybody better than Marc. I had a kid go to the NBA, and Marc was every bit as good as he was.

He was so strong, but he was very skilled, and being left-handed helped him. The ability he had to get to the basket ... his strength was unbelievable. And he was way more athletic than you thought he was, and he was a killer rebounder. He physically was so strong, guys would just bounce off of him. He was one of the first basketball players I saw who was a weight room warrior.

Life ain't fair for a guy like that to be gone. They don't make people much better than him. I got cancer myself, but I'm 63. He's young, and it don't seem right. The way he handled it is better than the way I handled it. I respect him for that. It's impressive.

Marc on the Saint-Etienne poster • 1996

CHAPTER 11

Narrator: *Three months after they married, the Davidsons moved to Saint-Étienne, France, so Marc could start his professional basketball career. They were either madly in love or crazy to leave everything they knew behind and start their marriage. It was actually a little of both.*

Marc: The Lord led us to France, and we just loved it.

They have several different levels of professional basketball there, and I was able to start in the middle and work my way up to Pro B, the second-highest level. So I'm practicing two hours a day and other than that, I'm home, and we had unbelievable quality time together. Wesley was born at the end of that first season, so before that, we were newlyweds, and a lot of days, we just got in the car and started driving. We had no idea what our destination was. If we saw something cool, we'd stop off and see it. We did all kinds of travel all over Europe. It was an adventure.

We had a studio apartment with no oven. The beauty of that first year was we grew so close because it was just the two of us. Living in a studio apartment, you have nowhere to hide. If you get mad at her, you are right there.

Lisa: There was nowhere to escape, so we quickly learned we had to figure out how to get along being together so many hours a day! But all I remember are the fun times. We recognized early on that the amount of time we had together was a gift from God. We've never forgotten that.

Marc: The team provided us with a nice Alfa Romeo car, and there were a lot of days we'd have morning practice and then we'd take off. We just started driving, and if you saw something that interested you, you stopped—Barcelona, Geneva, Paris. A lot of the time we spent looking for American food. There was a Burger King in Germany. It cost $20 for a hamburger, but it tasted good. The goal in Geneva was TGI Fridays, which was a little expensive but worth it, and there was a store that sold Lucky Charms for $13 a box.

Lisa: When we first got to France in 1995, we were Americans living in France. We were not ready to become French yet. We were fresh out of college, newlyweds. I didn't know how I was going to make meals that didn't include boxes of Kraft Macaroni & Cheese or Campbell's Cream of Mushroom Soup. We would go to Sam's Club and bring back some American "essentials" with us: JIF Peanut Butter, Velveeta Cheese and Mrs. Butterworth's Maple Syrup. When we went home for Christmas that first year, I forgot to bring back Velveeta Cheese, so we made the mistake of asking Georges, Marc's French agent, where we could find some.

Marc: He said, "We have 300 cheeses, and you are going to bring this 'sheet'?!"

Lisa: We went to France as American tourists, and we didn't really dive into the culture like we eventually did. That first year was like an extended honeymoon. Marc had practice two hours a day with one game a week. So we had a lot of time together! And I looked forward to seeing him play. The games were so much fun! But lots of pressure being the only American on the team.

Marc: It was my fourth game there, and we lost a tough game on the road. I had scored 27, and nobody else had scored more than 18. But when you are the only American on the team, you better win, first of all, and if you didn't win, you better score a crap-ton of points. The coach came up to me at practice on Monday and said, "In zeeze game, we really need you at cirty." I'm like, what does he mean by cirty? He wanted me to score 30 points.

I realized if you win and you score, they say you can carry the team. If you win and you don't score, boy, he's unselfish. If you lose and score, you are selfish, and if you lose and don't score, that's the worst scenario, he's just a bum.

My experience at Illinois prepared me for professional basketball. This was nothing, and the stakes were higher because it was my livelihood, but I loved it. I'm so thankful God gave me that perspective where it wasn't so hard. Other guys treated it like a life-or-death situation. I really didn't feel the pressure to perform.

Lisa: That first year was about finding American restaurants, bringing our American food and not embracing the French culture. A lot of American players we knew were not married, and the typical American doesn't live how we ended up living in France. For the first year, the biggest culture shock was the post-game restaurant meal with the team.

Marc: Part of your contract is about mingling with the sponsors and then going to a restaurant after the game, where the team took care of it. We didn't know what the heck was going on. We wouldn't get there until 11 p.m., and it was all about the white linen and nice cuisine. We would be sitting wondering when the food was coming, but France is about the whole experience.

Lisa: I think the only French we knew when we arrived in France in 1995 was from the childhood song "Frère Jacques," the 1980's song "C'est la vie!" and the clothing brand Esprit. And of course, "Touché, pussycat!" from Tom & Jerry. Marc had some teammates who spoke English, and some of the wives spoke a little English, too. But for the most part, when we were out of our studio apartment, we were completely immersed in French culture and language. It was the best thing for us so that we could learn French. As our French improved, our relationships with the French teammates and their families deepened, and our experience living in France deepened over the years too.

Marc: The French are an unbelievably hospitable people, and they were unbelievable to us. Eating with the French was a great cultural experience. That first year, I had a teammate who said, "Why don't you come over to the house for supper? Seven p.m." We show up at 6:45, and we're starving. I don't think we sat down to the table until 10. Then they'll get to the table, but the meal in France is an event. They would sit there for hours talking about anything and everything. The French love a good debate.

Every team we were on, we had teammates and fans who invited us to their homes, and we had meals together.

Lisa: We really did have to eat before we went to people's houses. When you are trying to strain to understand every word, it can be exhausting, but they are so laid back and understanding. That was so humbling for us, how welcoming they were.

CHAPTER 12

Narrator: When Eric Joldersma came to France in October 1999, he was a pure rookie after finishing his college career at Bethel College, Minnesota, the previous season. He was a 6-foot-6, 220-pound undrafted free agent on his first major trip away from home, which would be a little intimidating to anyone. That's when he met Marc in Prissé.

Whenever I think of Marc Davidson, the phrase "taste and see" pops into mind. First and foremost: The man had a supernatural passion and ability to taste things. Colossal amounts of things. A friend of mine often says, "Food is God's love made edible," and good governor, did Marc feel the love! One of my favorite eyewitness events of the gift in action occurred in Lille, France. The owner of a Pizza Hut there had the audacity to run an all-you-can-eat buffet (buffets didn't exist in the land of smokes and skinny people). Marc generously drove us an hour and a half to admonish said owner by crushing 20-plus slices in a free-for-all spectacle, eventually to an audience of amazed patrons and panicked workers. It was Marc in all his glory.

However, the "taste and see" that changed my life was Marc's relationship with Jesus. "Oh taste and see that the Lord is good: blessed is the man that trusts in Him," Psalm 34:8. If you don't know the Lord, I'm sorry to chuck a verse at you, as I understand that can be off-putting or feel condescending. Please hang in there open-mindedly; it's practical and functional.

When a steadfast, uncompromising and immovable individual truly "tastes and sees" Jesus, the results are beautiful. They're Marc. Whereas those characteristics typically lead to alienation and distrust, when they're devoted to copying the Man who made himself last, they give joy, life and security to entire communities. If Jesus would do it or want it done, Marc was doing it, no questions, no debate—final answer.

Marc displayed that (of course he did) the first time I met him. He made the effort to check in on a fresh-off-a-flight, bewildered 21-year-old kid in a French hotel in the loneliest moment of his life—despite the fact that the kid (I found out later, he knew then) was a potential threat to his employment as a professional basketball player. My very first pro hoops contract was as Marc's medical replacement—I play until he's recovered, then I'm out. However, if a replacement plays well ... contracts can get shredded, and drama can ensue. Uncompromising, competitive, injured Marc put all thoughts of self (and family) aside to make sure the dangerous new stranger was okay. Normal people don't do that, and self-centric pro ballers DEFINITELY don't do that. But Jesus would. So Marc did. Simply and wholeheartedly. And in those 10 minutes, he unknowingly provided the working model for what would be my 12-year pro hoops career.

And Marc modeled my entire life in the seven months that followed! His injury eventually ended his season, but he actually stayed in France to rehab it (still the only time I've heard of a team agreeing to this). He, Lisa, Wes and Will opened up their home to me. In a lifetime of blessings, this is one of the most generous gifts God has given me. Marc's mentorship to me was the most effective kind, the "taste and see" version. He wasn't loud with advice or guidance, he simply invited me into his life to check it out. I was a Christian and did truly love the Lord, but I was a 21-year-old professional hooper Christian who was still figuring out what that should look like. Basketball identity loomed large: points scored, autographs signed, etc. That all felt great. Before that could take hold, however, I was presented with true-life success inside the Davidson home. It felt safe, comfortable, and full of joy. Honestly, it was like I'd been eating hot dogs my entire life, and someone gave me a bite of steak. God was illuminating my dull light bulb.

This was "it." I didn't fully understand it, but I wanted it. Something about this family and the feeling in that home. To start, I can't put words to how Marc felt about Lisa. He openly treasured her, and you could instantly see he couldn't believe he got to live life with her. He loved the crap out of Wes and (Billy-to-be) Will and was truly excited each and every time he saw them, especially when coming home from practice. Quite simply, their lives were soaked in selfless love, a love they were capable of giving because of the One who gave it first. Their understanding of Jesus's initial love for them allowed them to supernaturally love those inside the family and out (until they had so many kids thru birth and adoption that there WAS no outside the fam). Whether you knew the source or not, their family was powerfully life-giving and benefitted all of us within their blast radius. The Davidsons still have this effect.

In large part due to Marc, basketball success was no longer a danger to my identity or self-worth. Jesus took center stage, and life got infinitely better. And as years clipped by, praise God, my life turned incredibly Marc-ish! I married up for my Lisa (Emily) the following year and started churning out kids, à la the Davidson model. We also eventually fostered and adopted a sibling set from Africa. But most importantly, the humble acceptance of the truly all-loving, ever-present, ever-involved God we serve continues to be the center of our blessed life.

Marc's all-in dedication to loving and copying Jesus resulted in a life that begged those of us who knew him to "taste and see" Jesus as he had, and to see that He is GOOD. I couldn't give a better compliment to my friend and mentor. All glory to the God who made him! God did great. So did Marc.

Marc and Eric with Billy and Frankie • 2005

BRAVE AT HEART

CHAPTER 13

Narrator: *As an example of God's hand guiding the Davidsons in France, there was a family of missionaries living in Saint-Étienne, and the wife had grown up in Marc's church, Helmar, in Illinois—and continued to attend! The Ray and Ruth Ann Gorrell family was on a furlough year during the Davidsons' first season, but they were there at the start of the Davidsons' second season with the same team.*

Lisa: We've just been in awe to see God's hand on our lives. To look back and see the places He has brought us and the people He has brought into our lives, they are all a part of His perfect, sovereign plan. And our connection to the Gorrells is something that only God could orchestrate!

Marc grew up in a small country church, Helmar Lutheran. His family was super involved at church, as Steph was the organist and Don was a Sunday School teacher. When the church doors were open, their family was there! One of the things they regularly attended was Family Night Mission. It was held one Sunday evening a month in the basement. It, of course, included a potluck dinner and some hymn singing with a featured guest speaker, usually a missionary that the church supported. One of the missionary families that Marc grew up hearing about and praying for was Ray and Ruth Ann Gorrell. Ruth Ann is probably 15 years older than Marc, and she grew up at Helmar. She attended Wheaton College where she met her husband, Ray, and together they have been serving the Lord as missionaries in France. So Marc grew up hearing about and praying for the Gorrells in Saint-Étienne, France!

Jump ahead to 1995 when Marc signed with an agent and we were open to go anywhere in the world for Marc to play! Marc had tryouts in Austria, Switzerland, Spain and France. Marc's agent also had connections to teams in Australia and New Zealand that we thought would be amazing, too. We were super excited and praying that we would end up in Spain, actually, since Marc and I both took Spanish in high school and it was my minor in college. So to be honest, we weren't hoping to end up in France at all. But God!! Out of all the countries in the world that have professional basketball teams, let alone all of the professional teams there are just in France, are you kidding me, the first team to offer Marc a contract to play ball is in Saint-Étienne, France?! The same Saint-Étienne, France, that Marc and his family and church had been praying for all these years that the Gorrells had lived there? Isn't God just amazing?

Looking back, Ray and Ruth Ann had such a powerful influence on how we viewed our life as Americans in France and as believers in a mostly un-believing country. Yes, they were missionaries, so of course their job, their profession in life, is to each day look for ways to connect with people so that they could have opportunities to share about Jesus. I'll never forget Ruth Ann telling me that she goes to the same cashier at the supermarket all in an attempt to develop a trust and a friendship so that she can share her faith with her! Isn't that how we believers are all called to live? So God absolutely wanted us around the Gorrells at the beginning of our marriage and the beginning of our time in France to help give us eyes to see and to seize opportunities to share our faith in our daily lives!

Ruth Ann grew up adoring Marc's mom and would tell us how much she looked up to her. Ruth Ann really took us under her wing when we were in Saint-Étienne. The Gorrells were so helpful and happy to share the tricks that they've learned to adjust to life in France.

I had no idea how to cook. I grew up with my mom making casseroles, so I thought I needed an oven to cook a dinner meal. I had the Helmar Cookbook that Marc's mom had given me with a bunch of recipes for casseroles. France doesn't have all the processed food that we do, so Ruth Ann taught me how to make a basic French roux, a super-basic sauce—and how to use it as the equivalent of cream of mushroom soup.

But we soon learned to love and appreciate French cuisine.

Marc: You can't believe how the French can take simple ingredients and make it taste like that. It's unbelievable.

Lisa: Where the Gorrells really helped us was culturally. They opened our eyes to fully experience the blessing of this opportunity we had to live in France. They helped us see the advantage we had being welcomed into the basketball community. Being a part of the team, we quickly formed friendships with Marc's teammates and their families and fans. It took the Gorrells years to develop friendships, and they helped us see how blessed we were to be welcomed into Marc's teammates' homes for meals right from the start. They helped us to fully dive in and embrace our surroundings. We learned to appreciate the culture, the people, the language—all things French.

Marc: Those subsequent years were so much richer because of that.

The Davidsons had already been attending the same church the Gorrells founded and lead with another family, which allowed them to make new friends. The Gorrells loved sharing Jesus and often used Marc's celebrity as a chance to introduce others to the Lord, even when the Davidsons had moved away in subsequent seasons. Marc's teams would play road games in Saint-Étienne, and the Gorrells would gather friends to go to the games and then for an outreach event and a meal afterward.

Marc: We'd go to their house after the game and have a meal, and I would share my testimony, and Ray would translate for me in the early years. By the end of my career, I was sharing my testimony in French. Who knows what God did because of those nights that the Gorrells put together? Lots of people heard the Gospel.

Later on, our kids loved going back and visiting the Gorrells. We would spend a night up in their attic after those Saturday night games. We'd stay up watching Disney movies, and Sunday mornings, we'd go to church with them. They had a little house church that met in their garage/basement. My dad even spoke at their church one Easter.

Lisa: They had a whole library of Disney movies on VHS tape, Ranger Rick and Sports Illustrated for Kids magazines, video games and American board games. Visiting the Gorrells was a little taste of life back in the States. We celebrated Thanksgiving and Easter with the Gorrells the years that we lived near Saint-Étienne. They were like family.

Throughout two different stints, the Davidsons spent eight seasons in France playing for four different teams. By the end of that time, they had become fluent in the language, enough so that Marc could deliver his own testimony and Lisa could later become a French teacher at Blackhawk Christian.

Marc: It took me probably three years. There was one year where I basically learned it. We lived 15 minutes from the gym, and we lived in the same apartment building as one of my French teammates. We had a half hour of basically school every day driving to and from practice, and I decided that was the only way I'm going to learn this. By the end of that year, I was very comfortable speaking French.

Lisa: He was around it every day, but I was at home with our kids. We had five kids in our first eight years of marriage. So I was at home a lot and wasn't having nearly the exposure to French like Marc was having daily. I am an outgoing person, so I looked forward to getting out to Marc's games and interacting with the players' families. I loved getting to know Marc's teammates, so for a lot of days, I would drop off Marc at practice and then come into the gym with the kids at the end of practice to let them run around while I'd get to know the players.

Marc: It's super important to not be self-conscious, and Lisa is not. She tried to speak it and understand it and ... you can't be afraid to say something wrong. You have to be a little fearless. In Saint-Étienne, there were players and wives who spoke English, and there was another family that spoke Spanish. Generally, they spoke enough English. With the basketball jargon, a lot of it was English with a French accent like, "Le pick and roll."

Lisa: Marc's first two seasons were in Saint-Étienne, where we had the blessing of his French agent and his family and a couple of American missionary families who spoke English. It took us two years to figure out how to live in France as Americans. Our third season, Marc played for a team in a little village in the foothills of the Alps called Pont-de-Beauvoisin, where we didn't have the comforts of American missionaries or teammates who spoke much English. But the team was so wonderful, from the president to the physical therapist to his teammates' families. They really embraced us and welcomed us into their homes. That really pushed us to dive in and appreciate French culture and our relationships with our French friends. Personally, that's where our French really took off and we learned to live more like the French do versus Americans living in France.

During these early years, we really understood the blessing it was for our parents to give us their blessing to go to France. They were so excited and so proud and happy for us. We went to Europe and got pregnant right away, but our parents were completely, 100 percent supportive, and that was really helpful. They never gave us a guilt trip that their grandchildren were a continent away. They helped model for us what we are now doing for Will and Sarah and now Frankie and Anna: supporting, encouraging and praying.

Marc: I think for us, being married was a huge advantage. If I had gone by myself at that stage of my life, I'm not sure I would have lasted. Going over there as newlyweds was such an adventure. I'm so glad we got to experience that together.

Lisa: Many of the Americans that play professionally in France are single, so Marc was most definitely not the normal American professional basketball player in France!! Most of Marc's teammates were married with children, and so we were able to make these wonderful friendships as a family with his teammates' families.

Ray and Ruth Ann Gorrell

CHAPTER 14

Narrator: *After playing collegiate basketball at Lewis & Clark College, Mike Gonsalves moved to France in 1982. Originally from Oakland, California, he was tagged with the nickname "Speedy" Gonsalves and eventually became a coach in France, where he continues to live. He met Marc and Lisa when they first arrived in Europe. In fact, Gonsalves was the first American Marc met in France, during a preseason game when Mike was coaching the opponents. They quickly built a lifelong friendship.*

It was one of those things where there are not five or six Americans on every team, so when you do finally come across another one, you stick together after the game to find out about each other. "How are you doing? Is the family adjusting OK?" things like that. A couple of weeks later, we were invited to Marc's friend's house for a meal after a game.

I quickly learned after meeting Marc and Lisa, any of their friends are really good people. They draw you to them. They have an impact on people that is lasting for a lifetime. I'm still in contact with a lot of my former players in France, and the news has gotten out about Marc's health, so they are always asking me for updates. The impact he had on teammates is long-lasting. Even Lisa.

I remember it was weird because he had that workman type of mentality. He would rub the bottom of his shoes with his hands and then rub his hands on his jersey. His jerseys were always dirty because he had that workman mentality. That told you what kind of player he was.

We never played together because I'm quite a bit older. I coached against him, but we kept in contact. I had an opportunity to recruit him in 2000, but he had an injury with his foot and went back to the States. Then I brought him back (2003-2006), and there were three seasons he played for me before I got fired.

When that happened, he kept telling me I had a raw deal, and in France they are professional, but at times they do things that are not very professional. The owner of the club was bringing in a new

BRAVE AT HEART

coach, but he wasn't qualified with the league. I still had to coach one more game knowing I was fired. We could have played an NBA team, and you could tell Marc was going to make sure we weren't going to lose that game. We were in the midst of a five-game losing streak, so that didn't make coaching easy, but he had 25 points and nine rebounds, and we won 98-96.

Whatever he had to do, he was going to win that game for me. It was one of those things where he wasn't going to let the other team beat us. He felt it was a raw deal, but it's how you bounce back from those problems you have that make the real difference in life.

When I recruited Marc, I kind of knew a little bit about his family, but I didn't take them fully into consideration. When they showed up, they impacted everybody around them—the club, the community, everybody. It's a whole package with Marc and Lisa and the boys.

Marc is a man of faith, but it's real interesting because he never imposes that. We had a real good player who was Muslim, but they were probably the two closest players on the team. They accepted each other for what they were and who they were. He made other people around him better, including me. I learned a lot from him.

Here in Europe, and especially in France, we get a lot of foreigners who come over, and sometimes you get the ugly American, but Marc just kind of blended in, and Lisa is definitely the MVP of the family. Marc would be in the gym with his sons, and they would be doing all kinds of activities. He invested in the whole project.

As a player, he made everybody better around him. There are so many individual stats involved that everybody gets into their own game, but with Marc, it wasn't just the stats he put up; he was all about the team. He's very conscious about other people around him.

Marc was one of those players who is almost position-less, like a Swiss knife. There were so many things you could do with Marc, inside and outside on offense, and defensively, he could guard anybody. He's very versatile, such as even though he's left-handed, he would shoot free throws right-handed. He was an extremely good rebounder and a great passer. He probably couldn't play point guard because of quickness, but he thought like a point guard, setting everybody up. He did everything.

He was extremely athletic for his size because he was as wide as he was tall. Marc was explosive, and I think that's why he had problems with his feet and wore them down. He is just an extremely good basketball player. Nowadays, players are good at specific things, but you build a team around guys like Marc. He was already a coach, and he could do anything on the floor.

When I talk about former players, it's sort of like your kids and you don't want to have a special one. When I look for players now, I look for the next Marc. I might have come across one or two guys who were kind of like Marc, but they don't have the human skills, too. You would definitely break the piggy bank to get somebody like Marc. He's a winner.

Marc and I still stay in contact, recently a lot more often just because of the health issue. If we didn't have the basketball type of relationship, if I had met him off the floor, we'd still be friends.

Marc (#15) with Coach Mike Gonsalvez and the 2005-06 Charleville Étoile team

CHAPTER 15

Narrator: *At the end of five seasons in France (during his second season for Prissé), Marc suffered a foot injury that required surgery, so the Davidsons decided to come home. Marc became a coach, athletic director and teacher at Macomb Christian School, a small school in Warren, Michigan, for three years. Eventually, his foot got healthy, and he returned to France for three more seasons to play for his friend Mike Gonsalves.*

Marc: When you start coaching and being an AD and you are at the school all the time, you start to think, "Wow, we had it made because we had all of that family time in France." Now at Macomb, I'd leave the house in the morning, and the kids would be asleep when I'd get home at night. I thought, "Shoot, we can go back to France and play basketball and be with the kids all day long again." So that's what we did. It was the perfect situation to raise children.

Lisa: Marcus was born while we were in Michigan, so we returned to France with four children aged 6 and younger. We had a new appreciation for family time. We love America. We love American life, but we sure could see the difference between our life in France and our life in the States. We were blessed with the most amazing community at MCS as they welcomed and embraced us. It was a very special three years for us. Marc counts two of the friends that he met while at MCS, Darren Coplen and Dan Payne, as two of his very best friends to this day. When we were in France, Marc was home all but two hours a day for practice. And then as athletic director and varsity basketball coach at MCS, he was gone 12-14 hours a day. So it was a no-brainer when he got the phone call from Mike Gonsalvez to come back to France to play for him. We had bought a house there in Michigan, so that was something to consider, something that could have potentially held us back. But we prayed about it and took steps of faith to move forward and sign the contract to return to France. Soon after we put our house on the market, the Lord provided a buyer for our house, a foreigner moving to Detroit to work for GM, who gave us our asking price! We weren't expecting to get our asking price or for it to sell that quickly, but the Lord did it again! He answered our prayers "above and beyond anything we could ask or imagine" (Ephesians 3:20).

Our last three years in France, Marc played for Coach Mike Gonsalves for L'Étoile in Charleville-Mézières, two and a half hours east of Paris near the Belgium border. We were warmly welcomed and embraced by Mike and his wife, Catherine; the players and families; and the basketball club. We understood the privilege of this opportunity, for Marc to be able to come back and get paid to play the game he loved. And we also embraced the unique opportunity we had as our French improved, to be more intentional about making the most of every relationship that we were blessed with.

We lived in a little village called Fagnon, a picturesque French village. Wes, Will (then called Billy) and Frankie attended the two-room schoolhouse at the center of the village. Wes was 7, Will was 6 and Frankie was 3. They started the year all three of them together in the petite classe to learn French with the youngest of students. By Christmas, they were fluent. The French school day was from 8:45 to 11:45, then we would go pick up the boys to come back home for lunch for one and a half hours, and then they would return to school from 1:15 to 4:15. And there was no school on Wednesday afternoons. C'est la vie! Since we had a taste of the hectic pace of life back in the States, we fully embraced the French village life, slowing down and enjoying the simple things and so much precious family time.

We loved our life in France. We lived there for 10 months of the year and then came home every summer and Christmas and spent it with our families. We were getting more and more comfortable living there. As our French improved, we were making deeper friendships with Marc's teammates' families, and the boys were making friends at school and playing on teams that were part of Étoile's club. We loved our life so much that we were open to extending Marc's professional career there. The club started the paperwork for him to become a naturalized French citizen so that he could play not just as an American but also as a French player. Since he was getting older, this could extend his professional career.

But God had another plan.

In June 2006, we returned to the United States for our summer back home with family. Almost immediately, Marc got a phone call from his alma mater, Trinity International University. They reached out to him to let him know that the men's basketball head coaching position was open, and they wanted to know if he would be interested in interviewing for the job. He had always said that ultimately his dream job would be to coach in college.

Marc: There were very few jobs that I would have left France for.

Lisa: We prayed over this decision. We were torn between the pros and cons of taking the job at TIU or returning to France. The perks of playing in France as a foreigner is that the team paid for our flights, our housing, our utilities, our car, our car insurance and medical coverage. So even though Marc wasn't making a ton of money, we had all of those basics paid for. The biggest pro was all of the family time. Marc had practice two hours a day and one game a week, so we had so much time together. The major pro for TIU was that we would be an hour from our family. The major con at TIU was that it paid about $35,000 a year salary. For a family of then 7, that seemed impossible for us. Throw in the fact that TIU is literally down the road from Michael Jordan's house, that made it impossible for us to live near campus. But the Lord made it abundantly clear and gave us such peace to trust Him, and Marc accepted the position. Just six months after making the decision to return to Illinois, we found out Marc's mom's melanoma had returned, and she passed away the following October. We are so incredibly grateful the Lord orchestrated all of those things so that we could be home with Mom and the family that last year of her life.

Marc: I am so thankful we were able to be with her in those last months. We just had some special times, and I have no doubt that was part of God's plan. I'm thankful that God closed the door in Europe so we could be home for that.

Lisa: Trinity is in Deerfield, Illinois, a very affluent suburb of Chicago. We were living in a home in Gurnee, Illinois, which was 20 minutes north, not counting traffic. Wes, Will and Frankie were attending Christian Life School another 20 minutes north of Gurnee in Kenosha, Wisconsin. Wes was in fifth grade and started playing school sports, and so we were feeling the pull of our kids' busy schedules conflicting with Marc's schedule at Trinity. The distance between Kenosha and Deerfield made it difficult for Marc to be able to make it to their after-school activities.

Marc: The job at Trinity was like a dream job, but I could tell pretty early on, our kids are still little, and I got spoiled in Europe being with my kids all the time. I felt like my wife and kids were off doing their thing, and I was off doing my thing. I wanted to be more of a presence as a husband and a father.

Lisa: Marc's mom was diagnosed with melanoma skin cancer originally in 1983. She was a teacher at Aurora Christian, so I grew up hearing her share her and Marc's dad's testimonies each year, thanking the Lord that she was in remission and cancer free. When Marc and I started dating in 1990, I grew to love her in a whole new way. I remember her sharing with me on one of their trips to visit us in France that if melanoma comes back, it usually comes back with a vengeance and metastasizes. I remember being so scared because I loved her so much and I couldn't imagine life without her. In December 2006, they found a spot on her lung, and the Lord brought her Home eleven months later, on October 30, 2007.

We thank the Lord that we were home and not in France during that time. Our two years at Trinity when Marc was coaching were so amazing. Some of his biggest impacts on his players have been with those teams.

Like Marc's dad, Steph was such a hero to so many people, yet even more so to us. She was the most generous, thoughtful, giving, encouraging person. So to be blessed with her as our mom, mother-in-law, and grandma to our kids, we were the most blessed that she was ours and we were hers! She loved and made family time a top priority, loved family get-togethers and went all out planning family vacations. She really was the glue that held our family so closely together! So to see the Lord carry us through that time when her cancer came back, it built our faith to keep trusting the Lord to do it again for whatever lies ahead in our future. I remember being amazed at the peace and strength that the Lord was so evidently giving us throughout Steph's cancer.
Her visitation was an incredibly amazing day. So many people

came to say how much they loved her and how God had used her in their lives. That was such an encouragement and helped us to look at her life and death from an eternal perspective. That built my faith so much. I know it also showed us just how much of an eternal impact one life can have on an entire community. We will never forget that—wanting to make our lives count and be used for God's glory, to point others to Jesus, like Steph so beautifully did.

Marc: Soon after my mom passed away, my dad asked me to take over his basketball program at Aurora Christian. He was ready to retire from coaching. It was not viewed as a transition, part-time, one-year deal (though that's how it turned out). He said his prayer was that he could pass down his program to me. So we came home and did that in the 2007-2008 school year. It was an answer to prayer that we could go back home after being away all those years.

Lisa: And it was an answer to our prayer, too, over the struggle we were feeling that Trinity was so far away from our kids' activities up in Kenosha, Wisconsin. As much as we loved our two years at Trinity, it became apparent that we wanted something different for our family. Taking a job at Aurora Christian would mean Marc would work at the same school our kids went to. What an answer to prayer! And it had the added blessing of finally getting to move back home near our family.

It was such a sweet year in so many ways. We were finally back home, especially meaningful to be near family after Steph passed away. Marc worked at Aurora Christian as a PE teacher alongside his dad, who was the athletic director. His sister, Mindy, was the athletic secretary, his brother-in-law Marshall was Wes's sixth-grade Bible and history teacher, Marc's dad coached Will's fifth-grade team, and Jimmy was in the same preschool class with his cousin Hauk. We were surrounded by old classmates who were also sending their children to ACS then, too. We were back at Helmar Lutheran Church, Marc's family's church that had so faithfully prayed for and loved us over the years. It was such a sweet year.

Marc: But 2008, that's when the economy tanked, and people weren't re-enrolling their kids for the next school year.

Lisa: In April, they called Marc in and told him that he was one of eight most recently hired people that they had to let go. That was so painful and didn't make much sense in our own understanding. We had finally moved home and had just bought a house in October, and then this happens in April. People rallied around us, but it really did just come down to them needing to cut back on their budget. The school had recently renovated their secondary school, so they had to cut back somewhere, even if it meant letting go of their prized alum.

Marc: I was angry, and I felt justified in my anger because I felt angry for my dad. I was upset for him because Dad had given everything to that school. They had no sports in that school when he got there, and he built it. They did him wrong, because they never even talked to him about needing to let me go.

Lisa: They told Marc that he could still coach the varsity and receive the $1,500 coaching stipend, so we were encouraged by some to just wait around until something opened up in the area. But I love that Marc and I pushed each other to trust the Lord and wait on Him, to wait and see what He would open up. Within a few days, word had spread and a former principal at ACS reached out to Marc. He was in Marietta, Georgia, at Dominion Christian High School. They were adding a junior high to their high school and were looking for teachers—and a junior high basketball coach.

So we jumped on a plane and went for the interview to go check out Dominion. We went more for the opportunity to make sure it was a "no," not really anticipating the Lord would move in our hearts to go there. Of course, it really wouldn't make much sense to move 700 miles away when we just bought a home. But we were blown away by the staff, the campus was beautiful and the school was growing. We could feel the southern charm on our visit. It was a very special place with a very specific need that would answer their prayer and ours. God again amazed us and made it abundantly clear to take that step of faith and trust Him. That meant trusting Him with the house that we just bought. With the financial crisis of 2008, not only did Marc lose his job but it also meant that our house was not worth what we bought it for just six months earlier. But God, once again, provided Ephesians 3:20, above and beyond anything we could ask or imagine. When we had a realtor walk through our house to get it ready to list, she said that her son and his wife were needing to rent a home, and she felt like our house could meet their need and ours. Just amazing. The Lord did it again.

Marc accepted a position at Dominion Christian School to teach middle school Bible and history as well as boys PE. He would also be the eighth-grade boys basketball coach and assistant to the athletic director. How incredibly blessed I am to be with a man who didn't think it was beneath him to coach a team of eighth-grade boys even though he had just been coaching his TIU team in the NAIA national tournament two years prior to that!

It is so incredible to look back over our lives and see God literally open and shut doors and lead us to where He wanted us "for such a time as this." We can look back on our 26-plus years of marriage to see 17 moves in two countries and four states for four professional teams in France, one college coaching job, five high school varsity coaching jobs and one middle school coaching job. We can see how to some it may look like the back side of a quilt that makes no sense, but to us, we see the beautiful handiwork of God, taking us exactly where He wanted to use us—more specifically, for WHO He wanted to cross our paths with. I am more convinced of that than ever before.

Two of Marc's players from Trinity, Chris Schmidt and Eddie Pascual, came down to Dominion, and Chris is still there today. All that is to say that I love how the Lord blessed me with Marc to lead us to trust God and His bigger purpose and plan. We had people who love us and who we respect so much who were telling Marc to just take a job at Home Depot if he had to, just to find some job during the day so we could stay "home" and he could coach at ACS. But we are so grateful for the peace God gave our hearts to trust Him and walk by faith rather than by sight, not needing it all to make sense. We are both convinced it was all a part of ultimately getting us here to Blackhawk.

Marc: After two years in Georgia at Dominion Christian, I got into Lakewood Park in Auburn, Indiana. But I was basically living there as the AD and coach, so I started looking for a coaching job without being the athletic director, and the Lord opened the door at Blackhawk Christian School in Fort Wayne, Indiana.

I've been at Blackhawk for 10 years, and we've just had an unbelievable experience there.

Marc with the Lakewood Park seniors • 2013

Blackhawk vs Lakewood Park post-game huddle • 2015

BRAVE AT HEART

CHAPTER 16

Narrator: *Chris "Truck" Schmidt played for Marc at Trinity International University, but he also became one of Marc's dearest friends. At Marc's suggestion, Chris followed the Davidsons to Georgia, where he continues to live with his family today.*

I was sitting next to my girlfriend, now wife, in the basement of a dorm at Trinity International University when Marc called.

"Hey, Truck, I want to talk to you about something."

I'd known Marc for three years at this point, but when you spend two basketball seasons under a coach like Marc, three years is life changing. He had a way with building relationships that set him apart.

He and his family of seven had recently moved to Georgia, where he'd taken a job at Dominion Christian School in Marietta, Georgia, as a middle school history and Bible teacher. There was a vacancy in the middle school, and Marc was reaching out to suggest I apply for the position.

All through college, I'd anticipated teaching at a public school, as it's all I'd ever known growing up in rural Wisconsin, but I trusted Marc. I spent time praying, applied for the position, interviewed for the job and moved to Georgia in less than two weeks. The move was a huge step of faith for me because I didn't know anyone in Georgia outside of Marc and Lisa, but I had learned from Marc to be open and obedient about what God is calling you to do, and it was clear God was calling me to Dominion. Moving to a town I'd never heard of, away from friends, family and my soon-to-be fiancée meant Marc, Lisa and their boys quickly became like family. They allowed me to stay with them temporarily while I looked for a place to live and regularly welcomed me into their home.

My wife and I had just gotten engaged, but she was living with her parents on a military base in Japan, so I spent a lot of time with the Davidsons at their house, teaching Wes and Will at Dominion, and hanging out with Frankie, Marcus and Jimmy, battling it out for bragging rights at a basketball card-based game they created called "Luck Ball."

I had first met Marc and Lisa in 2006 when they moved back to the US from France and accepted the men's basketball coaching position at Trinity. Lisa and the boys were an active part of the program, riding the bus to away games, hanging out in the gym and hanging out with the team in their home. The two years we worked across the hall from one another at Dominion allowed me to see Marc lead and love his family well from a different perspective as our relationship transitioned from player to roommate to coworker.

Marc called Lisa his queen and treated her like one. He respected her and loved her unconditionally. He never stopped pursuing her and lived out Ephesians 5:25, loving her the way Christ loves his own bride, the Church.

I didn't know it at the time, but doing life with the Davidsons greatly influenced the way I would later lead and love my own family. When his boys would get in trouble, he was stern but loving. He would correct them and pray with them. He would lead by example, and they would follow. He would play games, read, watch sports. If he was going to the gym, they would want to follow him. Marc taught me how to be a godly husband and father by modeling it. He demonstrated this in his relationship with them but also in his decision-making.

After my senior year, Marc stepped down as head coach at Trinity. My teammates and I were fortunate to play under him for the two years he coached our team, winning the CCAC conference championship and advancing to the NAIA playoffs, and his resignation caught me by surprise. Different factors influenced his decision to step down, but the reason that stuck out to me was a desire to find balance in coaching and spending time with his five boys, who were all younger than 10 at the time. That decision really spoke to me, especially as a college kid, about putting your family first. We all can get caught up in our careers and forget where our priorities lie. Marc's was clear: family came first.

BRAVE AT HEART

One of my favorite memories with Marc was Friday morning basketball. Every Friday morning, a group of guys got together at a local church to play basketball at 5:15 a.m. Marc and I guarded each other, every game, every week, getting to bang on each other. The morning always started with a devotion, and I loved hearing his insight on different Scriptures that were shared. I'm more of a processor, so I like to sit back and listen to what others have to say. One morning, he talked about a sermon he heard, and a phrase he mentioned has stuck with me to this day. The main thing is to keep the main thing the main thing. He hadn't come up with that, but I had never heard that saying before. What are we making the main thing in our life? Is it our relationship with the Lord, our family, our careers, idols? There are many Scriptures that talk about how we should do that, but Mark 12:30-31 comes to mind: "Love the Lord your God with all your heart and with all your soul and with all your strength. The second is this: 'Love your neighbor as yourself.' There is no commandment greater than these."

It was convicting to me and has stuck with me for the past 12 years. Since Marc's passing, I have probably heard 10 other people use that saying. A great reminder of what our focus should be set on.

Marc never met a stranger. He treated everyone with respect and kindness. Whether it was the janitor at an opposing team's gym or the waiter he was trying to convince to hook him up with a free appetizer, he was always friendly. He was definitely intimidating when you first met him, but you could not have asked for a nicer person to have a conversation with. Somewhere in the conversation, he would drop a quote from Seinfeld or The Office. He knew when to be serious, when to be easygoing and also how to find the happy medium.

It's impossible to share my testimony and where I am today without mentioning Marc in that story. He prayed over my wife and I during our wedding, came to visit us after our first child was born, brought the twins to visit after their adoption, allowed us to rent their home when they moved from Georgia to Indiana, and hosted my family in their home in Indiana. He coached me at Trinity, we coached together at Dominion, and we got to play basketball together on a summer league team. He has been an integral part of my life and has helped shaped who I am today. He helped me be a better believer, husband, father and coach. For that, I am forever grateful for the relationship we had.

Marc and Lisa could have been happy anywhere, and they made an impact everywhere they went. God kept opening new doors for them to walk through in different parts of the world. Their obedience to the Gospel created waves that impacted many lives for the kingdom of God.

To me, Marc set the standard of living out a life that glorifies the Lord without concern for his own comfort or cultural norms. You have to keep your priorities straight with all of the distractions and temptations that are set before us every day. There is so much crap going on and blurred lines that it makes being a Christian challenging. One thing is for sure, Marc was going to keep Christ the main thing in his life, followed by Lisa and then his kids.

When we were at Trinity, every Friday during preseason conditioning, we would run hills at the local forest preserve. It was a long hill that started out with a slow incline and then got very steep the last 50 feet. It didn't just test your conditioning but your mental strength as well. We would probably run around 25 to 30 hills for the day. We knew it was going to be tough. Our reward for finishing was having the weekend off and then going to get smoothies as a team to recover. Marc would run those hills with us to lead the way. He wouldn't ask us to do something he wouldn't so.

He set the tone for every person who had the privilege of knowing him. That hill represents the Christian life. Living life as a Christian is no easy task and, at times, can be very tough, with some even losing their life to present the Gospel. Marc's time was cut short, but he sure left a big impact and was not ashamed of sharing the Gospel. One thing I can say for sure, he has conquered that hill. Now he gets to rest with our Maker for eternity!

CHAPTER 17

Narrator: *Everywhere the Davidsons landed, no matter how short the stay, they always developed lifetime friendships that continued decades later. That is partly because of the impact they had on others, an impact that influenced lives and faith for the better. Denise Thrower's family was one of those relationships during the Davidsons' two years living in Georgia.*

Marc Davidson was, is and always will be to me and my family a champion cultivator for my son Darius and for countless other students, players and mentees across the world. The significant seeds he sowed into many hearts will live on throughout eternity, since the Bible reminds us that only what we do for Christ will last.

Marc lived as a master gardener with the purpose of cultivating every child's life that he encountered for the glory of God and the ultimate good of mankind. I will attempt to elaborate on Marc's unique abilities by describing his impact on my son Darius and our family.

It is due to the Davidsons' relocation to Georgia in 2009 that we have had the amazing privilege of knowing them, and it was none other than a divine appointment from heaven. We had believed in God for providing a Christian education for our children, and it was our oldest son's first year at Dominion Christian School. Although it was the Davidsons' first year there also, they greeted our family as if we had known them a lifetime.

My son was shy and had reservations about attending middle school since he had been previously homeschooled. Marc effortlessly made him feel welcome from the very beginning. He seized every moment and made himself a willing vessel to serve, even in the midst of his own transition. Greatness was seen in him by how he chose to place others before himself. He never knew a stranger, especially when it came to students and young people. He always made sure they felt valued and appreciated, much like Christ makes us feel when we come into the family of God: no strings attached, only raw, authentic love and acceptance.

Anyone could see that Marc awakened with a purpose in his heart daily to position each young person in his class or on his team in a posture to win. And not just to win in the classroom or on the court, but to win in life by getting to know their Creator and Lord Jesus Christ. He vividly displayed the importance of salvation to his students, including my son. You see, Darius had always liked sports but never really engaged in playing with confidence before he met Marc Davidson. Marc had an amazing, creative way filled with wisdom from above to bring out the best attributes in each child that he was around. He saw abilities in Darius that my husband and I didn't know were there.

Marc studied his players and learned what worked best to motivate each one individually, and he applied this concept as he pinpointed and targeted the gifts in his players/students, knowing exactly what to do to stir them up. He even gave my son a nickname, "D-Train," which we still use to this very day! Whenever Darius heard coach Davidson yell "D-Train," he lit up from a mile away! He knew it was "go" time, and he turned up the intensity on the court to another level.

My family and I have lived in the deep South all of our lives. As minorities dwelling in the birthplace of Dr. Martin L. King Jr., we have longed to see the day that his dream would be fulfilled in our state, our country and our world. We immediately felt the embrace of Jesus Christ as we met Marc, Lisa and their tremendous children. Our son not only gained a godly coach and instructor in Marc, but also a best friend for life in Will Davidson. We saw and experienced Dr. King's dream come to life as we watched our son Darius develop the best friendship he's ever had from then until this very day. We marveled at Marc as he built "content of character" into his own boys and every other young person at Dominion Christian School.

We as families on the red hills of Georgia, children of former slaves and slave owners, were encouraged by Marc's love and ability to see us as merely people, regardless of color. All we ever encountered was Marc depositing the power of God's love and encouragement into our son's heart, as we witnessed him do to all the players on his team. Marc focused on developing students who would become kingdom-minded individuals with an understanding of their eternal foundation in the anchor of Jesus Christ and a motivation to love all people.

Darius was the recipient of lifelong, valuable lessons, constantly the beneficiary of watching Marc, and this was during the delicate middle school years. He taught Darius how to maneuver through tough situations and how to shift fear into faith on the court, which translated into the classroom, as well. It never ceases to amaze me how someone could use their skillset with basketball to influence the next generation in so many ways. Coach Davidson saw potential in all his players, even at humble beginnings.

I witnessed firsthand Marc's patience with my son, who was new to the school and organized sports. Marc never yelled or belittled any of his players, which is rare for a coach. He used every mistake on the court as a teachable moment. Darius soon realized Marc wasn't just any ordinary teacher or coach as he experienced nurturing that he had never received before. Marc showed his players how to stay strong under pressure, yet how to rely on each other to gain ground. He taught them how to use the gifts of athleticism for the glory of God. He ministered to each boy, caring for them individually, depositing seeds of encouragement into their hearts, showing them how to play with strength and excellence, yet humility all at the same time.

This remained in my son's spirit as I saw him bloom and grow. I watched him under Marc's leadership begin to thirst for righteousness, on and off the court. I saw my son develop confidence in his walk with God while he gained greater skills in basketball. Marc walked out kingdom principles based on the Word of God that was beyond beneficial to Darius and our entire family for life.

Marc used the finest attention to details when guiding his players. He taught my son and other athletes, mentees and students that they were hand-picked by God, chosen to be here for a purpose. He helped Darius to discover one of the most important concepts in life: The secrets to significance are not found in the things of this world, they are only found when one seeks heaven. He showed his players how to shine while enjoying basketball and how to humbly follow Christ while doing so.

He was also a balanced leader. Darius gained the ability to make mistakes under Marc's leadership without harsh criticism or negative chastisement but instead with justified, loving correction, which made him feel like he had room to expand and improve on a daily basis. He knew that he didn't have to perform for Marc in order to gain his approval, which is contrary to much of what we see in sports. He clearly understood that Marc loved and accepted him no matter what and only wanted what was best for his healthy development. This unique gifting Marc displayed with all his students and players set him apart from the rest. It's a huge portion of the reason why my son not only flourished in middle school but is still thriving today.

Marc's courage kept him well grounded and stable in his convictions. He taught his students the truth of God's Word through the power of the Holy Spirit, regardless as to whether it was popular in the world's viewpoint. He helped his players gain a firm, strong foundation in their manhood as they watched him father his own children and treat his wife like a queen. Many of his mentees and players, including my son, have graciously grown into faith-filled warriors, which is what God intended them to be.

Marc told them to speak the best of each other, teaching his players the reassurance that nothing would be too hard for them, that there were no limits with how high they could go in Christ. The mental toughness my son developed at Dominion Christian under Marc's leadership caused the pests of self-doubt, fear and timidness to flee. It enabled him to ignore later situations during high school when he faced jealously from other players or was even called a ni**er and told to go home during an away game. Darius was able to stay positive through it all due to Coach Davidson showing him how to combat unfavorable pests with the love of Christ and the power of God's Word.

Marc knew how to get to the root of his players' and students' hearts through modeling prayer, hard work and dedication.

My son Darius grew by leaps and bounds during those essential middle school years with Marc. He began to believe in himself and expanded his athletic and academic goals. He went on to high school to become the leading scorer on his team at Excel Christian and set a record with the most points ever scored in a game.

Although Marc and his wonderful family moved away, he was still encouraging to Darius across the miles, even recommending him for a basketball scholarship to Truett McConnell University here in Georgia, where he was able to continue to thrive both athletically and academically. Darius graduated last year from Truett (2021) and enjoyed every moment of his college career. All because one man cared enough to pour out his very best for others; one man dedicated his life to making a difference for my son and countless others.

Marc, Darius and Will • 2009

Darius and Daylen at Will and Sarah's wedding • 2020

CHAPTER 18

Narrator: *Perhaps you've seen the meme, "I was raised to treat the janitor with the same respect as the CEO." Well, Marc Davidson lived this theory, as shown by his relationship with Bob Weis. Weis came to Aurora Christian School during the late 1980s, when he went from working in the much wealthier Naperville school system to assuming the title of Building and Grounds Supervisor at Aurora Christian. In other words, as he proudly said, he was the janitor, with the impossible task of upkeeping a dilapidated building far past its prime.*

On one of my first days on the job shortly before school opened, I was going around replacing burned-out lightbulbs. There was one over the stairwell that was beyond my reach. It was about a 20-foot drop to the terrazzo floor below. I needed to take off the huge white globe to remove the bulb. Marc was playing ball in the gym (yeah, imagine that), so I went down to ask for his help. He was all sweaty but didn't hesitate when I approached him in the middle of a game. Marc followed me to the second-floor landing, and when I told him what I needed, a look of terror spread across his face as he backed up against the wall and said, "I'm sorry, Mr. Weis, but I'm afraid of heights."

Many years later, whenever I saw him and no matter what he had accomplished, Marc always called me Mr. Weis. I could never get him to change that, and Lisa was the same way.

He was respectful to everyone. Even after the most heated game, I never heard Marc put down an opponent or speak poorly of one. If a questionable call was made by a referee, he occasionally displayed a brief smile and a furrowed brow, but he accepted the ref's ruling. Marc was just classy. I know he inherited that from his mom and dad.

My best friend at Aurora Christian was Don Davidson, Marc's dad. He has an imposing presence, but his ready smile and the attention he gives everyone makes him very approachable. Don knows the Bible inside and out. His ability to grasp the meaning of Scripture and include it in a conversation without it appearing to be preaching is amazing. The reason he can do this is due to the countless hours he devoted over his lifetime to studying God's Word. From all the interviews I have seen of Marc, he followed his dad's model and utilized every platform offered to him to share God's message and give Him the glory.

Don and Marc both shared a couple of hours after school—Don was his coach, and Marc was just one of his players. On the ride home and the rest of the time, Don was Dad, and Marc was his son. Having been around coaches for a lot of my life and seeing dads coaching their kids, that fine line is very difficult to walk, and in many cases, relationships suffer.

Marc provided thrills galore on the court. He was so dominating, but at other times, he was so gentle and caring. He tried to learn every one of the 700 kids' names in his K-12 school so he could address them whenever he saw them. Everyone knew who Marc Davidson was, around town and from other schools, too. Marc was the star, but he never saw himself that way. He took a genuine interest in other students, including the younger kids, to learn who they were. Marc made it apparent that everybody in his eyes should be treated the same. No one made Marc do this, but he just felt God laid it on his heart.

In my era, certain kids who were treated as outcasts were determined to have "cooties." Kids with cooties were treated differently due to circumstances often beyond their control. It may have been how they talked, what they looked like, how they dressed, or some other issue others considered taboo. Apparently, Marc never heard of cooties since I'd often seen him in the lunchroom or in the bleachers before school talking to these kids that no one else seemed to notice. Yes, this occurs even in Christian schools. When Marc entered the lunchroom, he didn't always sit with the other players, cheerleaders or the "in" crowd. Like Jesus, he didn't mind associating with ones who offended the Pharisees but often sought out the kid sitting by himself who appeared ignored by other students. He'd eat with them and get to know them. Pretty soon, other kids were accepting them, too, and invited them into their groups.

Even during fifth-grade boys basketball B games, I recall Marc encouraging players with little or no ability to keep playing hard.

He could smile at some of the bad plays, but he tried to build them up and focused on the positives.

One of my favorite memories of Marc was before one game even started—taking a page out of Hoosiers—Marc, his cousin Mike Mann, and Jay Hall, all varsity players in uniform, and teacher Scott Etchison, an ACS teacher, sang the national anthem before tip-off. Then they did it before every home game the rest of Marc's junior season. What a guy. I think Marc sold popcorn at half-time as well.

Once, ACS was playing the Ottawa Pirates at home. Ottawa's center was an all-state tight end. He was as tall as Marc but outweighed him. Don shared with me the player had a potty mouth, and Marc told him, "You're too good a player to need to use that language." The guy never said a word the rest of the game. Marc used a compliment to make his point.

At halftime of home games, Don invited the visiting team to join in a short devotion before going into the locker room. Marc picked up on this tradition as well when he coached. These devotions were led by players, cheerleaders, pom squad members and other students. Usually, the ones leading were nervous reading what they had prepared before strangers and a large crowd. Marc, however, was in his element and used this opportunity early in his career to share Christ with others. What struck me was not just his sincerity and ability to convey God's message, but also his willingness to overcome his shyness and allow himself to be in an uncomfortable situation for God.

I never heard Marc brag about his many accomplishments. If I said, "Great game, Marc," he'd simply respond, "Thank you, Mr. Weis." Never once did I hear him make fun of an opponent or put down another team—unless it was the White Sox.

Marc was a great passer and made people around him better because he was always facing double- and triple-team defenses. I believe Marc still holds the IHSA career record by a large margin for rebounds. He would have had even more impressive statistics if Don hadn't sat him for half a game during many blowouts. He never complained but instead cheered on the second and third string.

Don knew my financial situation left much to be desired, so he asked me if I wanted to help seal coat one Saturday. He did this business during the summer. My job was to run the blower to clear the parking lot of debris. The lot had concrete barriers in front of the parking spaces, and they had to be moved to do the job right. I tried to lift one end and about put myself in the hospital. Marc said, "Don't worry about those, Mr. Weis, that's my job." He proceeded to pick them up by himself and carry them off the lots so we could continue. He was an animal even back then.

A couple of times per month, I lead devotions at an assisted living center near my home in Corryton, Tennessee, and I once used Marc as my topic. What I remember best is how he acted off the court. Marc was always so humble about his accomplishments. He never drew attention to himself. What sticks in my mind is how he treated the underdog. Maybe that's from being a Chicago Cubs fan.

Now the reason I told you about Marc is, despite all his rewards and successes, the things that still stick in my memories of him are his heart and character and love of the Lord. He was open and honest about his prospects in battling cancer. Like Shadrach, Meshack and Abednego, who were told they would be thrown in the fiery furnace, Marc shared that he knew God could deliver him from terminal cancer, but if not, he would still give God the glory.

Watching Marc's health deteriorate was heart wrenching. Multiple times a day, I'd pray for his healing so he could continue to use every opportunity to share God's message. Foolishly, I thought if somehow Blackhawk Christian School could win one more state championship, what a movie that would make. In retrospect, what better ending could there be than to know that Marc is no longer suffering and is face-to-face with the Jesus he proclaimed all his life.

CHAPTER 19

Narrator: *During his 20-plus-year coaching career, Marc received only one technical foul. That's particularly amazing considering he measured 6 feet 6 and over 250 pounds for most of that career—much larger than the average official, who was almost always looking up at him. But Marc never used his size to intimidate anyone.*

And that one technical? It came during his first season at Macomb Christian School in Michigan during the 2000-01 season. That team won only two games that season, partly because it only had seven players. During one game, a second Macomb player had picked up his fourth foul during the third quarter in a game against Franklin Road Christian.

Marc: It was a foul I didn't like, and I think I said, "You have to be kidding me." Honestly, I was so embarrassed I wanted to crawl into a hole. I said that night, "I'm never getting another technical foul."

We've talked about the eternal perspective and the biggest thing that influences my coaching. When you have that perspective, you are able to maintain a real even keel, emotional presence instead of a roller coaster that is all over the map. I think kids need that. Dean Smith said that things are never as bad as they seem after a loss and never quite as good as they seem after a win. When you are in it for the long haul and doing it for eternal results, it changes everything in what your perspective is on why you do it.

There are different ways to approach it. Some coaches are screamers, and they try to scare kids into doing what they want. Sometimes, I have these kids for 10 years starting with Future Braves. Over the long haul, you have to build that trust and that relationship. That's a much more powerful motivator, when you understand there is a relationship there and my coach cares about me and believes in me and trusts me and wants me to develop as a young man of God more than he does as a basketball player. When kids understand that, it's a gamechanger.

Kids can understand that's really what you are about, and it's not something you are just pretending to be about. Kids can pick that stuff up pretty quickly.

Lisa: I just love how Marc is the picture of living out your faith in your profession. I believe that God has used Marc as inspiration for people to see how they can use their gifts and talents and the things that they are passionate about, use what God has given them to impact the world and talk about Him. You don't have to be a missionary or a pastor to do that. That's what we believers are called to do, whatever we do. I just think it's beautiful for kids to see that you can do what you love and what God gifted you with to impact the world around you, and in the most incredible way, a way that impacts eternity.

It would be easy to say Marc worked hard to treat every one of his players like his own son (though there were times when his own boys felt they were pushed a little harder), but that wasn't an act or a contrived part of Marc. It's just who he was.

Marcus: Sometimes you think something is just normal because you are around it so often. I know my dad has always been a coach, and I never really considered how wonderful it was until recently. You meet AAU coaches, and it's not the same. It's an incredible thing to see: Are you trying to coach young men, or are you just trying to win basketball games?

Coaches can have such egos. They get so caught up in wins and losses. What does it profit a man to gain the whole world yet lose his soul? The true measure of how a coach has done is the degree to which he has affected his players, their lives and their walks with Jesus. We've gotten to see that impact by all the former players who have reached out.

Lisa: So many players over the years have talked about what a great godly man and husband and father Marc is and how they recognize those qualities that they value. I can't tell you how many former players have communicated to us how he helped them become better husbands and fathers by his example.

Frankie: When people see Blackhawk, they expect a kind of behavior, but also those teams in the past wherever we were, when people see those teams and the way that they play, they understand there is something different about them and the way they carry themselves. When people come in, they buy into that.

For the most part, people come in and understand this is how we do things. There are some things we do and some things we certainly do not do. Just to be able to see that modeled by a coach ... you couldn't think of a better example of what my dad has done and how he carries himself.

Lisa: Marc's dad has had the greatest influence on Marc as a coach and ultimately as a husband, father and man. Don intentionally designed the jerseys at Aurora Christian to have the word CHRISTIAN across the chest. He wanted everyone to know that his team represented and played for Christ. That attitude and mindset has most definitely impacted the way that Marc has played and coached. We as believers are called to live lives that are set apart—in the world but not like the world—and that should be evident in the way we live, coach and play. Marc's had the blessing and opportunity to create this kind of culture at Blackhawk and the other schools that we've been at. He has stressed to his teams that they should be different from other schools in how they play and carry themselves. Not everybody who has played for Marc has decided for themselves to follow Jesus, but Lord willing, they will, and they'll see the incredible blessing of surrendering their life to Christ and ultimately living for Him.

Part of Marc's example has been fulfilled during his illness. The Blackhawk Braves played Barr-Reeve School five times during recent seasons, and they won all five times, including at the 2019 state championship game, the Hall of Fame Classic and Barr-Reeve's own tournament. When Marc got sick, Barr-Reeve donated the proceeds from a game to the Davidson family—something the University of Saint Francis in Fort Wayne and Leo High School did, as well, for the family.

Marc: I go to 2 Corinthians 12: the thorn in the flesh. My grace is sufficient for you because my power is made perfect in your weakness. I've always known that but never made the connection. I never like to admit my weakness. Now you are at the point where I have weakness in bunches. I have found out that's a good place to be.

We want to hang on to life with a death grip, and the Lord wants to pry our fingers off and hold it with an open hand. Coming to grips with my weakness was hard, but it was an invaluable lesson because that's where His strength shows up. It's such a freeing spirit. It's more a work on your heart. "Lord, I can't do this. I literally cannot do this." God loves to come through for His people. He has done that so many times. Maybe not in the way we expect, with a complete healing, but He comes through in these daily battles where I know I don't have the strength, and that's where God shows up ... being able to surrender and embrace my weakness because it drives you to the heart of Christ.

The way that people have reacted and reached out is just another reminder that it is Christ in me. I try to tell that to people every time they say I inspire them; it's Jesus in me. God can use anybody and anything. He can use a bush or a donkey. I'm not going to flatter myself to think it's anything about me. It's in spite of me, but never because of me, that God works. It's not anything we bring to the table; it's the power of God coming to the table and working through us.

Pastor Ron Williams told me at the start of this that I'll come across three types of people on this journey: people who know what they should say to you, and they say it. Then there are people who aren't sure what to say, so they don't say anything. And the third are people who should never say anything to anyone under any circumstances. I have had lots of just very raw conversations. It's refreshing when people are real instead of showing pretense. Some people kind of come with all these clichés, and I'd rather have real.

Lisa and the boys at Marc's game at Levallois • 2005

CHAPTER 20

Narrator: *After being part of Blackhawk Christian's staff for four previous years, Mike Lindsey was an assistant coach for all nine years that Marc was at Blackhawk. Their friendship grew well beyond basketball into a brotherhood.*

I was part of the selection committee when the job came open. We had some really good candidates, and we hired Marc. It was about a week or two after he got started, and he said he wanted somebody on the team from the previous staff, "and the administration said I ought to talk to you." I figured I wouldn't be coaching at all but said sure, let's do that. We had a very similar background, coming from small schools and marrying our high school sweethearts. We just had a lot in common.

Marc immediately articulated some things that I always thought should be the way to do things. Our goal is for our kids to be tough and selfless. In his mind, toughness is how much frustration and disappointment you can endure without showing it and letting it affect your play. It is just an incredible way to focus that. In our world, toughness is often reacting and kicking something and acting like a fool, but this was the other way around. How much can you take without reacting? Marc articulated that in a way I had never heard before, which I was buying into immediately. A lot of it is selflessness and focus on the team.

We wear our Lord's name on our uniforms, and a lot of people come in our gym. Sometimes, their only experience with the Lord was going to be watching our team play and seeing how we react. There was a dual purpose of being a better team but also being a better example for what our Lord is calling us to be in our world.

After the season was over, Marc spent every day for two hours with the kids (in the Future Braves program). It was easy to attract kids because he was in PE with them and they saw him everywhere, but he was talking to them on their level and often got down on the floor with them. There might have been a couple of kids out of that group who played for us a few years later, but there were 50 kids in the room absorbing everything he was saying. It was just phenomenal.

It took a little time for some to buy into that culture. Marc's ability to get the kids' trust was something to watch. He's just brutally honest with the kids on their playing time and what their roles are going to be. Kids may not appreciate that at the time and may not agree with it, but you can't say he wasn't honest with you.

During the nine seasons we were together, I can't think of more than a couple of kids we cut from the team. Those two kids needed to go do something else with their gifts, or they were better at other things and decided to concentrate on those things. He always found a place for people. I don't think we cut anybody the last six or seven seasons. Kids tended to cut themselves if they didn't want to be a practice player on the scout team. We've been fortunate every year to have a group of kids who want to do that, and it's made our team better.

The best thing I can say about Marc is he valued every kid, whether it was Caleb Furst or the last guy on the roster. He treated them the same and had the same relationship with them. He was pouring into those kids regardless of their basketball ability. He was honest and raw with them, so kids trusted him.

There was another aspect of Marc I always appreciated and respected. During his first year here, we were at a girls game, and a student walked in and sat down. This was an exchange student, and Marc said, "I think this is his last day here, and I don't think he knows Jesus. He's going to know Jesus before he leaves this school." So Marc went and sat next to him and started witnessing to him, giving him the plan of salvation and making sure that student knew the truth.

That scenario repeated itself often. He'd have a senior, maybe not even a basketball player, and Marc was going to talk to him. We'd be at a shootout basketball tournament, and maybe it would be a player he developed a relationship with through AAU. "That kid needs the Lord, and I'm going to go talk to him." He wasn't an intimidating person, but he knew if he walked up to somebody and started talking, they were going to listen. The way he could connect with people was unreal.

This winter, I got a call from a friend, and he's telling me this story about how his brother was at a local gym with his son watching a ballgame. He didn't know Marc or anything about him. The brother called him later and said, "The weirdest thing happened to me today." Then he talked about how this guy came up to him and said he needs Jesus in his life. My friend tells me how his brother has been an outspoken atheist for all of his life and is really struggling with some things. The brother is like, "How is this happening? How does this man, who I later find out is dying from cancer, find out I need somebody to talk to me?"

Marc met the man two or three more times before he passed and developed a true friendship.

That's the kind of stuff that happened all the time with Marc. I observed that a lot, where Marc sees somebody, and he knows they need somebody to talk to them or call them out and hold them accountable.

He was that way with everybody, and you could see it in the way he valued every kid in our program. When you are not real with them, kids catch on pretty quickly. His ability to talk to them and in some ways give them bad news as far as their playing time ... We had lots of kids who were leaders on our team who never saw meaningful minutes on the floor, but everyone listened to those kids and followed what they said. That type of leadership became our culture.

We have some kids who we know aren't always going to play a lot of basketball for us, but Marc would sometimes say, "That young man needs us more than we need him. We have to figure out a way to keep this kid engaged." He didn't want to cut anybody, and we carried 15 players for a couple of years because Marc wanted to keep them and teach them life.

We're in a world where a lot of times, you see the public person and then the private person. Marc is one the few people who, when you pull the curtain back, the private person is even better than what you saw in public.

CHAPTER 21

Narrator: After Marc's introduction to Indiana high school basketball during two years at Lakewood Park Christian, it would be easy to guess the Davidsons left for a better coaching situation at Blackhawk Christian. But that's not really the case, in part because Lakewood Park had beaten Blackhawk Christian during those two seasons. In actuality, Marc was also the athletic director at Lakewood Park and was getting worn out working six or seven days a week at the school, including almost every evening. The funny thing is, Blackhawk Christian wanted Marc to again be athletic director, coach and teacher, but he turned that option down when he joined the Braves in 2013.

Marc: I had been an athletic director back in 2000 at Macomb Christian School in Michigan where the school was small and the basketball program was not good at all. The first year, we won two games, beating the same team twice. As the AD, if I had known that, I would have scheduled them for a lot more games.

When I got to Lakewood in 2011, Indiana high school basketball was a big deal. I didn't know it was that big of a deal, but I had coached in college, so I figured it would work out. The piece that snuck up on me was the athletic director part, being in that building a whole bunch and putting in a ton of hours.

I knew I wanted to coach without being an athletic director but still stay in the classroom. The Blackhawk job came open, and I had developed a relationship with Steve Wild, who was the athletic director at Blackhawk at the time. Linda Pearson was the head of schools, and we sat down for breakfast. Steve was stepping away as athletic director, and I told her I wasn't really interested in being AD, but they had a PE opening, so that worked out really well. I accepted the job.

Lisa: What was interesting to me is that when we were at Lakewood, Blackhawk was their No. 1 rival. What was so crazy is that our boys used to come home and play "Lakewood vs. Blackhawk" upstairs in the loft, and they would say they were Blackhawk players Teagan Wild or Joey Morlan. Little did we know we would be there someday and love those boys and their families.

Lakewood is such a special place with special people. They have major school spirit, and they loved and accepted and embraced us amazingly well, and it was hard to switch to Blackhawk.

Marc: The Lord wanted us at Blackhawk, and we've been so blessed there. It felt like home early on.

Lisa: It's just been amazing how God has moved in people's hearts over the years to make it possible for this family of seven and then nine to live on one salary! God has provided every step of the way. On paper, there is no way that we should have been able to keep me home with the kids and make ends meet on Marc's Christian school salary. But the Lord provides. It's so humbling to see people say so many times, "God prompted me." I want and pray that we too will respond to God's prompting us to be cheerful, generous givers.

Originally, the Davidsons did not join Blackhawk Ministries but instead attended Pine Hills Church near Huntertown. But then the boys got involved with the Blackhawk youth group, and Pastor Kevin Rivers came to Blackhawk.

Lisa: It just shows the amazing community that we have at Blackhawk, church and school, that it was sweet for us to be in the building six, sometimes seven days a week.

When Marc came to Blackhawk, the twins had just turned 3. We put them in preschool and signed up for three mornings a week. Then the director asked me if I would like to be an assistant. I did that for four years and got to know a lot of the Blackhawk preschool families.

Then the French position opened up, and they asked me if I'd be open to it. It was three periods a day, and I had learned French by living in France. It was awesome that the Lord cracked open that opportunity. I love being in the high school to be in teachers' devotions and in meetings with Marc and being able to watch our older kids around their peers.

Marc: One of the things we've noticed about Blackhawk is there is very little turnover when it comes to staff. It's such a great work environment, and that's what creates a solid school. When you have teachers coming and going every other year, that can be a red flag about a school. People just seem to stick around at Blackhawk.

All of our kids' relationships with the staff have been special. The teachers are like Jimmy's friends. It's just neat the type of relationships he's built, and you don't see that all the time.

Lisa: Another blessing for us is to be in such an amazing community at Blackhawk with so many male teachers. That is pretty rare for a Christian junior high and high school, to have so many head-of-home male teachers. They have been huge influences on our kids' lives!

Marc: The Lord has given me peace, and a lot of it is in understanding that our five boys will step up with the twins and with Lisa. Our male staff members … that gives me a peace just knowing they are going to be in our children's lives and the type of men they are. When you are losing a male presence, just knowing you have so many teachers who are willing to step in there and speak life, hope and truth in my kids' lives, that gives me peace.

Lisa: Wes and Ashton's Bible teacher from Blackhawk, Steve Webster, married them during COVID-19, so that is really special. Will has come home at summer and Christmas and met with different teachers over the years to get their advice; Jay Sefton was instrumental in helping Will make the very hard decision to stop playing basketball in college. And Jimmy has boardgame nights and fantasy football leagues with other teachers. We've seen our teachers cheer our boys on in basketball but also care deeply for them off the court. And of course, now we've seen the entire Blackhawk staff rally around us through Marc's cancer journey. We've had the blessing of the entire Blackhawk school family reaching out to us since Marc has been a primary PE teacher, has had intermediate students in basketball camp and the Future Brave basketball program, has been a junior high and high school PE and health teacher, and has been the varsity head coach.

During his tenure at Blackhawk, Marc helped the Braves become a Class A powerhouse again, rebounding from 7-16 to 16-10 and winning the sectional in his first season. It helped that Wes and Will were added to the roster.

Marc: They had really good teams through the early 2000s. They won three regionals in a row and advanced to the state finals in 2004 under coach Gary Merrell. He helped lay that foundation, and they had that ebb and flow of talent.

When we made the move, Wes was going to be a junior and Will a sophomore. We had Joey Morlan and Riley Reimschisel and a solid core there to build on. We had some really good teams.

We gradually started to play more of the bigger schools. That started with Jeff Kowatch coaching way back then (during the 1990s). That was a nice little step. When we got there, we decided we were going to play anyone, anywhere, anytime. We got virtually every Summit Athletic Conference school on the schedule.

I love the fact that we are independent because we can play who we want and custom-build our schedule. We've been intentional about playing not just good teams but different styles of play. For us, it's all about preparation for the state tournament. We want our guys to be able to face any kind of adversity.

Maybe the downside is we don't have those natural rivalries. Our rivalries shift from year to year, which is fine.

When we played against Lakewood Park, those were emotional nights. We love Lakewood, and we'd like to think that is reciprocal. You love those people, but they are trying to beat the snot out of you.

Lisa: Wes loved Lakewood, but he also loved Blackhawk. When it was time for us to order his letterman's jacket, he wanted one sleeve North Carolina blue for Lakewood and the other sleeve royal blue for Blackhawk. He truly loved both schools so much.

In his first year with Blackhawk while playing at Lakewood, Marc gathered the team after the game, and everyone got back to the locker room.

Marc: I usually don't say a lot after the game. Your emotions are high. I start talking for just a couple of minutes, and I look around and, "Where's Wes?" It was a huge crowd, so Coach Lindsey goes out and finds him, and he's out there talking to his buddies, because the Lakewood Park fan section is right next to the locker room.

You can imagine the old man didn't like that very much. I just made it clear to him that you go with the team after the game. In hindsight, he wasn't doing anything intentional, but I had to make an example. We may or may not have dented a locker.

What was rewarding was the kids that grew up in the program. There's always an assumption that private schools are always out recruiting, and that kind of stuff has gone on, of course, but the reward for us is seeing kids who stay in our program. There were always these fans chanting, "Stop recruiting!" when Caleb Furst was a big star for us, but Caleb was at Blackhawk since preschool.

Lisa: I'll never forget when we were playing Argos in the regional championship game at Triton High School in 2019, when Caleb Furst was a sophomore. Their student section was chanting, "Stop recruiting!" and our students came back with, "Here since preschool." That makes us laugh to this day.

Marc: We won the sectional the first year we were at Blackhawk in 2014. You had a kid like Joey Morlan, and he really helped, because his freshman and sophomore years, he was being touted on all the recruiting lists of top players in his class. He did a lot in terms of helping get our program on the map. When you have kids who have talent and then buy into what you are trying to do, that really is how you build it. Joey was talented, and he was committed.
Joey graduated in 2015, so there was a couple of years' gap before Caleb's first year in 2018. Frankie was the bridge between Joey and Caleb, and by that time, we had some good momentum going.

It wasn't until 2018 that the Braves were able to break through and win a regional title. That started them on a dominating three-year run that led to state titles in 2019 and 2021, with the end of the 2020 tournament being wiped out by COVID-19.

Marc: I was at a point where my perspective on coaching was that it's about the kids. I think I remember Bobby Knight when he coached the Olympics: They didn't give medals to the coaches, and he loved the idea, and I love that idea. It's all about the players. Just being able to have that perspective, it makes you happy for the kids when they see how hard work pays off.

It's temporary. It's rewarding and it's fun, but it's not the end-all and be-all of our existence. It can open so many doors for great conversations about meaning and purpose, and we tried to capitalize on that with our players.

Lisa: One of the things that I love about Marc is his eternal perspective, which is what drives the way he coaches. The second thing I love about his coaching is he's not an idiot who separates how he coaches from how he is off the court. I love the way he carries himself, and I'm so proud of that.

Marc is competitive, but that doesn't mean he acts like an idiot and stomps his foot and yells and screams. His players and students respect him so much that they don't want to disappoint him.

Marc: Amos Alonzo Stagg had a quote when he coached at the University of Chicago where he said, "We won't know for probably another 20 years what kind of season this really was."

We have an alumni game every year, which has been fun. We've started alumni open gyms in the summertime, Sunday nights at 7 p.m. The guys know I'm going to be there, and the ball is going to be out. That's been a neat tradition, and Wes loves rallying the troops. Sometimes, it will be open over Christmas break. We have a huge group text going with every player I've ever coached here. "Hey, Coach, I'm in town this weekend, can we get an open gym going?" The fact that those guys want to maintain that is really cool.

That's one of those situations where even if you don't see somebody for a year or two, you pick up where you left off. Those have been a lot of fun. To see the kids initiate that is really special. It's always a way to keep tabs on those guys. We're playing basketball, but it's not really about basketball. We're connecting and doing life together.

Lisa: Marc and I have been especially blessed because ever since we've been at Blackhawk, he's had at least one of our sons on his team and several years where we had two playing for him on the same team. And those teams have been beyond just his players but our kids' best friends, too. That just deepens the relationship with the team and the kids and the parents. You love each other's kids. Every single team has just been such a blessing. Of course, the postseason success and run for the state championships were so very, very sweet and special, but every single step along the way has had its own special place in our hearts.

Marc: What says something about our culture is the last game. I've been in a locker room after a last game about 40 times. Once you get into high school and college and beyond, that last game ... those can be heavy scenes in a locker room. My dad always said you never forget your last game. Almost every team ends on a loss, and that's hard in itself. There were every bit as many tears in 2019 and 2021 as there were in the years when we ended on a loss. It's just that feeling that this group right here is together for the last time. You put so much into it.

The really cool thing in 2019 and 2021 was how many of our guys said they wished they had a practice to come back to on Monday. You don't want it to be over. Those have been some really special moments in those locker rooms, just great opportunities to talk about perspective.

Wrapping up practice with Blackhawk's 2017-18 team huddle and prayer

CHAPTER 22

Narrator: *Caleb Furst became the major star around which Marc built the basketball program as well as the most honored and recognized player in school history. The Braves won state titles in 2019 and again in 2021, the same year Caleb earned Indiana Mr. Basketball honors before he received a scholarship to Purdue University.*

When I reflect on the years with Coach Davidson as my coach and friend, there are many, many different stories that help express his character and who he is at his core. When thinking through these stories, and which ones have stuck out the most to me and had the biggest impact in my life, all the stories throughout the years have one common denominator: They all help to show the way in which Coach Davidson has lived for God above all else.

The first story that has been in my mind is not so much a single moment in time, but rather a series of different events throughout my senior year during the 2020-2021 season. This took place almost immediately after Coach Davidson received the initial diagnosis for his cancer in the fall of 2020. However, with this diagnosis also came a blessing: Coach Davidson had received a larger opportunity for him to share his faith in Christ and the Truth of the Gospel that he had built his life upon.

Throughout this season, there were many different times that Coach Davidson had the chance to point people toward God that he otherwise would not have been able to do had he not had cancer. The most notable moments to me were during our state championship run. After many of our games, the opposing coach would ask to pray over Coach Davidson in the middle of the court. On multiple occasions, Coach Davidson used this opportunity to share a bit of his story with the opposing team, and most importantly, he took this time to tell them about our Savior, Jesus Christ. Not only was this an incredible chance to minister to the other team but also for the hundreds to thousands in attendance to witness it, as well.

This type of boldness and strength that Coach Davidson had been filled with, despite the cancer, was apparent the entire season.

I can specifically point toward a time during team devotions when I mentioned how it was amazing to see the strength that Coach Davidson lived with, and his response was, "This is not my strength. On my own, I am weak. This is Christ working through me, and it is because of Him that I am strong." This sentence alone, in my opinion, perfectly sums up the testimony that Coach Davidson's life has always been for the Lord.

Even before becoming diagnosed with cancer, his testimony for God has always remained the same. One of my most vivid memories of this goes back to our 2018-2019 season in the locker room immediately after we had won our first state championship. After the game, we huddled up in a circle with our arms on each other, as we had always done. This time, however, Coach Davidson took our state championship trophy and laid it down right in the middle of our circle. He then proceeded with this: "This trophy right here is really cool, but at the end of the day, in the grand scheme of eternity, it means nothing. One day, it is going to be dust. Everything in this room will be dust. The only thing that will remain is our Savior. Our relationship with Him is what is eternal and is what really matters."

As he said these things, I remember thinking in the moment, this is a man who truly loves God.

Even since I have graduated from Blackhawk Christian, regardless of the fact that we are not together as much nor are we able to communicate as much as we did when I was still in high school, Coach Davidson's influence in my life has become greater than ever before. Being in college has given me the opportunity to openly confess my faith and live it out like I have not had the opportunity to do up to this point.

Coach Davidson has had a massive influence on the boldness that I live with in Christ, due to all that he helped instill in our basketball teams each year. Even now, as I have watched Blackhawk's games live-streamed this year, read articles and watched interviews with Coach Davidson, the way he has continually glorified God's name has been a great encouragement and example to me and so many others.

The more I have reflected on my time with Coach Davidson, the more I have realized that he not only has done his best to lead us to become a great team or great individual players. More notably, he always led us in a way through his words and actions that would help us become good friends, loving husbands, caring fathers and, most importantly, great men of God.

Marc and Caleb with the IHSAA Class 2A 2021 Boys Basketball State Championship trophy

CHAPTER 23

Narrator: *As competitive as Marc Davidson was as a coach, he was even more fierce as an individual athlete, but in a way that few in northeast Indiana ever got to see. Starting in 2006, he began building himself into one of the strongest men in the state and maybe even the world.*

Marc: After I retired from playing in France in 2006, I think I played in one men's basketball league game when I realized I had to do something else. I just have to compete, but playing basketball just wasn't the same. I had a former player, Adam Cora from Trinity, who had gotten into Strongman competitions, and he suggested I try it. I was pretty much hooked instantly. Strongman scratched that itch for me.

I did my first contest in October of 2013 because I had just turned 40. I just loved it. I zeroed the deadlift, which I've done many times. One of the things I like about Strongman is you are going to fail over and over, but you have to have the wherewithal to get back up there and take your swings. I just think that's healthy. It was the first individual sport I had ever competed in, and that's a different dynamic, too.

The beauty of Strongman is that every show I've ever done, I've made new friends. It's just a neat community, because even when you are competing against somebody, you want to see them do well, because that is going to push me to do more weight. There's something really healthy about it when you are legitimately happy for them and cheering for someone you are competing against.

Maybe because Marc was a relative newcomer and hadn't torn up his muscles for years, and maybe because he couldn't compete during the basketball season, his body had plenty of time to heal as he participated in six to eight events a year. He increased his weight from 240 pounds to 315 pounds as he built up, loving how unique powerlifting was from basketball competition.

Marc: It's totally different. For me, it's been kind of refreshing. I love the dynamics of a team sport, but I had never done an individual one before. Team sports tend to lend themselves to more excuses. You can point to a teammate or a ref or whatever, but there is something really honest about Strongman. The bar is there, and you are either going to move the bar or you are not. I love that challenge, and you can set gradual milestones along the way. When you hit a milestone, it feels really good, but it's never over. They keep going up and never ending.

I love the training and the discipline that is required. When you are on a team, there is accountability from your teammates. But when you are in an individual sport, most of the time you are training by yourself, so getting your butt up and getting to the gym is basically what it boils down to.

Lisa: I loved how much Marc loved it. It was definitely an atmosphere and a crowd unlike any other we had been in before, but I could see the connection and brotherhood that Marc had with these guys. It was beautiful. I know sometimes Christians can get caught up being inside our Christian bubble, and it's good for us to be outside of our bubble. It was good for me to see Marc have a love and a heart for these guys who he had nothing in common with other than Strongman, but that was enough to make a brotherhood.

To have their lives look so different but for them to have a love for each other, that was convicting. Just seeing how welcoming, encouraging and open that Strongman community is has been awesome to be a part of. The places that we've been able to go together ... to see how much it meant for him to compete and do that has been wonderful and was so good for our marriage to get away by ourselves, especially now that we realize what a gift Strongman became to us.

Something I learned from Marc's time with Strongman is the beauty and blessing of cheering on my spouse, even when it's not something I enjoy. To be honest, I didn't really love the Strongman competitions. It was a lot of sitting around in a usually steaming hot gym and blaring loud heavy metal music, all to watch Marc compete for maybe one minute in each of the five events. But I knew it meant a lot to him, and I wanted to be a part of something he enjoyed so much. I was blessed to meet some incredible people that I never would have met if I hadn't tagged along with Marc. For those first competitions, it took everything in me to go, but I am so thankful that I did, and competition weekends soon became something I looked forward to. Our last carefree getaway, just the two of us, was actually at a Strongman competition in Ohio. It was on August 14, 2021, my 49th birthday. I remember fighting the selfish instinct of thinking the last thing I felt like doing on my birthday was sit at a Strongman competition. But I am so incredibly thankful for that sweet day Marc and I had together with the most cherished memories of what came to be his last Strongman competition followed by a beautiful night in downtown Dayton, just the two of us. I have learned after many years of marriage that there is joy in loving Marc more than myself. It took me a while to learn that, but I am so thankful I did.

Marc: The trick for me was basketball season. For a high school basketball coach, the time you put in is ridiculous. I don't think people understand the time you invest, even in the offseason. During the season, it is just nuts. I tried to think this through; how am I going to do this? I don't think I can compete during basketball. Occasionally, I'd do a local show just to keep my hand in.

In some ways, it is probably good to give your body a little bit of a break, but when you have a show on the horizon, that just injects intensity into your training automatically. I have found that sometimes you have to sign up for a show to get yourself going. It definitely helps, because now you have very specific goals and you have to get to here on this and there on that.

The other thing that surprised me going through this is when it's game day, you are just stronger. That kind of snuck up on me. There would be shows I was prepping for, and I couldn't hit one rep during the training, but sometimes during the show, you could hit three reps. You get the adrenaline flowing a little bit.

Lisa: He is so disciplined. He loves to compete and train and work out, so I have learned over the years that is an important part of him. I have come to understand that, and I absolutely give him my blessing to go do it.

Marc: I like both aspects, training with a group and training alone. To me, that's just like a time of solitude where you can get away and be quiet. I even used that as a prayer time to connect with the Lord, and there's a Scripture that says we present our bodies as living sacrifices, holy and acceptable to God. This is an act of worship, and if we look at it that way, that weight room becomes much more than just a gymnasium but literally an arena to worship and recognize His place in our lives.

When we pursue Jesus with all that we have, with all of our heart, soul, mind and strength, He empowers us to be a better spouse, a better employee and a better friend. He gives us the ability in all of these other areas to be our best, so it's not like there's a trade-off. He elevates us in all of these other areas, and that's what brings the balance.

The Scriptures over 300 times give us the command, "Do not be afraid." That's not by accident. He made us, and He knows that we have a propensity to feel fear. He knows that. That's why He put that in there over and over and over. You can't miss that. I'm not afraid, and I have zero fear whatsoever. That's the peace that God brings. When you get yourself right with the Lord, it brings a peace you cannot even explain.

Competing in the Farmers Walk at a Strongman Competition

CHAPTER 24

Narrator: *The odd thing about Marc's friendship with fellow Strongman competitor Jes Reeve is that though they both trained in Fort Wayne at the time, neither knew of the other before they met at a 2015 competition in Kentucky. Reeve lived in Albion, Indiana, and Marc trained in the Blackhawk Christian gym, but once they met, the men formed a strong bond through competition and encouragement.*

I didn't even know he was from Indiana, but I might have overheard him talking to somebody else. At that time, we had a very small training group of Strongmen. In this sport, you need someone to push you, and Marc is that guy, being 6-6 and 300 pounds and a former Division I athlete. I asked him where he was training, and then I don't think I saw him for like a year after that. I said, "Why don't you train with us?" and he said he didn't have time and explained what his life was like.

He was down there by himself. We just started talking, and the Strongman community is so small, you're talking less than one percent of the people in the world who do it. Then there are guys who take it seriously, and you notice those kind of people, and you talk to them. I could see his potential just watching him, even knowing he didn't train and that he was unfamiliar with implements.

The respect you get from watching someone pull or set a stone and pass out almost or—sorry—crap their pants or blow blood vessels in their eyes or pull tendons, it takes a different person, and you have to respect that. That's what drew me to it. I don't know why I'm that way, and I don't know why I get that rush of picking something up. I can't explain it. It's a respect you give to those guys when you watch them do it. I don't know if it's a barbaric thing or what. You just know they have no quit and would stick with you through thick and thin.

I saw all that in Marc, and I just wanted to push him. I knew what he had and what kind of heart he had because I could see it. It takes me about five minutes to watch somebody in the gym to see if they have it, that maybe they love the sport or if they are there to do it for some other reason. Weightlifting is the loneliest sport in the world, and Marc knew he was never getting famous doing this, but you could tell he just loved it.

I never pictured myself as a mentor to Marc because him just being around made me a better person in general. I've had five or six people ask me the last few months, why did you get to know Marc? I never thought of it. Our paths crossed for a reason.

Another odd thing about their friendship is that Marc and Jes competed against each other only one time because of their age difference, as Jes was a few years younger than Marc. They went head-to-head during a competition in Ohio in 2021. Jes won the log press, setting a national record, and then the deadlift. Marc rallied to win the sandbag carry and set a national record in the farmer's carry, setting up the winner-take-all sandbag toss. Marc's effort hit the bar and came back toward him, and Jes's toss cleared the bar for the victory. It was around that time the men became brothers. And it ultimately would be Marc's last Strongman competition.

I told him I was going to beat him at Ohio in sandbag toss for height even though he's 6-6 and I'm 5-9. I told him, "I know I'm going to beat you, but this is the last time I'm going to beat you, because I'm going to show you how to do it for next time." To see the fire in his eyes at that time was fun.

Once you get to know someone, you see their heart. There ain't no quit in him, and you want to be around people like that. It just draws you to them. When you get that level of respect for someone, they feel like family to you. If Marc needed anything or if he got in trouble or his wife got in trouble, I'd put my life on the line for him. I'd do anything for him. Not that many people would really do that for you. They think they would. You think maybe you have friends who would die for you ... until that time comes. We'll see. To have friends like that is pretty cool, and I hope everybody gets someone like that in their life.

There are certain people who text me "Brother," and that makes me hold up a second and read that. Over the years, it has been overused a little bit, and maybe I never thought of them that way, but I view Marc as a brother for sure, and I'd do anything for him or his family, now and forever. I promise him that. I guarantee that.

Marc: A loyal friend is hard to come by. When you get that, you recognize it. When you have a brother like that, you don't (have) to see him every other day. You just pick up where you left off, and you have each other's back. If something good happens to him, I'm just as happy as he is. If something bad happens, I feel that with him, too. That's what being a brother is about. You kind of enter that world on both sides through the good and the bad. That's something I appreciate about Jes. He's loyal as there is. You go through stuff through thick and thin. It's just that strong bond.

Jes: It's not like we spent a ton of time together. Most of the time, we're in the gym trying to hurry through a workout to get home for something. We might have had 45 minutes together at a time. It's not like we had time to sit back and shoot the bull for 2 hours. I respected what he was doing, and he respected what I was doing. I went through a ton of training partners, but he stuck. There's just no quit in him, and we have that the same.

I've never seen Marc in a bad mood. He's always got that little grin on his face before he competes. God is too deep in that boy's heart to ever look nervous. I've never been around too many people in that way as far as my faith and growing up, but Marc approaches it different than some. When he talks, people listen. Not many people can do that.

I told Marc awhile back that there are two people in my life who I never heard say a bad word about anybody. One was my grandpa, and one was Marc. If more people tried to live their lives that way, it would be a different world. It's hard to do, but he does it, and there's a good reason why. His dad instilled that when he was young.

I thought about that when Marc got cancer, and it doesn't make any sense. It's always the good guys. I had another buddy say, "Hey, Jes, you have to look at it a little different. You know how many lives Marc is going to affect if he does pass away early before his time?" I thought that was pretty stupid, and told him to shut up, but then I started thinking about it over the next few weeks. It's affecting me and I just don't know how, seeing him being so comfortable in his faith and trusting God. I can't explain it. He's so confident the Lord has him. Not being scared in these days is not easy. There's a lot of things to be scared of, but there is no fear in his eyes, and I respect that. That's how I want to live my life. I can always be better. Every time I leave Marc, I'll tell you what, I feel like an underachiever.

The number of people thinking about that man every single day right now is crazy, and I'm one of them. There isn't a day goes by that I don't think about him. It might be short, don't get me wrong, but he definitely kept me moving in the gym the last few months.

Marc and Jes after Marc's last Strongman competition • August 2021

Marc won 3rd place at Strongman Corporation Master's Nationals in Las Vegas • 2018

CHAPTER 25

Narrator: *A topic Marc pondered in his heart for many years is something he calls legalism, and it's a struggle he sees among many Christians. In a way, it's about taking the side of the older son in the "Prodigal Son" parable.*

Marc: This actually is something I started thinking about at an early age. When we talked about the "Prodigal Son," a lot of people who grew up in church were probably more like the older brother and openly jealous. The danger with that is you develop this attitude where you almost end up comparing yourself to others without even really thinking about it. It becomes this comparison game. Even if you do have a sin, you say, "Well, at least I didn't do what he did." You try to justify it.

Part of it for me was realizing I had a legalistic mindset growing up. I was not the prodigal son, I was the older brother, always thinking I'm doing the right thing. "God, I'm serving You, so therefore You should bless me." That fed into my issues when I was in college because I thought, "Lord, I'm living for You, and my teammates are out partying and this and that and the other. I'm trying to serve You and be a light for You, so I deserve better."

That is just the height of pride. Larry Crabb, one of my favorite authors, calls that a demanding spirit. We go to God, "Because of my efforts and my goodness, You should fix stuff for me." That is not Biblical. The Lord had to really break me from that mindset, and that was a long process.

I very naturally have a legalistic bent—where I'm keeping score, and as long as I'm living better than you, God should bless me more. I had so much pride that God had to deal with, pride about things I didn't even know about.

I think where we start to learn is when we go through adversity. If you don't go through adversity, you feel like, "Hey man, God is blessing me because I'm being obedient." That's just not a good place to be because that disrespects God's grace.

The other danger with that is I'm relying on my goodness and my obedience, and therefore if something difficult comes in, I really feel like it's God's responsibility to fix it, to make it better. I read Romans 8:28 a million times growing up. When things would go bad, you just say it's going to work out for good. What I believed that verse was saying is God is going to swoop in and fix it.

The more I read through the Scriptures, example after example shows something different. What it actually says is, "And we know that all things work together for good to those who love God, who are called according to His purpose." Look at Hebrews 11 and the hall of faith. These are the heroes of our Christian faith, and God did not swoop in and fix it for them. None of them received what had been promised in this life. It was about eternity. I remember my preacher in Georgia, he said Romans 8:28 should never be taught without attaching Romans 8:29 with it, which says, "For those God foreknew, He also predestined to be conformed to the image of His son."

The good that God wants to work—in other words, Romans 8:28—is 100 percent true. It's a promise, and He's going to work it for good, but the good does not necessarily mean He's going to just fix it. The good is He's going to conform me to the image of Jesus. That's what God wants to do, and that might mean walking me through something that is really hard. I didn't understand that because when things go wrong, you think, "I'll pray, and God makes it better." That's not the way that it works. God will oftentimes lead us right into hard things. Right through it.

In Philippians 3:10, Paul said, "I want to know Christ and the power of his resurrection." If we stop that verse right there, everybody says, "Amen, sign me right up." But then Paul says, "And the fellowship of sharing in His suffering," because that's how we learn to become like Him. But until you experience adversity, you don't understand that. You just think you are being rewarded for your obedience and good behavior.

Lisa: When you accept that and embrace it instead of fighting it, it changes everything. Instead of fighting it, you say, "Okay, God, this is what You are allowing, and I'm going to trust that You will work this together for my good and ultimately Your glory."

Marc: In Shattered Dreams, Larry Crabb wrote, "As long we view our purpose on this earth as being to have a good time, to have soul pleasure exceed soul pain, God becomes merely a means to an end, an object to be used, never a subject rightfully demanding a response, never a lover longing to be enjoyed. Prayer and worship become utilitarian, a cunning strategy to get what we want rather than a passionate abandonment to someone far more worthy than we.

"Happy people, though they are right to be happy, face a subtle danger. They tend to spiritually gloat to publicly express gratitude and praise for the good things they enjoy while privately thinking these blessings are their due."

That just hit me between the eyes because that was me.

Marc with Blackhawk alumni • January 2022

In the Blackhawk locker room with his 2021-22 team

CHAPTER 26

Narrator: *Lisa Morlan has been a Blackhawk Christian parent since her sons, Joey and Zac, entered kindergarten, and they are now in their 20s. (Joey became an assistant coach on Marc's staff in 2018.) She also attended Blackhawk from third grade through eighth grade before going to Northrop High School. In addition, the Morlan family has been part of the Blackhawk church for more than 40 years, all of which gives Lisa an interesting perspective on Marc's impact on the school and the church, and especially on her kids.*

We knew of Marc because he coached at Lakewood Park, and he came to Blackhawk the summer before Joey's junior year. When Marc came, he was this larger-than-life guy who did the Strongman competitions, and the kids just connected with him right away. He was this big guy, but he was a gentle giant, even on the court coaching. He would get onto the kids and challenge them, but he was approachable and accessible, and he lived what he spoke. He didn't speak one thing and then step on the court and all of a sudden become this raging, crazy coach. I think the kids respected him for that.

I saw Marc instill a confidence in the kids he coached because he didn't over-coach them. Marc just let them play, and the kids knew what their roles were and what they could and couldn't do. He encouraged them and wasn't super critical. He was like that with all the kids. "This is your strength; go do it."

His absence is just felt on these guys' hearts because they loved him so much. You don't always love your coaches because you don't always develop those kinds of relationships. You always want your kids to know they can depend on their coaches, and they all did with Marc. I've watched my kids depend on Marc for so much through high school and college. When Joey was playing in college, Marc may not have been there physically, but he was always there watching on the computer and sending notes of encouragement after games. He always stuck with his kids, because they were always his kids.

And then to get to watch this last year where Marc depended on Joey, and to see how Joey stepped up to help with practices in the fall when Marc was in Arizona ... It was just all that Marc instilled in Joey, and it just made me so proud to know that ... Joey just loves him so much, and he just loved being able to help in that situation.

The other thing that is cool for me is that I first became closer to Marc because of when he came to Blackhawk. I coached the eighth-grade boys basketball team, so I was on his coaching staff, and we got to talk basketball and offenses. I once had a parent conflict, so that night, I called Marc and let him know what had happened. I never felt like I was a female coaching a boys sport, but I did that time. Marc called the dad in the next day, and he quoted Bible verses about what being Biblical means and respecting authority. He supported me 100 percent, but he brought it all back to Biblical things.

When I coached Frankie the next year, Marc never, ever said anything about any part of the coaching. It was always 100 percent supportive. About the only thing he ever suggested was to inspire me to be more eager to share my faith and pray with the kids.

Zac, who is 2 years younger than Joey, played basketball when he was in eighth grade, but he never played for Marc. He was in the program for a year; Zac was 6 feet 5 and a big, but it just wasn't his thing. He got involved in theater, and he was in all the plays, and he is amazing with computers.

Like he was with so many of the Blackhawk kids, Marc was still interested in Zac even though he was no longer part of the basketball program. The whole school goes to the plays, and Marc would tell Zac, "Z-Mo, that was amazing! You made that play so much fun!" He always gave Zac the affirmation that he gave his players.

It wasn't just the basketball players he was invested in; he was always invested in the other kids, as well. That always made me feel so good. Zac was kind of a quiet kid in high school and didn't find his niche until he got involved in theater. Then his senior year, he took a weightlifting class with Marc, because not being an athlete, he knew Marc would always challenge him. His best story about Marc is that they went somewhere where they were getting rid of one of those huge Universal machines, and they had to take it all apart to get it into Marc's van and take it back to school. He and all the boys carried it upstairs and put all the pieces in the weight room.

Marc quickly realized he had no clue how it came apart or how it would go back together. Zac comes into weightlifting class, and Marc said, "Z-Mo, I have no idea how to put this together." So Zac goes online and finds the schematics, and he was in charge of rebuilding that machine. Marc told me, "It would still be sitting there in 800 pieces if Zac hadn't done that." I think back as a parent about the confidence that gave Zac, and Zac knew how proud Marc was of what he did.

Before that, during Joey's senior year in high school, Marc asked Zac to become their videographer for basketball. It gave Zac a place of belonging, and without really thinking that was what he was doing, that's what Marc did.

He was always willing to do things like that for kids, because doing what was best for the kids was the most important thing to Marc. If that meant having 15 players around, and even if that one kid really struggled athletically, if it would help that kid, then that's what they did.

I told Joey the other day, "I've seen you do more than just live your life in the last year. I've seen you, through helping Marc, live your faith." He did a devotion for the team around Marc, and now he's the one who is doing devotions about the kids, and the kids are reaching out to him. I attribute that to Marc's coaching and building relationships and being there for the kids.

You don't just step up and do what Joey did for the heck of it, you do it because the person you love so much instilled that in you and needs you.

Even though they are 25 and 23, Marc was still impacting my kids. The last thing he said to my boys was, "Always follow Jesus." As he's on his death bed, he was telling my kids one last time, "Just follow Jesus."

BRAVE AT HEART

What has made my heart content is the understanding that we need to appreciate and love the ten years Marc was a part of our family, not be sad about what we missed and what could have been. We need to be happy for the time we had with him.

Marc with Zac and Joey Morlan

CHAPTER 27

Narrator: *After COVID-19 halted a chance at back-to-back state titles in 2020, Blackhawk Christian was fired up for a chance at another title in March 2021, this time moving up to Class 2A. The 21-3 Braves were playing great basketball, beating some very good teams on the road over the season's final two weeks. Then, two days before senior night, Marc was told the cancer had spread to his lungs. That led to a conversation with God as Marc set up the orange traffic cones in the school parking lot at about 1 a.m.*

Marc: That night was raw, really raw. We had a really sweet prayer time after the game, players prayed over me, parents did, colleagues did. It was really powerful.

I'm walking around out there crying out to God. The thought that came to my head was, "There's more for me to do. There's more." I know He can heal me from this if He chooses, but I was pleading with Him. "God, in Your mercy, I want to be around, please."

As Marc and Lisa have done throughout their lives, they leaned into their faith. It's one reason why they chose to settle down and build careers at Blackhawk Christian, a place where they are encouraged to testify to others. Marc saw his illness as an opportunity, not to deal with his own adversity but to help others with theirs. During an interview the week before the state title game, Marc told how even more he was utilizing his favorite Bible verse, Colossians 3:23: "And whatever you do, do it heartily, as to the Lord and not to men."

Marc: I've used that verse so many times on myself, on my kids, on kids that I've coached. ... Everybody has heard me use that verse, usually with the little things, the simple, the mundane, the routine, that there's a purpose in everything and doing it well. I've been using that verse lately to relate to big things like dying. That's a big thing. I'd never thought of Colossians 3:23 as it relates to dying until about three weeks ago, and I've been thinking about it a lot since.

I think it was C.S. Lewis who said, "He speaks to us in our comforts but screams at us in our pain." I've always known God is with me, but right now, it's so much more palpable, and you can feel He's with me. All of the truths that I've known for many, many years, it's like they are all in bold print with exclamation points and highlighted and underlined.

I think about joy, which I've always talked to my family a lot about. I've always been told that joy is not dependent upon your circumstances, and I've always believed that in my brain. But right now, I feel it in (my heart). I'm overflowing with joy in the midst of this. I'm more aware of this joy than I've ever been going through this. From the time of Jesus, faith causes people to scratch their heads and say, "What is this? What kind of joy is this?" When you are going through something that is tough, you experience joy in a new way.

We talk a lot about the promises of Scripture, the promise of peace that surpasses all understanding, the promise of joy even in hard times, the promise of eternal life in Christ. We also have the promise of trials. Jesus said, "You will have tribulations." It's not if, but when. He also said, "Take heart because I have overcome the world." A lot of times we don't talk about that promise of suffering, but it's reality.

There's a Scripture that says, "When we are weak, then we are strong." The more you are in athletics, the more you are going to get humbled. It just happens, but I think God allows those things to ultimately point us to Him and to realize we were created for more than just this. That's something I try to express to our players, because when you are an 18-year-old high school kid, you think it's all about right here and right now. I'm just trying to get them to understand a bigger perspective and realize that ultimately, we were created to enjoy fellowship with our Creator.

When I got my initial diagnosis, I felt incredible peace from the beginning. We've had so many scans and reports and updates along the way. One scan, we got good news, out of how many? Literally every other one from a medical standpoint has been bad news.

When I got the final diagnosis, after the doctor delivered that news to me, I was not one shred more discouraged. It did not bother me in any way. The Lord has my days numbered, and that's not going to change. That just gives you an incredible peace.

The fight for self-sufficiency is something I've battled. I'm super independent. I wouldn't say it right out, but there have been a lot of times in my life where I spiritually kind of coasted. "I have a handle on things, and I'll call you when I'm in a jam." That's the posture of where my heart has been. There's something in all of our flesh that says, "I'm fine and I can do this." My experience in college helped me to realize I'm not fine. I need some help. It was so freeing to be able to admit that. Now I find it so much easier to live a life of God dependency rather than self-sufficiency. My natural bent is to say, I got this covered. The Lord has driven that from me, to where I know I'm lost without Him. With Him, we can do all things.

We talk about the freedom of surrender, but there's freedom in obedience, too. The answer is yes, now what is the question, Lord? That is the attitude I always want to be at, but I haven't always been there. They say God is way more concerned about our availability than our ability. He just needs somebody who is willing. You follow the Spirit's leading, and when you are living in obedience, you are more aware of those things.

The Spirit is prompting us all the time, but a lot of days, we are too busy doing our own thing to hear His voice or sense His leading. When we are fully surrendered, He creates those opportunities all the time. Faith is spontaneous. It's just like you get the interruption to your day, but God is saying you have to set this aside and do this right now. You can live there, and it's a powerful place to be. I think I learned that even in coaching. I knew God had called me to coach, and all the stuff I had been through was preparation for me to coach and mentor young men. Experiences I had opened my eyes and made me more sensitive to a player who is struggling. Now that's on my radar, and I can tell them I've been there.

God opens those doors, and those opportunities are all around us. When those kids walk in the doors, even at Blackhawk Christian School, they are coming in with hurts and stuff that we don't even know about. I always pray the Spirit helps us to be aware and know what is going on around us—for me these last months, especially. Like Peter said, "We cannot help talking about what we have seen and heard." God has brought me here, and He has been so good to me. The peace He has given me, I can't help talking about that. I just think there is such a freedom in that when we can learn to walk in obedience.

Success in the Christian life ought to be a measurement of obedience. That's what we are called to do. When you are living in tune with the Spirit, you allow Him to lead. In our flesh, we want to take the wheel and be in charge, but the Spirit has a way of prying our hands off of our stuff and so we can surrender and let go so we can walk in obedience. When you get to that point, there's no pride because you understand this is 100 percent the Holy Spirit of God working. This is not me, this is the power of God, and it really removes any kind of pride. You understand it's only Him and only because of Him. And that's a good place to be.

Marc helping harvest grapes in his coach's vineyard near Prissé in Burgundy, France · September 1999

CHAPTER 28

Narrator: *As the athletic director at Blackhawk Christian, Joel Cotton was not only Marc's boss but also his friend. Even after the basketball season ended, they communicated regularly as Joel checked in on his friend and kept Marc up-to-date about the search for a new coach.*

I had the privilege of knowing Marc Davidson on a personal level for six years. As a new athletic director in 2016, I showed up and met Marc for the first time, in the gym of course. As with anyone who had the opportunity to meet Marc, the first thing I noticed was his physical presence. He was a tall, strong and commanding presence in person. I found out over time that this physical presence was a small glimpse of the depth of his spiritual presence. There were many different settings where I was able to see Marc's presence spread into the lives of those around him.

Present in the locker room
"Therefore encourage one another and build each other up, just as in fact you are doing." **1 Thessalonians 5:11**

The locker room is a sacred place in basketball. The most intimate moments between team members and a coaching staff take place in this space. It is private, and it can be powerful. Marc used this space in such a unique and personal way by empowering his players and coaches to encourage each other through triumph and defeat.

After each game, the team circles up and wraps their arms around each other for a session called "Put-ups." This is a time when members of the team and coaching staff take turns offering to "put-up" or encourage someone else in the circle. This goes on as long as the moment demands, and Coach Davidson made it a priority to allow this space for the growth of relationships on his teams.

I was present in a few of these locker room settings, and they were some of the most powerful interpersonal conversations I have ever witnessed. I saw teenage boys pouring out their hearts to each other and to their elders in moments of raw emotion. I heard boys telling each other how much they love each other. I heard coaches telling the boys how much they had learned from their students. None of this comes naturally from young men, but it was encouraged, supported and even demanded by Coach Davidson as a staple of his locker room. I am convinced that these relational moments on his team strengthened his groups more than anything else that he could do on the court. Players and coaches can sometimes hide their true feelings behind their skill or accomplishment or failures. In these moments, there was no hiding, and Coach Davidson made sure that they were going to make encouragement a priority in the relationships of his team.

Present with children
"Jesus said, 'Let the little children come to me, and do not hinder them, for the kingdom of heaven belongs to such as these.'" **Matthew 19:14**

Marc Davidson exemplified what Jesus is saying in this short verse from the book of Matthew. He was always present in the moment with little children in his presence. I remember talking with him as he monitored his study hall on several occasions. He would be sitting at a table in the back of the commons, and we would be in conversation on something basketball-related. Often, a class of preschoolers would come down the hallway on their way to the gym for an indoor recess, and Marc would immediately turn his attention from our conversation to this line of preschoolers and proceed to fist bump them, call them by their names or nicknames, and smile and encourage them. He saw these kids and prioritized knowing them by name and acknowledging them. I don't know that most of us would stop a conversation mid-sentence and do the same, but that is what Marc did. And I can't say that I was offended in the least bit. In fact, it was challenging to see what was truly most important in that moment.

This impact on children I witnessed firsthand on many occasions with my own children. The Braves baseball team played at Parkview Field a few years ago, and we were invited into the club-level suite to watch the game. As my family entered the suite, Marc was sitting and watching the game. Immediately, he saw my three children and greeted them with those same fist bumps, names and nicknames, and words of encouragement. Furthermore, I think his attention totally diverted from the game itself to having personal interaction with my three kids for the next several innings. This was unique considering Marc's status as a high school coach and administrator, physical presence and obvious difference in age. He transformed into a child in those moments, and I am forever grateful because I know my children felt loved, respected and empowered by someone that could give those gifts to them.

Even on gameday with his game face on, Marc would not hesitate to stop and acknowledge my children. We were at Grace College this season minutes before the game, and our family was sitting a few rows behind the bench. It was literally moments away from tip-off, yet Marc stepped a few rows up in the bleachers to fist bump and call my kids by name and even ask them about what else they had done that day. Putting aside the game plan and game face in those moments brought this parent to shock and awe in a most powerful and impactful way. As Jesus did, Marc always let the little children come to him and did not hinder them, recognizing that the kingdom of heaven belongs to such as those.

Present in his task
"Whatever you do, work heartily, as for the Lord and not for men."
Colossians 3:23

It became well known in these last couple of months that Marc loved Colossians 3:23 and lived this out during his life. He worked hard at whatever he did. He let his very life be used as an offering to God to use his talents and abilities FOR the Lord's work. He did not do anything for the approval of men. He did not seek any attention for the glory of himself. He tried to point everything and everyone to God. He was always present in the task that was before him.

In the first few years of knowing Marc, I would describe his task as being a teacher, a coach and a Strongman competitor. These things occupied his time, and he worked hard at all three of these things and used them for the purpose and glory of God. However, these three things also were simply earthly tools that Marc used. The greatest tool and gift that God had blessed Marc with was the gift of evangelism. He would not shy away from sharing the name of Jesus with anyone he encountered through his earthly tasks. This, too, became more publicly known during his last year of life through his cancer battle. Marc used his coaching platform to bring the Gospel of Jesus into the mind of both teams and coaches by having team huddles at center court after each game. Though his physical strength was failing rapidly, he prioritized this task because he was convinced that God would use this platform to bring others to know Him.

As his physical strength and body failed him, Marc could have easily and understandably started to fade away into a more private space, but he vulnerably showed all of us an undying commitment to live out his God-given task in the time he had left on earth. He truly worked with all of his heart to glorify his Lord and Savior Jesus Christ while on earth.

Marc and Joel celebrating with the team after Blackhawk's 2021 semi-state win

CHAPTER 29

Narrator: *One thing getting sick re-emphasized to Marc was the need to have an eternal perspective on life. It's something he lives and talks to others about all the time, including to his players. Part of that is discussing how he debated and initially felt anger at God over his diagnosis.*

Marc: To me, that was part of learning how to pray. I've never prayed as earnestly as I have the past year and a half. I've been praying virtually my whole life, but not to the depth He has taken me. I think part of that is He wants us to be real. And so, I definitely wrestled with that. I go back to Jacob wrestling with God for an entire night, saying, "I'm not going to let go until you bless me." I don't know if I took it that far, but I think God wants us to pour our hearts out to Him anyway. He knows what's in there, and He's not going to be shocked. I do think it's okay to be angry, and there are things that should make us angry. Even with cancer, that's the result of sin and the fall, and it's not God's plan. I think it's healthy to be angry at those things and what sin and destruction have brought into this world.

My pastor used to talk about bitterness and not allowing the roots of bitterness to spring up in yourself. He described bitterness as a nursed anger. We can be angry, but God wants to help us through that. He wants to help us process that. He's done that for me, I know.

The really hard piece in all of this is family, and there I really struggled. If I were a single man, I think I'd have a very different view on this. Feeling the responsibility of wanting to be there for my wife and kids, that weighs on me. You immediately go to, "What is going to happen to Lisa, and what is going to happen to the kids?" The Lord really spoke to my heart and brought me to a place of peace to where I know He's going to take care of everyone. I've been able to rest in that. I do think it's okay to be angry, but God wants to move us from that and help us grow through it. It definitely helped my prayer life to really get real to where I haven't prayed like that before.

I go to 2 Corinthians 4:18: "Fixing our eyes not on what is seen but what is unseen. What is seen is temporary, and what is unseen is eternal." That's our challenge because in our flesh, we want to see the here and now and deal with the tangible things we can see and touch, but the Spirit is calling us into this spiritual realm where we are trying to see from God's perspective. That has helped at least get me closer to that direction and seeing things the way He does.

The Scripture 1 Corinthians 13:12 says, "For now we see in a mirror dimly, but then face to face. Now I know in part; then I shall know fully, even as I have been fully known." Now we see dimly, but one day we are going to see things clearly as they really are, and we will be like Him because we will see Him as He is. On some level, we are not like Him because our view of God is somewhat distorted. As we deal with trials and wrestle through anger, I think He helps us develop that perspective where we can get closer to see how He really is, and that's how He makes us like Him.

Lisa: I think about what Marc shared in the locker room after winning last year, that someday this is all going to burn up, and this trophy doesn't really mean much in light of eternity. Some may think that is such a killjoy attitude at that moment—let the kids celebrate—but I think that it was such a beautiful opportunity for Marc to share that this big accomplishment, as amazing as it was, won't bring lasting joy. God gave Marc that eternal perspective before we even knew anything about his cancer! And so of course it has guided how he lives and coaches every day, to point his players toward living lives with an eternal perspective.

Marc: We did that in 2019. I shared the same verse in 2021. In 2 Peter 3:11, it says, "Since everything around us is going to be destroyed like this, what holy and godly lives you should live, looking forward to the day of God and hurrying it along." If you back up to 2 Peter 3:8, the verse says, "A day with the Lord is like a thousand years. The Lord is not slow in keeping His promise. He's patient with you, not wanting anyone to perish. Since everything is going to be destroyed in this way, what kind of people ought you to be? You ought to live holy lives." My point to them, when we had the trophy on the floor, was, "That's a beautiful trophy, fellas, but you know it's going to be destroyed one day." I just wanted them to get the perspective that it's so temporary, and we've done other things to remind them of that in the past. I just wanted them to understand that eternal perspective. That trophy is never ultimately going to satisfy you; your relationship with Christ is ultimately all that matters.

Lisa: Coming from a place where Blackhawk had all this success—both the 2019 and 2021 state championships—and here they are at the pinnacle, literally right after winning state, back in the locker room, and Marc knows it doesn't bring lasting satisfaction or joy. Winning state had been a lot of these boys' (and their family's) dream come true, including our family! But even the next day, you realize that it doesn't bring a lasting satisfaction. Sure, it feels good to know that we held the prized title of "state champs," but there's got to be more to life than just chasing after dreams and working hard to achieve them. In the middle of their victory celebration, Marc pointed his teams back to Jesus. He kept the main thing the main thing. Only what's done for Christ will last. Keeping an eternal perspective changes everything!

We have been so blessed to have people reach out and send texts, Facebook messages, emails and cards in the mail letting us know how God has used Marc to encourage them and point them to Jesus. Just yesterday (the day after Marc relinquished his coaching duties), a friend reached out and shared about her husband, who isn't a believer. "About two weeks ago, he came to church with us. He pulled up the Bible app. The seeds your family has planted extend much farther than you know, sweet friend."

Hearing that makes me say, "OK, Lord, You've got this. You are at work beyond whatever we can imagine and doing so much more than what we can see." My feelings turned from feeling cheated and robbed of precious years with Marc to, "Wow, Lord, I am humbled and honored You are using Marc in such a huge way." To trust Him with how He is using Marc's cancer to impact lives for eternity, that eternal perspective, that brings me peace to know His bigger purpose and plan. The pain of walking through this with Marc still hurts, but I trust what God is doing and know that He is the God who makes beauty from ashes, the kind of beauty that lasts for all eternity.

Marc: You have a sense of anticipation, of "OK, God, what are You going to do today? We are along for the ride. Show us what You want to do through us." When you live with that sense of anticipation, it's exciting because you know He's at work.

Lisa: I had another friend share a conversation she had at bedtime with her 8-year-old daughter, who Marc had in gym class. She shared the beauty of this conversation because her daughter saw Marc on Sunday and realized how much weight he has lost. "Mom, I know with a million billion percent that Coach Davidson is going to be with Jesus. I'm going to be sad, but we talked about it today, that with Jesus in heaven is where we want to be. I'll see him there one day." The beauty of seeing what God is doing with an 8-year-old's heart is amazing.

Marc: The last four years, I got to teach the kindergartners and first graders, and then seventh through twelfth graders, so I know every kid in that school. It's pretty neat when you get to touch that many people and get to know them.

There's a tendency to procrastinate when you feel like you have time. When you know you don't have much time, you understand the urgency of the Gospel. That person is in my life for a reason, and they need Jesus, but we have a tendency to say, "I'll get around to it." You understand that urgency of the Gospel and the urgency of making amends. If you have something against somebody or they have something against you, you just want to deal with that immediately. Don't put that off.

Lisa: The eternal perspective for me is also knowing and understanding that healing is coming either on this side of heaven or the other. Maybe some people don't feel like prayers are being answered, but we know healing is coming.

There have been dozens of times during their lives when the Davidsons can point to how the eternal perspective helped them trust God in confusing, uncertain times, such as coming home from France to coach at Trinity before Marc's mother was diagnosed with the cancer that would cause her death, losing a job at Aurora Christian, becoming convinced to adopt the twins and trusting the Lord's time on when to adopt, etc.

Lisa: I think about Joseph in the Old Testament, looking at his life and what he went through. We can see the end of the story and say, "Okay, it was worth it. God's hand was through it all. He did work all things together for good and for His glory." There was a lot of yuck and a lot of pain, but we can see the beauty of God's plan through all the pain. We've been so blessed from the get-go of our marriage. Right from the start and every single year, we have had to wait to see where we'd end up, if Marc would re-sign with the same team or if we would move to a new one.

I remember especially having such peace at the time when Marc lost his job at Aurora Christian, knowing this didn't catch God by surprise. He allowed it for a reason and for a purpose. It seriously filled me with such hope in the midst of such confusion. "Where does He want us? If not here, where?" We would have missed out on so much if we had been grounded in our own plans instead of trusting Him and His plan for our lives.

Marc: My surgeon texted me the night before my surgery and shared 2 Chronicles 19 with me. Jehoshaphat was leading the Israelite army, and there was a massive army that was after them and was about to annihilate them. He prayed and said, "I don't know what to do, but I have to keep my eyes on the Lord." The Lord said, "This battle is not yours, you don't even need to fight. You stand your ground and watch My victory."

I initially thought wanting God's victory was watching Him heal me. I still pray for that, but there have been a million little victories over this whole journey. I'll just sit back and say, "God, I can't believe the things You are doing. I don't want to miss all those victories because I'm thinking about healing." He's done a big shift in my heart on that. I don't want to miss all those other things that He's doing.

He's opened my eyes to say, look at all the victories that Jesus is doing.

Lisa: God has been in it every step of the way, there's no doubt about it.

CHAPTER 30

Narrator: *Gary and Lotus Furst have known Marc Davidson from when he started as the head coach at Blackhawk in 2013. Their son, Caleb, was in the fifth grade at that time, and he was already tall. Under Marc's tutelage, he became Indiana's Mr. Basketball in 2019. The Fursts' three sons—Nathan, Caleb and Josh—all attended Blackhawk. Caleb and Josh played for Marc while at Blackhawk, but most importantly, they learned life from him.*

Gary: According to Mark Twain, "The two most important days in your life are the day you are born and the day you find out why." Coach Marc Davidson knew his "why," or his purpose. Marc knew his ultimate purpose was to walk and talk according to the teachings of Jesus. The book of James provides that faith without works is dead, and Marc "worked out" his faith through specific actions between the lines on the court but, most importantly, outside the paint. When asked to reflect upon Marc's life and his journey, he consistently demonstrated and exemplified three attributes: He was fearless, he was a fighter and he was consistently faithful.

Fearless – With respect to fearless perspective, I never knew of anything that Marc wasn't willing to go ahead and attempt to conquer. There was not a team inside or outside of Indiana that he wasn't willing to go ahead and play. He leveraged our school's independent status to play a variety of teams and was willing to play any time at any place. Marc did not want the team's success to be confined to a 1A or 2A bubble. Marc knew the only way you could grow was if his players were stretched, and he was really willing to stretch the boys in that regard.

When Caleb was entering his freshman year of high school, Marc planned an overseas trip to Macedonia. Admittedly, I was concerned about Caleb traveling overseas, even if he was going with the team. I'll never forget that Marc put me at ease when he said (in only the manner in which he could): "Gary, I'll be with them all the time, and just remember, for anyone to get to them, they'd have to go through me." Marc's comments were reassuring not because he literally was a strong man with a huge physical presence, but because I knew he was even stronger and more determined on the inside.

I also witnessed Marc fearlessly and intentionally pursue some students "on the fringe" or who others had perhaps given up on, given their behavior issues. Marc never gave up on them. I watched him from the sidelines engage and invest in them. I witnessed Marc, with his big physical presence, just walk over and put his arm around those kids, look them in the eye and engage with them. Marc met all kids, but especially "at-risk" kids, where they were located. Marc never saw a soul that he was unwilling to invest in. He understood that everyone had intrinsic value and worth. Marc never gave up on others and fearlessly and tirelessly pursued those at risk so that they may find the purpose that Marc had discovered.

Fighter – Throughout his life, I witnessed Marc being willing to fight for what is right. He had a strong sense of integrity and would do what was right at all times. Sometimes, I believe that some people may think Christian athletes are timid or that they are weak; however, humbleness and meekness do not equate to weakness. One of Marc's favorite verses was 2 Timothy 1:7, which provides: "For God did not give us a spirit of timidity, but of power, of love and self-discipline." Marc was anything but timid, and he believed that the basketball court was a means by which to mold and grow boys into men. The success that he and the Blackhawk program had provided a platform for him to share his testimony and his "why." And, while we'll never know Marc's impact absent the success and winning record, two state championships provided him with a platform to share with others his story, his purpose and his desire to fight very hard until the end. Because he stayed focused on fulfilling a higher purpose and working as to the Lord in all things, he fought extremely hard and held others to a very high standard of excellence.

Marc's high standard of excellence and his eternal calling made him a seasoned fighter who at times may have seemed more like a military drill sergeant rather than a basketball coach. I saw him "lay into" Caleb and Josh a number of times from the sidelines. If, for example, Caleb wasn't ripping rebounds like he was capable of doing, Marc made sure Caleb (and others) knew about it. Marc's standard was absolute aggression, and the one thing he didn't have any tolerance for was half-heartedness. He inspired his team to give it their all, at all times, and fight to win while playing with purpose.

Lotus: Marc always wanted excellence out of his players, and he could get Caleb to pretty much do anything with the right inspiration. I remember a game at Fremont. Caleb had been sick that week, but Marc didn't know that. Caleb was loafing, and we were already going to win that game anyway, but Marc called a time-out and lit into Caleb, not in a bad way. Part of the reason Marc could do that is because Caleb knew that Marc loved him. He loved all the players so much that they all wanted to do their best for him, but he wanted them to do their best because they were there to glorify God in their play. Caleb took with him that desire to strive for excellence and for a higher purpose.

Gary: Faithful – The baseline for all of Marc's actions or his "why" was his faithfulness to his Lord. How he went about coaching and living as a fearless fighter was driven by his eternal faith perspective. He didn't want his faith to be heard; he intentionally wanted to live it. He gave his Lord and Savior all the glory. He did so not only on the "peaks" (e.g., immediately after winning state championships). He ran the race and wanted to finish strong and expressed a desire to sprint to the finish line. That's exactly what he did in any valley and even as he entered the "valley of the shadow of death" (Psalm 23:4).

After Blackhawk lost the regional final this past year to a very talented team, Marc was consistent. Marc, the team, the parents and the fans had it scripted differently, and there was great disappointment and sadness in realizing that was Marc's last game as a Blackhawk coach. It did not seem right for Marc's last game to end in defeat; however, Marc remained consistent in this valley. He ended with a loss, but he was nevertheless faithful and consistent throughout and still had an eternal perspective.

Lotus: Marc's actions and leadership also influenced Caleb during a valley of life. I heard Marc's voice when Purdue lost to St. Peter's to end Caleb's freshman season. I really didn't get to talk to Caleb after the game. I eventually called him later that night, and I said that I was so very sorry. While Caleb was extremely disappointed, his response echoed his former coach when he said, "Mom, there are much more important things in life than winning a basketball game. That is not how we are defined." I immediately texted Lisa regarding Caleb's response because it reminded me of Marc's example. She simply responded that there was "no greater joy than when you see your children walking in and living out the truth."

Gary: The last time I saw Marc was on the Friday before he passed away. In that circumstance, Marc continued his faithfulness. I went to his house to provide something to his brother, Matt, who was visiting with their father. I ended up getting there a little later than I anticipated due to traffic. As they were leaving and during the additional window of time caused by the delay, Lisa called us back in and said Marc wanted to talk to me. They had invited me into the house, as well. What I observed was Marc saying "goodbye" to his dad and his brother for the last time. In only the manner in which Marc could do, he did so by hugging them and praying for them. In some respects, I felt as though I should not be present during such an intimate moment, but it created a lasting impression upon me. Marc was literally in the valley of the shadow of death, but he was not walking, he was sprinting to the end. When it was my turn to talk to Marc, I said, "Marc we're going to do this differently and we're going to pray for you now." Thereafter, Marc gave me one of his big ole hugs, and I told him that I loved him and appreciated the investment he had made in others and, in particular, my family.

Marc Davidson was a great role model and has influenced at least two of my sons more than any other person. Words cannot suffice to express our gratitude for what Marc has meant to our family. He taught, showed and modeled to them how to be a Christian man. He taught them how to serve and lead. Marc led, coached and mentored others with a servant's heart and knew how to inspire and make them better because he wasn't ashamed of his relationship with his Lord and Savior. Beyond a shadow of doubt, I know Marc heard, "Well done, my good and faithful servant," shortly after entering heaven's gates.

Lotus: The way he invested in our boys, my children would not be the same people they came to be if it hadn't been for Marc's efforts with them. He molded Caleb into a man, and it was such a blessing that God gave us Marc—who went to a Big Ten school and played at the college level—so he could share those experiences with him. Caleb had a lot of peaks and valleys during his freshman year, and he handled that all so well. I believe that Caleb's response to those circumstances was a direct result of Marc's training. Marc talked to Caleb all those years about his experiences as a Big Ten player at Illinois and how he made basketball too much of an idol at that time. Marc reiterated that he and Caleb were meant to define the game, not have the game define them.

Marc has really influenced boys to carry on his legacy as young men. I know that there will be a positive ripple effect over the years from these young men that he has coached. As a woman, I hope people have expressed how meaningful it is to watch a man love his wife the way he loves Lisa. The way he would go up to her and embrace her and give just a soft kiss on her forehead after games. He's always spoken so well of her in anything, calling her Queen. It was sweet, and I am thankful that I and others got to witness his love for his bride.

Marc at Caleb's signing with Gary and Lotus Furst • November 2020

CHAPTER 31

Narrator: *One of the most amazing things about Marc and Lisa's relationship is that even after 32 years, he felt and wasn't afraid to show that seeing her always excited him as much as it did when they started dating. He often told her that he loved her more than ever. Here are Marc's observations about Lisa.*

Marc: I was really introverted as a kid and did not talk to girls hardly ever. I didn't know what to say to them, so I just kind of avoided them and threw myself into basketball. Lisa, of course, was very outgoing, which obviously for me was a very attractive trait because I knew if I had to carry the conversation, I was going to run out of things to say pretty quickly.

The timing of it all was neat because she was a statistician for the baseball team. We'd sit together on the bus, and we became great friends. We had known each other through classes, but that baseball season was really instrumental. That was my junior year, and she was about to graduate.

We started passing notes back and forth in class, and we'd sit together on the bus. I had never had feelings for a girl before, but it really started as a friendship. It didn't hurt that she was drop-dead gorgeous. That's really when it started to bloom.

It kind of snuck up on me. I just knew very quickly that I loved being around this girl. I loved it. We just started dating and hanging out and being friends. Then I got to know her family. I had known her dad from volleyball games and such.

After she graduated, Lisa had gone to North Park College for one semester, and then she went to the College of DuPage. She came down to Illinois with me my sophomore year. We actually lived in the same dorm, Weston Hall, on different floors.

After we got back together, it became really clear that she was the one. I do not want to live my life apart from her. That was February of 1994. I had no doubt in my mind, but of course, I had really hurt her. I knew it wasn't going to be, "Let's get back together and no problem." That first phone conversation was a couple of hours, and I'm apologizing and telling her how much I need her and want to be with her. She was naturally very hesitant, and I didn't blame her. I knew I had to prove it to her to rebuild that trust. I told her I'm willing to do whatever I need to do, because there is no doubt I want to be with you. I knew I was such a better person because of her, and I knew I wanted to be with her forever. It was a process to earn back her trust.

I think we both knew what we had was so special and how good we could be together. I even think that helped her parents because they were so welcoming to me, and they didn't have to be. They could have just grilled me, but her dad didn't give me a hard time at all, and I deserved it. We knew how special we were, and her parents knew that. We were so good together.

It's just one of those things you smack yourself in the head and say, "You're being an idiot." Sometimes, you don't always realize that. We don't always get things right. I didn't want to lose what we had. We had to make this work. She finally came around and took me back.

I wasn't 100 percent confident going into that first conversation. There were tons of prayers, and having Mindy there was helpful. She was helpful for both of us through that. Mindy handled that well. She wanted to smack me upside the head, but she didn't take that approach. She took that softer, gentler approach.

It wasn't, "Let's give this another shot and see what happens." I wanted to be with her forever. I just felt like it was pretty seamless. This is right. She's the one, and there's not a doubt in my mind. Once I was there, there was no question, and I was just praying that I could prove that to her.

As for talking to her dad about the proposal, I remember picking up her mom and dad from the airport after they had been on a vacation in March 1995. I was borrowing my buddy's car, which was a stick shift. We were in neutral as we're sitting in the parking lot of the airport. "Now that I've got both of you guys here, Mr. Bartley, I love your daughter, and I want to spend the rest of my life with her, and I'd like to request her hand in marriage." Dad is patting me on the shoulder, and Mom is reaching up and hugging me from the back seat. We take off, and I put it into first, and Dad puts his left hand on my knee several times with hard slaps. "We would be delighted to have you as a son-in-law," and every time he hit me on the leg, the car would dart forward. It lightened the moment. It was a special time. Her parents are amazing, and I have always loved her parents.

Lisa's dad is a fellow bargain hunter, and he had a connection to a guy with diamond rings. Dad and I went to see his buddy in downtown Aurora and picked out the ring. Once I got the ring, I was like, I'm not hanging onto this baby for long.

She had no clue. I never wanted it to be an obvious night where you are going to propose. I wanted to surprise her. This was Friday, April 7, 1995. I wrote a poem on yellow notebook paper. I put blood, sweat and tears into that poem. It was a legit poem, a page and a half long.

She drove up from Champaign, Illinois, where she was student teaching, and we went to a Christian concert, Clay Crosse and Kathy Troccoli at North Central College in Naperville. Then we went out to eat at Bennigan's. It was super late at night, but she hadn't had a chance to eat all day, and then we went back to the Bartley residence. Her parents were in bed.

Lisa went up to put her sweats on, and she was sitting in a chair in the living room below the front window. I came over, pulled out my poem and got down on a knee. I stammered through it, fighting back tears, but I couldn't wait to give her that ring. It took me a minute or two, and it took me a while to get through because I was struggling. I was so excited. It shocked the crap out of her. She had no idea.

She said yes, we hugged and kissed. Unforgettable moment.

I had absolutely zero reservations. None. I knew I wanted to be with her, period.

I think it's a process, you learn your spouse and you learn each other as you go, and that makes marriage so much sweeter and richer. We're still learning each other. The more you get to know each other, the sweeter it becomes.

Tommy Nelson says you have your honeymoon, then you have a period of disillusionment and then you reach commitment. You have to fight through that disillusionment phase. Who is this person? Once you reach commitment, it's such a beautiful place to be. You realize neither of you is perfect.

I hate when people say this is 50-50. It's 100 percent of her and 100 percent of me and 100 percent of Jesus leading us. That's the beauty of it. She sees life in a different way than I do, and I have so learned to value the way she sees things. She will see things that I never would have seen, and it's been so helpful for me, and I'm thankful for her perspective. My natural bent is to be extremely task-oriented, but she helps me see different things. She has helped me so much in seeing things from a better perspective and seeing a different way.

I've just really learned to value that, and it has become a precious thing. She has made me such a better person.

Lisa and I have learned to disagree, though it doesn't happen often. We see things differently and don't always agree, but we have gotten really good at being able to talk things through and work things out. When you know you are committed, you can have hard conversations, and it's okay. You are a team.

I love marriage, just love it. You hear people always spouting out these statistics about the marriages that don't make it. I hate that because this is God's instituted plan, and it works. I just feel like marriage itself is under attack.

One thing I have shared with all of my boys and with a lot of different people is the idea of the pyramid. The marriage pyramid looks like this: On the top, Christ is at the head, and that's what the Scripture teaches. The husband is at the base on one side, and the wife is at the base on the other. I tell young people, as you get closer to God, what happens to your relationship with your spouse is it becomes closer. We are living that right now. Both of us, our strength in Christ and our faith have grown exponentially as we have pursued Him together, and it has brought us closer. It really welds that relationship; without suffering, I don't think you can get to where Lisa and I have arrived.

She has that adventuresome spirit that I love. If she didn't have that spirit, I probably wouldn't have played in Europe or done a lot of things that we've done. Every step of the way, God has been right there.

She's always had that selfless servant's heart. That just has been magnified. I look at what she is doing and think, "How in the world are you doing everything?" She's been with me every step of the way, helping her mother get acclimated to moving to Fort Wayne, still teaching, doing everything around the house, still getting meals and in the middle of the night, she's over here grading papers. How are you doing this? To me, her selflessness and unbelievable care and love have been magnified. I've always known she's had that, but it's at a new level, and I'm seriously blown away by her.

We were so close before, I'm not sure how much closer we can get. This experience has taken us deeper. Our love is deeper still. We've always been such a team, always, but it's definitely gotten deeper.

She is such a giving person and has always been that way, so selfless, and she puts my needs and the needs of the kids before herself all the time. Just to watch her take care of me, take care of the kids, and then at night, I'm trying to sleep and the kids are crashed, and she's trying to get her grading done and her lesson plan done. She has just blown me away at getting everything done, and she does it with a smile and a joyful heart. It's like, how do you do this?

I've just seen the Lord at work in her, and she's such a woman of faith, and I know God is giving her a platform through this, too. She's had amazing conversations with friends and students. She just has a way of connecting with people. She's such a great listener, and she's so empathetic. It's been amazing to watch, not just the things she gets done, but the spirit in which she does it. It genuinely brings her joy to serve, and that has been inspirational to me, and to be the recipient of that has been unbelievable.

CHAPTER 32

Narrator: *Mindy Johnson is not only Marc Davidson's little sister (younger by two years), but she was also Lisa's roommate at the University of Illinois, even during the six months when Marc had broken up with Lisa. Somehow, with God's grace, everything worked out. Mindy even ended up marrying one of Marc's U of I friends, Marshall Johnson, in a relationship that was sparked at Marc and Lisa's wedding.*

I realized recently that I'm the only one that holds the title "little sister" to Marc, so I knew I had to give my perspective.

Our family was close growing up as our cousins were our neighbors and we lived in the country on a gravel road, so we had each other to play with. Marc and I had a typical sister/brother relationship until high school. I knew very well how to annoy him, and I did it often.

He was always very into sports. He'd go out with his bat and swing the bat in the driveway for hours. He'd pick up rocks and hit those as well. During basketball season, it was all basketball.

My mom loved to tell the story that she had just brought me home from the hospital, her precious daughter, and Marc threw the ball at me and said, "Play basketball, baby." She told that story a lot.

It was Marc, and he loved sports, and he was very dedicated to practicing and improving. He would literally take the ball with him everywhere just in case he wanted to get out and dribble, which he did at gas stations or when we'd stop at church—anywhere, really.

He had absolutely no concerns about girls whatsoever—until Lisa. In fact, he literally had a rule where on a game day, he wouldn't even speak to girls because it would distract him.

He was funny and always had an incredible memory. He and I watched Karate Kid endlessly one year, and we could probably go through the whole movie quoting it. Until the last couple of years when he was sick, any time we'd hear a song from the Karate Kid soundtrack, we'd call each other. Usually, it was Bananarama's "Cruel Summer." It was just a way that we'd share fond memories of childhood together.

We started to get a lot closer during high school. He started getting interested in Lisa, and I think he needed my advice on girls because he had absolutely no experience dealing with them. He would actually ask me to pick out his clothes when he was trying to impress Lisa. He was smitten with her from Day 1 and smitten on his last day, as I watched him fight to stay awake and alert just to "be with her" a little longer.

When he was really struggling at U of I with basketball, I know it was really tough on him emotionally. We all knew he was struggling, and I focused on letting him know that I couldn't care less about the Marc who was only about sports. He was my big brother, and I simply thought he was the best because of being him. I remember praying for him a lot and wanting him to know that. I just knew he needed to sort through some things, but it was tough when he and Lisa broke up for several reasons: First, we knew how good she was for him. Second, she had become part of our family. And third, she was (along with my other sister-in-law, Julie) my best friend.

We had already decided that we were going to room together, so it wasn't even a question when they broke up. Lisa and I are kindred spirits, and she is easy to love, so I never thought twice about it.

I adored my big brother and only wanted the best for him, too. There is a sibling bond that we have that I can't really explain. I somehow knew eventually they'd find their way back. They both casually asked about each other, and it was always in love that they asked. It's funny, he recently thanked me for that time, and I just thought, well, my goodness, that was easy. You are both so easy to love, and I love you both so much. (I think I may have embellished a few of Lisa's dinner dates with friends to make it seem like it was a boy when it may have just been friends, but—hahaha—it worked.)

One memory we just spoke about that was pretty cool is we both remember coming home from school one day in high school, and it was just the two of us. It was stormy but not pouring rain, just the sky was weird. We were almost home, and we spotted a tornado. We were out on a country road and just stopped the car and got out and sat on the hood of the car to watch it. I don't know ... it was weird because we weren't afraid. It was just a really cool thing to witness that kind of power. We both remembered getting home, and my dad was absolutely terrified about where we were and the tornado. I think it annoyed him that we were so cavalier. It was something Marc and I talked about in his last days, a cool memory that we both never forgot.

Marc actually was the catalyst for my husband and my relationship. Back before I started at U of I, Marshall and Marc were friends from InterVarsity, a Christian organization at U of I. They had a group of buddies from InterVarsity that would get together before classes, and they called themselves the Breakfast Club. Well, Marshall and Marc got to know each other there, and Marc mentioned to Marshall and me separately that we should meet. My first Sunday at U of I, Lisa introduced us, and we were just friends for 2 years, but Marc must have known something because we've been married for 25 years now.

The six of us—Matt and Julie, Marc and Lisa, and Marshall and I—are literally best friends. I think it's difficult for people to understand how close we are. I do believe a big part of that is our faith in Christ. We've literally grown up spiritually together, and "as iron sharpens iron, one man sharpens another" (Proverbs 27:17). It's been the six of us in Christian education, raising our children together, helping each other, loving each other. We all like to spend time together. I am so grateful for that. I recently thanked my brothers for picking the best girls in the world to be my sisters.

I really want to add this: As proud as I've always been to be Marc's sister, it was never because of the achievements. Through the cancer, that was even more evident, and I saw him grow exponentially spiritually. He was just really focusing on eternity. I saw him be humbled physically but to see it as the Lord's strength on display instead of focusing on his own weakness. My kids were able to see him absolutely LIVE OUT LOUD all that we talk about with our faith in Christ. That is something I thanked him for over and over in the past year. I was never prouder of him in all his life than in the last months.

I am so grateful to have had him for 47 years as my big brother. I will miss hearing him say "SISTA!!!" loudly in his raspy voice, but thank you, Lord, for the assurance of salvation. Because of Jesus, I will see him again!

Marc, Mindy and Julie • October 2021

Julie, Mindy and Lisa • 1994

CHAPTER 33

Narrator: Lisa truly is Marc's "Queenie." She supported him in so many ways, including his faith. She would have been justified to keep him all to herself over his final two years, but she always encouraged him to share his message with others, even until his final days. She's the definition of wifely grace.

Lisa: I came to Aurora Christian in fifth grade. Marc was a grade below me, so he was a fourth grader, but I don't remember noticing him until he was in sixth grade. He was just so cute. That hair and those long, floppy bangs, which he kept that way until high school.

He stood out from the rest of the boys. He was so tall; he was like a man amongst boys, and all the girls had a crush on him. He was the stud athlete that was just amazing at everything. Even though he didn't really talk to girls, he was friendly with a big smile and sparkle in his eye, but I don't remember talking to him until I was in eighth grade.

At that time, I was in volleyball and he was in soccer. We traveled to Rockford Christian for a volleyball and soccer tournament, and we were on the same bus. I wanted to talk to him, but I was too nervous. In high school, we had classes together, pre-calc and geometry, and that was the first time I ever had a class with him. I was a sophomore, and he was a freshman. We started passing notes probably my junior year, so there was a friendship that started then. I remember having a couple of small conversations with him. This was in 1989, so this was way before texting and social media.

I just always thought he was out of my league. He also just had this element of mystery to him because he didn't hang out with girls. You could tell he didn't feel comfortable talking to them, really. It wasn't until my senior year that we really started to interact, and I could tell that he talked and smiled at me differently than he did other girls. I had so much respect for him. Everyone in our school did; we knew what he stood for and believed in. He took his faith seriously and was not into any nonsense. That was not a part of Marc. I had so much respect for how he would give honor to God when he was interviewed. Little Aurora Christian was finally getting some media exposure, and here we had an underclassman talking about honoring God.

I thought he was so cool and talented, and he was the poster child for Aurora Christian. The whole school was so proud of him because he was fun to watch and absolutely dominated every game, and off the court, he was kind and respectful to everybody. He was humble and never carried himself like he was better than anybody, even after all of the attention that he was getting.

His dad was our principal and Bible teacher, and after my pastor, he was the second-most important spiritual influence in my life when I was growing up. I knew Marc was so much like his dad, and that attracted me to him all the more, knowing that was the kind of man I wanted to marry someday.

Even though I didn't know much about baseball, I asked his dad if I could be the stat girl for his baseball team. His dad was happy to let me have that role even though I didn't know what I was doing. I got to go on the bus and sit in the dugout with the team, and that was my opportunity to ask Marc for help filling in the scorebook. Our relationship just blossomed from there.

Marc: During a game, I would go over and talk to her, and that was extremely unusual for me. I saw it as an opportunity.

Lisa: Everyone was shocked that Marc was talking to a girl, and people could see that something more than just a friendship was starting. This was April and May, when seniors kind of think, "Really, do I want to get into a relationship with someone when I'm about to go away to college?" I was super excited about going to college in Chicago, but knowing Marc and the man of God that he was, he was absolutely someone I wanted to invest in a relationship with and see where it would go. I knew it would be awesome to end up with someone like him.

May 4, 1990, was our first date. We went to the old theater in downtown Geneva, Illinois, to see "Pretty Woman." That was the first time we held hands.

BRAVE AT HEART

He asked me to be his girlfriend on May 25, and he gave me his class ring. That was a big deal back then. It was so huge on my finger that I wrapped it in this North Carolina blue ribbon so that it would fit. I was so proud to be his girlfriend and so excited to be with him. We spent so much time together that summer. He'd milk cows early in the morning out by his house and then he would come into town to go to school, shoot around, work out and help with basketball camps. I had a summertime office job, and we would hang out at night. He surprised me on my birthday and took me to a Chicago Cubs game.

We had so much fun. His family invited me to go to family dinners and reunions. I would go to church with them at Helmar, and I remember people saying, "We've never seen Marc smile this big before."

One of the biggest perks of dating Marc was getting to spend time with his family. Matt and Julie were dating then, so we would often double-date. They were a year ahead of me at ACS, and Julie quickly became one of my closest friends. Mindy is three years younger than me, and she quickly became like a sister to me. She came to the University of Illinois when I was a junior, and we were even roommates my last two years of college.

It was really hard saying goodbye to Marc when I left for college. I'll never forget the night we said goodbye. We were both crying. When I went to North Park College, I loved it, but I was disappointed with all of the partying I saw going on. It really made me realize what a rare catch Marc was and made me want to be with him all the more.

I started at North Park in nursing and volunteered at Cook County Hospital on the pediatric floor. I was in the nursery, and it broke my heart to see the crack-addicted babies. There was a toddler I held that had been in a fire and had some damage to his vocal cords. I'd put him back in his crib, and he would be sobbing, and that broke my heart.

So after the first semester, I decided to switch my major to elementary education. I came home for a year and a half and went to the nearby College of DuPage.

Marc headed to U of I soon after he graduated from Aurora Christian in May 1991. Champaign was two and a half hours away from home, so we were officially in a long-distance relationship. And it made us even stronger. I went to every Illinois home basketball game. I would jump in the car and ride with his parents, and we'd go out to eat with Marc after games. Those were great memories.

I also went to many away games: Wisconsin and Minnesota, Indiana and Northwestern, Michigan State, Purdue. I had that bit of adventure in me. I didn't have much fear, so I wasn't afraid to drive by myself. My parents were so great at giving me the liberty and freedom to do that.

Marc's Grandmom Jackie ... she was the best. She loved us girls. There was Mindy, Julie and me, and her grandson Mike Mann was dating another one of my friends, Andrea, who he ended up marrying. So Andrea, Julie and I were dating Grandmom Jackie's three grandsons, and she was so concerned about our safety that she bought male mannequins and dressed them up in clothes so we could pose them as passengers in our cars on our trips to visit them. All three of us girlfriends felt very welcomed and embraced by the family.

Something I am so grateful for is that our parents made sure we were careful to guard every part of our relationship, and they were wise to hold us accountable so that we wouldn't slip into sexual sin. Marc and I both were committed to waiting until we were married to have sex. I do remember, though, thinking how much easier it would be for me to visit Marc at U of I if I could just spend the night in Marc and Corey's dorm room, legitimately just to sleep. But we all know how slippery that slope can get when we little by little cave on our convictions. If I was visiting Marc, our parents would ask where I would be staying. At the time, it felt like such an inconvenience, but we respected our parents and knew that their concern was from a place of love and wanting the very best for us, which meant helping us protect ourselves from temptation. There was one friend a couple years older than me from Aurora Christian who was also at U of I, and I would stay with her. I would go to InterVarsity with Marc on Friday nights, so I got to know a girl there, and I'd stay with her, too. I am grateful that even with the freedom we had being away at college, we still honored and respected our parents and trusted that setting those boundaries was for our own good. It wasn't easy, but we were committed to save that part of our relationship for marriage, and I am so grateful for the accountability we had. It made our wedding night and finally living together as husband and wife all the more special. What a priceless gift we were able to give each other!

My junior year, I transferred to U of I, and we were in the same dorm, Weston Hall. I was on the third floor, and Marc was on the second, and that was so much fun. I loved being at U of I in the dorm. We were right across from Memorial Stadium in the "Six Pack" (dorms), and there was always something going on there. I got plugged into InterVarsity right away. They do a great job connecting with people and inviting students into a small group Bible study. I loved to be in a place outside of the Christian bubble where people were following Jesus because they wanted to, not because it was expected or assumed. Marc and I loved meeting all different kinds of people on our floors. We loved getting to know people from all different cultures and backgrounds and beliefs. Our InterVarsity leaders, Mark and Kelly Ashton, challenged us to stay living in the dorms all four years of college because truly there is no other time in our life that we would have the opportunity to have conversations and relationships with people 24 hours a day, 7 days a week.

I loved being at U of I and was so thankful I was there. Marc was busy enough with basketball, and I was social enough that I think we had a good balance of time together and time with others. I could tell Marc was frustrated with basketball and disappointed mostly with himself. As for our relationship, we had so much fun dating in Champaign-Urbana. He would get per diem checks to cover meals over breaks and weekends, and we'd use those on our dates.

We had been a couple for three years, and then in the summer of 1993, after the year we were both at U of I together, my friends began getting engaged to be married that very next summer. I started putting that pressure on Marc, wanting to get engaged like a lot of my friends. But we were nowhere near ready to get married.

Marc actually broke up with me in July 1993. I was shocked because it was out of the blue. I cried the hardest I'd ever cried. He broke my heart, but I don't ever remember hating him. I never disparaged his character. He broke my heart, but I still thought he was an amazing man. I thought the world of him, but I thought, "OK, Lord, I'm going to trust that You've got the best for me." I truly wasn't trying or hoping to get him back.

I never would have said it at the time, but I did love him and put him in a place higher in my heart than I did God. I put so much of my value and identity in being Marc Davidson's girlfriend instead of finding my security and identity in being a child of God. I had taken a good thing and made it a god-thing. I realized I truly needed my identity and joy and contentment to be in Christ. He alone will always be there for me. Only God can perfectly love me, and that's when I came to understand that life-changing truth.

I honestly look back on it and am so thankful for the breakup even though it was the most painful thing I ever felt, because it made me realize Marc Davidson can't complete me. Only Christ can complete me. They say that there's a God-shaped hole in all of our hearts that only He can fill, and it is so true! We can try to fill that hole with great things, but only God can truly complete and fulfill our heart's longing to be loved. So after Marc broke up with me, I put God where He needs to be in my life: truly No. 1.

I didn't know what Marc was up to. He was at Trinity, and I was three hours away in Champaign. So I truly was moving on and trusting God with the future He had in store for me.

Eventually, with God's grace, Lisa and Marc were able to work out their relationship and get back together, stronger than ever.
Lisa: He is the real deal. This is where the rubber meets the road; when your life is out of your control and prayers are not answered in the way you are hoping for, what is your faith really made of? The Lord is his strength and his rock and his hope and everything. Marc's living that out at home and not just preaching it in the huddle, leading our family to trust in the Lord, too.

Mindy just brought up to me how disciplined Marc's been his whole life to add or drop weight and do all of these things physically. And now not to have any control ... he's at this surrendered place where he says, "My life is really yours, God. Use us to have an impact for eternity."

To see how God is using Marc now is so humbling and beautiful. I told him the other day I think he's the most blessed person I've ever known. What an incredible blessing to have people tell you the impact you have had on their life! So many people have reached out, including strangers and people we know on Facebook who we haven't talked to in years.

These people are taking the time to say how God used Marc in their life. Marc went into Christian education and has been committed to teaching and coaching in a Christian school because he wanted to make an eternal impact on kids' lives. And at the young age of 49, to be able to hear that is such a blessing.

I'm the most blessed girl in the world to have married him and have him be the father of our kids. It's been such an adventure to have him lead us as he follows Jesus. Our life is in God's hands, and to be able to see that play out, all the places He has led us to and through, has been amazing. I'm so grateful that Marc looks for the big-picture perspective and trusts in the Lord that He's going to lead us where He wants us. It's been a true adventure, and the greatest honor of my life has been to be his wife.

CHAPTER 34

Narrator: *The Davidsons decided before their marriage that they wanted a big family. Wes arrived 10 months after they were married and was followed on a semi-regular schedule by Will (called Billy when he was younger), Frankie, Marcus and Jimmy. Then in 2012, the Davidsons adopted Isaiah and Jaela from Ethiopia.*

Following are Marc and Lisa's observations about their children.

---- WES ----

Marc: We got married on July 16, 1995, then I headed out to Europe on August 20.

Lisa: Marc flew to Europe to try out for teams in Austria, Switzerland, France and Spain. He then was just waiting for a team to offer him a contract. We had just gotten married, and then we were separated by the Atlantic Ocean!

Marc: I said, I need to see Lisa, and then she flew over in early September.

Lisa: And that's when I got pregnant. Wesley arrived within our first year of marriage when we were in Saint-Étienne, not speaking much French and surrounded by French-speaking people. That was 1995, so before the era of having the internet to search every possible answer to our pregnancy questions. We didn't have a clue what we were doing. We had that book, What to Expect When You're Expecting, and we learned along the way.

Marc: Wes loves to be the center of attention. He still does, and we could see that early on. He would jump in front of the camera, where William would hide from the camera. Wes was all about, "Look at me and see me!" in a cute way. He's still got that life-of-the-party trait about him. He's super social, and he reminds me of Lisa the way he talks to people and connects with them. He's also very giving.

I asked him to help out at a basketball practice this morning, and he just brought an energy to the gym and got the kids fired up. If Wes is going to be there, you know he's going to infuse energy into whatever he has to give. It's just a wonderful trait. In high school, his teachers laughed because he was such a goofball, and he had a hard time taking academics seriously. In college, something flipped, and he figured out what he needed to do. There's a time to be serious, but he still is a huge jokester and loves to be the life of the party. He can be more serious than he used to be, but things are never going to get too heavy when Wes is around.

Lisa: He loves adventure and he's been blessed with so many opportunities to see the world. In high school, he went on mission trips with Marc to Ecuador and then twice to Panama. At Anderson, he went on mission trips to Atlanta, Dominican Republic and Argentina, and cultural trips to London and the Grand Canyon. Wes loves to discover new places and new people.

Marc: Part of that is we moved so often as he was growing up. He just rolled with the punches. He didn't complain. He just adapted so quickly to new situations. For him, it excited him to step into a new situation. He went to Dominion in Georgia for his seventh- and eighth-grade years, and then to Lakewood Park as a freshman and sophomore, and then Blackhawk for his junior and senior years. I think for a lot of kids, it would have been difficult, but he'd get plugged in when we'd go somewhere else. His approach to those moves really helped the rest of the kids. It was harder for William and some of the other kids.

The other thing about Wes, he just handles things differently. He and William played on the same summer basketball team. Wes was going to be a junior and Will a sophomore. They played for the same coach, and he's a holler-at-the-kids type of guy. They were in a tournament, and they didn't play well at all. The coach sent out a text message to the whole team and just lit them up. Will is very conscientious, so he got that text and was down in the dumps, and that really ate at him. Will and I talked through it, and I go to Wes, "Did you get that text from Coach?" He gets this foggy look. "What text? Oh, that. Yeah, I saw that." It didn't bother him like it did Will.

This is the seventeenth home that we've lived in, and he's been in sixteen of them. By the time he graduated high school, he had lived in sixteen different homes in two countries and four states and had gone to eight different schools. Wes has this adventuresome spirit. He loves to see new things and new people.

Lisa: He's always marched to the beat of his own drum. He wore a headband through high school and college. His free throw routine was dribble, dribble, dribble, kiss the ball and then shoot it! That was just Wes. He has always stood out in the crowd.

When he graduated from high school, he sent out resumes to every normal, good-paying place he heard of. He didn't hear back from anybody, but one day, he got a letter in the mail to come in for an interview with Vector Industries, which we had never heard of. He got all dressed up and came back home telling us he was hired and going to be selling Cutco knives! I about died when he came home from that interview and asked if I would please share all of my contacts with him. Sure enough, there were many Blackhawk moms that opened up their home for Wes to come over and give his presentation and who now have Cutco knives today because of Wes. But we can see how God closed doors to other first-job opportunities to put Wes in a position that forced him to hone his social skills. He worked for Cutco for two summers, which was a great experience to prepare him for his communications major.

He's so fun, he's the goofy fun brother, but he'll put his siblings in their place, too, if they need it. One time in Georgia, Marc and I went on a date, and we didn't get back until late, after the kids went to bed. Wes was an eighth grader, and Marcus was a first grader. They got to goofing around playing football in the house, and Wes tackles Marcus and drives him into the couch. He sent Marcus to bed with an icepack. We noticed it when we got home and came in to check on the kids, but we didn't think much of it. We got up the next morning to go to Marcus's Upward Basketball game that Marc coached. We had no idea what happened the night before. Nothing was mentioned about Wes maybe being a little too rough tackling Marcus the night before, but we could tell Marcus was hurting. Marc only had five players that morning, though, so he had to put Marcus in. The way he was holding his arm to his chest, it was clear something was wrong. So Marcus came out of the game, and we headed to urgent care to get it looked at. To our surprise, he had a broken collarbone.

Marc: Wes had given him ice cream and read him Diary of a Wimpy Kid to get him to go to sleep.

Lisa: And also to bribe him not to tell me and Marc about the little-too-hard tackle. We all laugh about that now.

Marc: Probably the best thing Wes has done for his brothers and Jaela is that he has adapted to all of our moves. He just rolled with the flow and didn't get worked up about stuff, and that example for his siblings is really powerful.

Lisa: We were blessed with the way Wes did it. They really have been smooth transitions, and he's been a big part of that.

Wes had a lot of success on the basketball teams he was on when he was growing up. He was so fun to watch. He brought an energy to the teams he played on, and he was a key player to their success. Wes set the single-game record at Blackhawk with 42 points and the career-scoring average record.

Marc: While he was at Anderson University in Indiana, Wes was on the basketball team. He also was an RA one year and then on the Campus Activities Board, a Chapel Usher and then he worked for admissions and took kids on campus tours. He sucked every last ounce you can get out of a college experience. He just dove into Anderson in all these relationships and opportunities. We were just amazed at how he was able to do all these different things.

His major was communications, but he got three minors: history, Christian ministry and marketing. He found some professors that he loved, and he wanted to be in their classes.

Lisa: Ashton is his wife, and she is awesome. She grew up at Blackhawk and was in Will's grade, actually, so it makes it extra special that she's known our family for years. Wes always had a crush on her in high school even though she had a boyfriend. When the two of them broke up her freshman year of college, Wes reached out to her as a friend. She went to Indiana Wesleyan University, which was about 30 minutes from Anderson, so they were able to find time to see each other quite a bit. It took a year or two, but then it switched to more than friends. They fell in love, and they are so fun to watch together.

She keeps him humble. She's spunky, herself, so they are so good together.

Marc: She lets him do his antics, and she rolls her eyes and laughs.

Lisa: They got married in May 2020. That was when the world was still shut down from COVID-19, so they weren't able to have the wedding or reception like they had originally planned. A close family friend, Lisa Morlan, told her dad about our dilemma, and he offered for us to have their wedding in his backyard. It was the most magical wedding. There were 39 of us, and it was a beautiful, intimate setting, in the middle of his backyard that was full of blossoming trees. You never would have known we were in the middle of Fort Wayne. It really emphasized what the wedding day is all about: the two becoming one. Nothing else mattered. We were just overjoyed to be able to gather together and celebrate the Lord bringing together Wes and Ashton.

It has been so amazing how Ashton quickly became a daughter to us. We love her heart for the Lord, for Wes and for our family. I am so grateful for Marc emphasizing over the years that our kids are supposed to leave us and cleave, cling to their spouse and become their own family. Wes and Ashton have done that, and it's so beautiful to see them choosing to follow the Lord for themselves.

---- **WILL** ----

Marc: Will is 15 months younger than Wes, and he is your classic overachiever. He aimed for perfection and would follow through on stuff. We'd be driving home from school, and he'd have his books out with his checklist. He's very task-oriented and driven as an athlete, a student and a follower of Jesus. He's the opposite of Wes as far as wanting to be the center of attention. He'd rather run away from the camera.

Lisa: I, being an only child, was amazed at how different kids who are raised in the same home with the same rules and structure can be! It all points to how God designs each of us uniquely. It's so evident to me now as our kids are older, I can see how God gifted our kids each differently, but I love to see that at their core, they have the same convictions and beliefs.

Marc: Will could talk at an early age and was so smart. He loved reptiles. When we moved from France to Michigan, we got a Planet Frog habitat and got him a tadpole. We finally got him a bearded dragon when we moved to Gurnee, Illinois.

Lisa: We were pretty certain when he was 5 that he would be a herpetologist when he grew up. He loved to read and learn. He loved to go to the library with my mom and check out books. He was born with a thirst for knowledge.

William would get every award growing up as far as academics, character, athletics, citizenship and spelling bee. Blackhawk has an awards ceremony on the last day of school, and an award for excellence is given for each subject. Will received so many of those awards his senior year. He was also named salutatorian of his class.

Marc: Will was gifted not just academically; he was a really good athlete. Sports came so easily for him. Wes and Will played on the same baseball team. William was younger than Wes and made the all-star team, and Wes didn't. They were probably 11 and 12. I was so proud of both of them, how they handled that. Will was like, "Wes, you so deserved it, you should be in there." At the all-star game, Wes was cheering for Will and handled it so well. Wes had his little notebook keeping score and cheering for his brother, and William was over there high-fiving Wes. It was just beautiful. That incident kind of summarized their relationship because they were just there for each other.

Lisa: Will had a hard decision to make about where to go to college. He loved the academic rigor that Wheaton College is known for, but he received a full-ride academic scholarship to play at Marc's alma mater, Trinity International University. After much prayer, he chose Trinity. He had such special memories from the two years that Marc coached there, when he was in third and fourth grades. He also had two cousins, Matt's children Luke and Macy, that were also attending Trinity at the time, so that was a big draw, too. After weighing the pros and cons and much prayer, he chose Trinity.

Will's freshman year at Trinity was special, and he got significant playing time. He loved his coach and teammates. They had a very special season, making it all the way to the NAIA national tournament in Branson, Missouri. But even after the incredible year he'd had, he still felt a strong desire to transfer to Wheaton.

Marc: He ended up going to Wheaton and majoring in history, but the best thing that came out of Wheaton College for Will is Sarah. She is amazing.

Lisa: Will didn't meet Sarah until he was in grad school. He had finished undergrad at Wheaton and returned for one year of grad school to get his master's degree in education.

When he was student teaching, he had to quit his on-campus job at the Office of Campus Outreach. He went back to the office to see who had replaced him, and it was Sarah. He met her in October, and I noticed over Christmas break that he was constantly texting her. Will invited her to his cousin Luke's house for a Super Bowl party in February 2020. After the game, they sat in the car, and he told her he was interested in being more than just friends. We could tell the moment we met her that she was genuinely a beautiful person inside and out, and her love for the Lord was so apparent.

Just a month after they had made things official, COVID-19 sent everybody home, which meant Will moved back home with us in Fort Wayne and Sarah went back home to Virginia Beach. They quickly began a long-distance relationship, both taking turns making the 11-hour trip to visit each other. Things got serious pretty quickly! They got engaged that September and were planning on getting married the following June.

But everything changed after Marc's diagnosis in late October 2020. Will was teaching at Hope Academy in Chicago, and Sarah was working and taking grad school classes at Wheaton. They both were experiencing quarantines and attending/teaching school virtually from their apartments. So in early November, just a week after Marc had surgery to remove his kidney and tumor, they decided to get married in 41 days, on December 13. Marc's dad married them. It was beautiful and so special after the world had shut down during COVID-19—and even more special with Marc, with the wedding being just six weeks after they had found his initial tumor.

They started looking into Christian schools in Latin America where they could teach. They found job openings at Asunción Christian Academy in Asunción, Paraguay. They were intrigued by Marc's stories of the couple of weeks he had spent in Paraguay back in 1993 visiting family members who were missionaries there. After weeks of praying, Will and Sarah felt peace about choosing ACA.

They left in July 2021 for Paraguay, where Sarah has been a first-grade teacher and Will has taught junior high and high school Bible and history. They teach in English, and they go to a Spanish-speaking church. They have fully embraced their life in Paraguay and have gotten very involved with the people they've met. They are so loved by their students' families!

Marc: Sarah's mom is from Korea, and her dad is from Wisconsin. They met as single missionaries in the Middle East, got married, and Sarah was born there before her family moved to Virginia Beach when she was 4. She took a gap year after she graduated from Regent University to teach a year in an international Christian school in her birth country before she came to Wheaton.

Part of what attracted them to each other is they both have this love for other cultures. When you've been to and lived in other parts of the world, you get it—and then throw in that eternal perspective.

Will and I have had some really good talks. He is still very conscientious. He is such a good writer and has a blog,

"Meditations of a Christian Millennial." He just has a mind, and he understands God gifted him with a mind he can use.

Lisa: That Bible verse is so true: There's no greater joy than to see our children walking in the truth. There is no greater peace than hearing and seeing our children making our faith their own. We desperately miss them and would love for them to be at all our things, but it brings us great joy to see and hear all the ways God is using them in Paraguay.

---- FRANKIE ----

Lisa: Frankie is almost three years younger than Will. It's just so fun to look back at the videos and remember how he was that cute, chubby baby who was kind of shy and would sit back and watch Wes and Will and all their shenanigans. He, too, was born in France, when Marc was playing his second season for Prissé. Actually, Marc was injured in October 1999, but the team was so amazing to let us stay until Frankie was born in July 2000. They were patiently and optimistically waiting for Marc to be able to play again. Marc's ankle wasn't improving after physical therapy, so he had surgery in February. He started thinking it was time to retire and head back to the States. So while we were waiting for Frankie to be born, Marc reached out to several Christian schools. He was interviewed over the phone and hired at a school we had never seen or been to, Macomb Christian, a small school outside of Detroit in Warren, Michigan. He was hired as the athletic director and head basketball coach as well as to teach some high school PE classes. We flew home at the end of July and drove to Michigan with three kids. It was a total leap of faith what we were stepping into. We had never been to Detroit, and we didn't know a single person there. But the Lord kept increasing our faith to trust Him with all of the unknowns our first five years of marriage. I am so blessed to do life with this man who together with me has trusted God to lead us each and every day.
The staff and families at Macomb were amazing. They immediately embraced our family, and they were in love with baby Frankie.

Marc: He was so cute and so chubby. We still call him Chubz to this day. His friends still call him Chubz.

Lisa: Frankie weighed 10 pounds when he was born, and he was even born three weeks before his due date! He was the cutest little chunk of a baby. Just so easy, laid back. There was always so much going on with two big brothers, and he was just content to sit back and watch. He's been an easy kid to raise.

Marc: He's really chill, and he reminds us of Lisa's dad with his laid-back temperament. He never gets rattled, just calm, and we can see it in his driving because he's always under the speed limit. He's a real calming presence and doesn't get worked up about much at all.

Lisa: He was always getting dragged to Wes and Will's stuff. He was just so easy that maybe he got lost in the shadows, but he was comfortable in his own skin. He's himself, and he's never tried to fit in to whatever everyone else was doing. His freshman year of high school is where he decided he was just going to be himself.

Marc: He knows he's different, and he's OK with that. He's grown into understanding the way God made him. He's very quiet and very introverted, but he just enjoys being different. The basement is his lair down there. He has 8-track, reel-to-reel and VHS tapes, and they are all throwbacks. He loves Nat King Cole and all these old-time singers, and he cranks up this classic old-school music. He's also Mr. Thrift Store. I think he gets that from his old man, who loves a bargain.

He bought a 1967 Ford Thunderbird, and this thing was a boat. Somehow, he's online and found this dude who loves Thunderbirds, so Frankie met up with the guy, who had a 2009 Cadillac GTS worth three times what the T-bird is worth.

He can fix things, and I'm not sure where that comes from. I was mowing in the fall, and the belt came off underneath, and the whole deck fell down. I'm looking on YouTube trying to find out how this belt goes on when Frankie gets home, and I ask him to take a look. I try to show him the pictures, but he wanted to figure it out. It took him five minutes, and I was going again.

Lisa: Frankie has always been a homebody. He hung out with his friends on the team but never outside of practice and school. He was a lot like Marc in that he did not talk to girls.

Marc: To people that don't know him, there are times when he could be perceived as standoffish, but part of that is him getting comfortable in a situation. Then he's much more relaxed. It's a challenge for him to jump into new situations.

Lisa: He didn't make varsity his freshman year, but he grew 5 inches between his freshman and sophomore years. He made varsity his sophomore year, and his junior year was when Blackhawk really started gaining momentum. His senior year was Blackhawk's first state championship, and during that 2019 championship game, Frankie became Blackhawk's all-time leading scorer.

Marc: He was the Journal Gazette High School Player of the Year for all Northeast Indiana in 2019. He was at the University of Indianapolis his first year in college and transferred to Grace College his sophomore year to major in history.

He was Player of the Year in the National Christian College Athletic Association. He was leading the nation in scoring for a while. Because Grace had some injuries, he had to score. He's not always assertive on the court even though he'll be the best guy out there. He'll just blend in. They played Saint Francis at Grace, and Frankie had 23 points at halftime and finished with 36. He's so skilled, but he has to get more aggressive. He's likable and respected by his peers.

Lisa: He's lighthearted, so usually he sits back and listens to our conversation and laughs. It's been awesome for us to see Frankie get more comfortable and spend more time hanging out with his teammates. A big part of that has been Marcus going to Grace, too. Marcus is so social. He's been the extra push Frankie needed to enjoy all the fun there is at college outside of class and the team.

One night in November 2021, Frankie and Marcus were invited by some of their teammates to hang out with them and some of the Grace College volleyball players. That was the night that Frankie and Anna met. Marcus said he actually talked to Anna more than Frankie did that night and that Frankie was pretty reserved, as usual. But Marcus started doing some investigating to find out more about Anna, and he learned that she was the same age as Frankie and was from Fort Wayne, too. And would you believe, she actually attended Blackhawk from kindergarten through second grade, so her family was good friends with some of our closest friends, including the Fursts.

Anna was still in volleyball season and Frankie's basketball season was ramping up, so they both had busy schedules but were talking more and more. In December, Frankie finally had a free night, giving him the perfect opportunity to ask Anna out for dinner. They went to a Mexican restaurant in Warsaw, and the rest is history.

Frankie and Anna quickly learned that they shared so much in common, like coming from close families, shopping for vintage things at estate sales and, most importantly, the same desire to honor the Lord with their lives. It wasn't long after their first date that Frankie brought her home for us to meet. It was pretty clear from the start that they had something special, and Marc and I could see that Anna was so good for him. They spur each other on in their faith, and it's been so beautiful to see what God is doing in and through them!

We are so grateful for the six months that Marc and Anna got to know each other. Marc quickly knew she was the one for Frankie. Truly, one of the sweetest gifts from the Lord was Marc getting to know and love Frankie's future wife before the Lord brought him Home.

---- **MARCUS** ----

Lisa: Marcus was born two years after Frankie, the only one born in the USA, when we were living in Michigan. He was the easiest baby, even easier than Frankie, just so happy-go-lucky. When he was born, the nurse told me he had dimples. He also was 10 pounds when he was born, and I remember him having the broadest shoulders and chest. He was a chunk, too. I would push him in a stroller at games, and he was always so happy. He was just one of those little kids who was dragged to all of his older brothers' things, but he was content as a baby to just sit back and watch Wes, Will and Frankie run around. Because he is so laid back, he is a natural peacekeeper, doesn't insist on his own way.

Marc: Socially, he's really good. He has this unique ability to connect with younger kids. At basketball camp, the younger kids just love him, and he does such a great job with them. Then he connects with his peers and older people. I tell him the Lord is going to use that in some way because he can connect with anybody and everybody.

Lisa: Marcus, like our other boys, has just been an unbelievable help to Marc over the years. They have all helped Marc run his summer basketball camps and also the Future Braves program offered after school for grade school kids. Marcus has Marc's gift of working so well with kids.

It has been so fun to watch Marcus play basketball over the years. He was at Blackhawk since the fifth grade, so he's grown up playing in the starting lineup alongside Caleb Furst and other teammates who have been playing together for years.

Marc: The kid can play. We played Northridge, who was very good, and Marcus finished with 37 points. This was against a good team. He's not a ball hog, but he was feeling it, and our guys found him for open shots.

He had a heart for the Lord at a young age, and it's been neat to see. He just loves genuine, real people and has an empathy for the underdog and those who might be overlooked.

Lisa: Marcus loves to be so involved and not miss a thing. He's been our kid that went to youth group every Wednesday night and the fall retreats and summer camps with church. He served at Fellowship of Christian Athletes Power Camp. Now it's just awesome to see him really get involved at Grace. Marcus is always down in the dorm lounge playing ping pong and Catan and hanging out with people. I love that he hangs out with all different kinds of people, not just his roommates and teammates.

Marc: He's unbelievably committed. They've all been pretty committed, but Marcus is just so driven, and it shows by the amount of time he puts in for basketball. If he had the body of Frankie, he'd probably be playing wherever he wanted to for college because of his skills, but he's 6 feet even. He's had to scratch and claw, and he's still doing that.

He's fighting for playing time at Grace. It's not easy to sit the bench, and he has not had to do a lot of that, but I'm so proud of him because he's all about the team, and he doesn't sit over there and sulk. As a dad, you want to see him persevere and stick it out and maintain that team-first attitude. He has showed a lot of resiliency. His role at Grace might be to be a great practice player and do whatever you have to do to support the team.

Lisa: Remembering the struggle that Marc went through at Illinois, we understand the pain and disappointment that Marcus is going through, not getting the playing time he's been used to having. But he's a freshman on a really good college team, and he's making the best of it. He loves that he's with Frankie and that they're getting these bonus two years together. He loves his coaches and teammates. But he's had to surrender his hopes and dreams with basketball much like Marc did and find his identity, contentment and true joy in the Lord, not in what he can do on the basketball court. We want that for all of our kids. That is what all of us need to realize, that we won't find true contentment and joy anywhere until we find it in Jesus and trust His plan for our lives.

Marc: Marcus is majoring in sports management, minoring in Biblical studies, and when I think about Marcus's career path, it has to be about people. If he was stuck in a business cubicle, he would be lost. He's going to have a lot of options; he's so gifted with people.

Lisa: He spent last summer living with Marc's dad, "Grandpa D," and carried on the family tradition of seal coating with him, and he loved it. As much as we'd love to have had him home with us, we know that the time he gets with Marc's dad is precious and priceless.

I call him our golden retriever because when he has a chance to come home, he makes the most of every opportunity that he can to be with Marc. He loves this family so much. He is so intentional about making time to talk with the twins and hang out with them. Marcus has been so relational, and he has conversations with them all the time. He loves to be at college, but we say the word and he is happy to change his plans and come home.

Marcus has such a tender heart now for Marc. He's sleeping down here by us, and he's been coming home at every opportunity so he's making sure he's by us. I've woken up to see him praying on his knees next to Marc.

Marc: That was just an awesome, inspiring thing to see, but that's just Marcus.

---- JIMMY ----

Lisa: Jimmy is two years behind Marcus, and he was born when we moved back to France and Marc was playing for Charleville. I had a scheduled C-section, so Marc was there for his birth and then went to practice that night. The first basketball game I brought Jimmy to was when he was three weeks old, so he has quite literally grown up in the gym going to basketball games.

I think Jimmy is the perfect blend of all his brothers. He has bits and pieces of all of them. He can be funny like Wes, smart like Will, super social like Marcus and not afraid to be different like Frankie. Jimmy has the ability to connect with little kids, his peers, teachers and his friends' grandparents. He went to visit Wes at college when he was in the fifth grade for Little Siblings weekend and became friends with Wes's teammates! Everybody loves Jimmy.

Marc: One of my colleagues at Blackhawk said Jimmy is Mr. Blackhawk. He's at all the events, and he's like the welcoming committee to new students. He's always helping them fit in.

Lisa: Jimmy has been at Blackhawk since second grade, so it's evident that his relationships are deeper. His friend group is so big, and he's so loved.

BRAVE AT HEART

When we went to Arizona, it was Jimmy's junior year. He loves school, so there was no way we were asking him to come with us to Arizona for six weeks. We felt such peace about leaving him home for those six weeks, because he's such a responsible, trustworthy kid that we felt comfortable letting him stay behind.

Nathan Hyde is a teacher at Blackhawk who also pastors a church in Auburn, and it was so encouraging to hear that while we were gone, Jimmy and his friends wanted to go visit his church one Sunday. What great joy to know your 17-year-old son, when left at home with all that freedom, is getting friends together to go to their teacher's church.

It's neat to see how each of our kids has flourished and come into their own when the older brother goes to college and they become the oldest kid at home. Jimmy has done an amazing job of stepping into that role. He's helped Marc so much at school and helped me so much at home. He's stepped up on the team, too.

Marc: He's the most vocal player I've ever coached. He's like a coach on the floor in that he talks and says the right thing. He's talking to teammates about where they need to be, rallying the troops, keeping everybody together. He has a great voice on our team.

Lisa: Marc has the players vote on the awards at the banquet at the end of the season, and Jimmy received the Braves Award, which is for toughness and selflessness. This year, he played so unselfishly. Growing up, he was the kid who shot three-pointers, but this year, he was all about getting rebounds and passing to other people.

Marc has always said of himself that growing up as a coach's kid was the best childhood he could imagine. All of our kids are gym rats, and at every opportunity, they've gone into school with Marc and shot around. They've done that for as long as they can remember.

Marc: We played a lot of three-on-three. When I would play with them, I would try to guard Frankie because we all had a hard time guarding Frankie. We just kept switching teams because it got to a point where nobody would guard him. It had to be half-court when I was playing because I'm not going to run up and down with them. We'd go to the gym all the time. That's just what we do. Life as a coach's kid is just the best.

In some ways, Jimmy grew up fast because he's always around his older brothers. It's neat to see him interact with his teachers. He'll invite teachers over to play board games. He'll be in a study hall with another teacher, but he will stand there the entire period shooting the bull with his teachers. He genuinely enjoys their company.

Lisa: Part of Marc's position at Blackhawk has been the assistant athletic director, but he could hardly do that this past year, so Jimmy was Joel Cotton's right-hand man this year. He never complained or acted annoyed that he was asked to help fill in and do some of the things that Marc couldn't do, like keeping score at games, etc. If Jimmy is there and there's a need, he steps up and never complains. He just does what is asked of him with a willing and great attitude.

It was awesome to see his brothers come back this year to see Jimmy play. For so many years, he's been the one tagging along to their games, and now they're coming back home to watch and cheer for him. He's the only one of our kids on varsity now, and it was so special for them to come back and be so proud of him. Their nickname for him is Steed. Back in 2011, Marc's brother, Matt, asked Jimmy, "What nickname do you want?" Jimmy was in first grade, and he came up with Steed.

Marc: I think he got it from Shrek when Donkey says, "I'm his noble steed."

Lisa: I never call him that, but Marc and his brothers do, and his friends and teammates call him that. At the games, I hear Wes yelling, "STEED!" with his booming voice.

Marc: Jimmy did have a brief rapping career, and his music was hilarious. His biggest hit was "Straight out of Reims," the city he was born in. Frankie is the creative genius, and he was the mastermind behind the whole thing. He would write the lyrics and the beat, and here's the little brother that they are putting on Instagram, and all of Frankie's friends shared it. He was "Steed the Artist," and he was like a first grader. He probably did four songs.

Lisa: It's been such a joy to watch our kids grow up together. I'm so thankful that our first five are so close in age. And I'm so thankful that the twins have gotten all of this love and attention not just from Marc and me, but their older brothers love them so deeply, too. We love to be together, and we are so incredibly blessed.

Wes and Ashton's wedding · May 2020

Will and Sarah's wedding · December 2020

CHAPTER 35

Narrator: *Lisa always had a heart for adoption. And after spending time in Zimbabwe the summer before her senior year in high school, the Lord put Africa on her heart. Marc's interest in adoption was a little more dramatic, coming at a Steven Curtis Chapman concert in 2007. The singer and his wife, Mary Beth, had adopted three girls from China.*

Marc: Steven Curtis Chapman wrote a song, "When Love Takes You In (Everything Changes)." There was a video of him with his children and showing orphans from all around the world. The Lord just put it on my heart. But the biggest thing was the financial piece. I remember praying that night, "Lord, we want to do this if we can ever afford it and You provide." Financially, things were tight with five kids already. It didn't necessarily make sense.

Lisa: We didn't know how we could ever afford it, but we trusted the Lord that if it was His will for us to adopt, He would make a way. And He did. Five years later, in February 2012, Marc's precious Grandmom Jackie passed away, and we received a part of her inheritance. So we started the adoption process that April.

Marc: The timing was good. We had just gotten to Lakewood Park, and our good friends the Chapmans had just adopted two boys from Ethiopia, and their friends Matt and Amy Swartz had adopted a girl and a boy from Ethiopia. It just became clear this is what we were going to do.

Lisa: But we had never considered adopting two children at the same time until we saw how great it was for the Chapman and Swartz families.

Marc: It was great for the twins that they had one another. Both of our friends had adopted two children, and they recommended that, and I'm so glad we did.

A lot of people talk about how their adoption stories take years, but we had the home study in April, and then in late July, we got an email called a referral, and it was little Isaiah and little Jaela. They were the sweetest little things, and I said, "Let's do this."

BRAVE AT HEART

Lisa: But there were still a lot more hoops to jump through. To adopt from Ethiopia, at least back in 2012, you had to make two trips. The first trip is a court date where you stand before an Ethiopian judge and declare that your intention is to adopt and care for these children, and the second trip is with the American embassy to get your kids the proper paperwork so that they can travel home. But in between the two trips, you are waiting for their birth certificates to be re-issued with our names as their adoptive parents. So it is most definitely a process with lots of waiting on the Lord and trusting Him and His perfect timing.

We could see God's hand all over our adoption process. All along, our prayer was, "Lord, give us who you want us to have." We had requested to adopt two children. We didn't request male or female. We wanted them to be younger than Jimmy, who was in first grade at the time. So we were kind of preparing for a preschooler and an infant. We had completed all the paperwork as quickly as we could, so then we were just waiting.

We asked our adoption coordinator in July to get an idea where we were on the waiting list, and she said, "You are like ninth on the list, and there's a rainy season in Ethiopia where the court shuts down in August through October. There's no way you're going to get referred a child before courts shut down in August." But God! On July 22, 2012, we received an email. Our hearts jumped at the subject line: "potential children ... medical report ... twins ... aged 2½." The only message in the email was, "Please let me know if you might be interested in these twins." Attached were four pages of medical reports. They wanted to make sure we were okay with their medical reports before we fell in love with them through pictures. We said yes, we were interested, and then they sent the first pictures.

Marc: God's plan.

Lisa: No doubt they were handpicked for us. But I have to be honest, the first pictures of Jaela, she looked so sad. I said to Marc, "I don't know if I have what it takes to have a sad little girl." And I'll never forget what he said: "Lisa, we have been praying all along that God would give us who He wants us to have. This is what we've prayed for. He's given us who He wants to be ours." And so ever since that moment, I have never doubted for a second that these twins were to be ours! That night, two hours after we got the email with their pictures, we told the adoption agency, "We are ready to move forward to bringing them home!"

The next day, our adoption agency emailed to tell us, "It is going to be impossible to get this case done before rainy season. There is no way to complete the (paperwork) within 2 weeks when the courts close, and we need that for court. Just do what you can, and we will hope they come home by Christmas."

But God again made a way!

Much to our surprise, we were given a court date on August 14, my 40th birthday! We got our court date before rainy season! It was the beginning of the school year, and Marc and I dropped everything to head to Ethiopia to meet the twins.

Marc: We spent four days with them, and they stayed with us in a guesthouse. It was so special connecting with them, but the hard part was leaving. We all sobbed.

Lisa: We took them back to the orphanage on our last day, and Isaiah was holding onto Marc so tight, sobbing.

Marc: He was grabbing my leg.

Lisa: The coordinator said there was no way we were going to get them by the end of the year, but on October 25, we received an email with the twins' new birth certificates, issued with our last name. They were officially ours, officially Davidsons! The next step was to wait for our appointment at the U.S. Embassy so that we could get them cleared to come home to the U.S. To our surprise, we got an email on November 28 with the subject, "Davidson Family, Cases Cleared," and were given an appointment at the American Embassy on December 3. Marc and I flew out of Chicago on December 1, arrived in Ethiopia on December 2 and went straight to the orphanage to bring Isaiah and Jaela back to the guesthouse with us, never to return to the orphanage again. We flew back home to the States and landed in Chicago on December 6. It was quite the whirlwind trip. Marc was the athletic director and head coach, so that was tough timing in the middle of basketball season. We had five kids at home and Marc's job to get back to, but most of all, we couldn't wait to get back home to introduce Isaiah and Jaela to their five brothers, who were eagerly waiting to meet them at the airport, ready to finally be the Davidson family of nine. Our forever family.

Marc: This was bigger than basketball. I missed one game, and I remember watching it on the webcast from Ethiopia. As much as I love basketball, nothing compares to this.

It was so amazing. We went back to the orphanage in December, and the kids know how it works. When we pulled into that gate, they came running out to the van. Isaiah and Jaela saw us and just marched out and jumped in. What struck me about that was they had nothing. They didn't have a backpack, clothes, toys—literally nothing. There are five million orphans in Ethiopia, alone, and the level of poverty we saw was unbelievable. That's a beautiful picture of salvation. When we come to Jesus, we don't take anything into it, and He gives us a name and makes us part of His family.

Phil and Shari Chapman—he was the superintendent at Lakewood Park—brought our boys to the airport. My dad was there with his wife, Sig, and Lisa's mom and dad. It was an unbelievable scene at the airport. I have a picture of me holding Isaiah, introducing him to my dad.

Marcus is the only one who we didn't carry through those airport doors to meet everyone because he was born in Michigan. Our parents met five out of seven of our kids for the first time at Chicago's O'Hare. It's a special place.

Lisa: When we were driving around Ethiopia, the twins just sat in our laps in the back seat. They probably had never sat in a car seat before, so when we got into our van and strapped them into their car seats with the five-point harnesses, they were screaming! That was really hard for our kids to see.

Marc: The first meal we gave them in America was McDonald's. We drove to Timothy Christian, where my brother is the superintendent, and we introduced them to Matt and Julie and their kids Luke, Macy and Joey before heading home to Indiana.

Lisa: To prepare for adoption, you have to read up on all the likely problems and difficulties, and it has just gone exceedingly, abundantly well beyond anything we could imagine. The twins are incredible. There are different theories on how to help your adopted children adapt to their new life. We had a busy life with our five older kids, and we just wanted them to learn quickly how we roll. Rather than sit home and cocoon, I immediately brought them to their older brothers' games and jumped right back into doing the things and going to all the places we had gone before. Those days were exhausting, but the twins did so great adjusting to their new life in America.

Marc: It's amazing to me how quickly they assimilated into our family. I believe that is a God thing, the way the boys opened up to them.

Lisa: The five boys have helped so much with the twins. I could not have done it with Marc's busy schedule without them helping.

Marc: And they do it so naturally. You can see it's a joy for them to be around the twins, to invest in them. They just love being with them. We've never sensed jealousy or the older ones thinking they are a nuisance. They want to be with them. For the boys, it happened so quickly that the twins were just part of the family, and it surprised me how quickly that all came together.

For us, it was immediate. We know they are the Lord's ultimately, but they were our children immediately. I think God just puts that on you because He's entrusting them to you. It wasn't like anything different than it was with the first five.

What I wish we had done right when we got them ... the first few weeks, they would be jabbering in bed, and I wish we had recorded it because it was the sweetest sound. It was just so sweet.

Lisa: Decembers are always crazy for us with basketball season and all that comes with the Christmas season. Add to that a quick trip to Ethiopia, jet lag and bringing home twin 2-year-olds that don't speak English! So those first couple of weeks were kind of a blur. It's amazing to look back at our first Christmas picture with all seven kids. Isaiah and Jaela have the biggest smiles on their faces just 19 days after we brought them home.

Jaela is the most amazing girl. I know I'm her mom, so I'm biased, but she is just the sweetest. We'll whisk away every so often and watch a girl movie, but right now, that's about all we do together that's super girly, just the two of us.

Jaela was hesitant with us at first when we were with them in Ethiopia. She warmed up to me first. She would sit on my lap, and we would watch Marc and Isaiah throw the ball back and forth, Isaiah giggling the whole time. I'll never forget when we finally saw her first smile. That was the most amazing moment! Isaiah right from the get-go had his smile and the sparkle in his eye even with the language barrier. He was 100 percent all in. Jaela didn't cry with us, but she was quiet and tentative.

Marc: Jaela initially was a little hesitant to come to me. When I would go to her on the first trip, she would say, "Em be," and we found out that means, "Stay away." By the end of that first trip, she was gradually starting to warm up. Once we brought them home and she warmed up, it made it so sweet. I remember the first time she embraced me, and it was amazing. Obviously, we loved having boys and that too was amazing, but having a daughter was just this totally new dynamic. I think that daddy-daughter connection is a powerful thing.

Lisa: It is just beautiful to see how she quickly became the sweetest, happiest, easiest girl I've ever known. She has a really great, understanding heart and is such a joy. If she wanted to pitch a fit and complain that we never do anything that she wants to do, being the only girl, that would be perfectly understandable, but she has never done that. Being in a family where boys basketball has been dominating our schedule, she has had a great attitude and has never complained. Jaela has amazingly fit into our family full of boys. She is so loved and cherished by us all.

You can tell Jaela's got six brothers. She's so tough and athletic! She tags along with them to the gym and is happy to shoot around with Isaiah or jump in on a game of PIG. This past year, she played volleyball, basketball and even gave track a try. She has a humble confidence and isn't controlled by fear or worry. We are so excited to see all that God is going to do in her life.

Her memory is unbelievable; she's like a sponge. She amazes us how quickly she can memorize a Bible verse. We tell her she has such a good memory that she could be a doctor, but she has no stomach for blood. She has the gift of recalling lines from a movie, just like her dad and brothers. Marc started calling her "Tutz" after hearing Kramer call Elaine that in an episode of Seinfeld. She can draw and sketch so beautifully, and she's so talented that she won the Amazing Artist Award in fourth and sixth grades.

Marc: She's unbelievably helpful. It's not like a shrug of the shoulders and, "OK, because you asked me to." It's almost like she can't wait to help you or do whatever. That's rare. Sometimes kids will do things just because you are asking, but she legit loves it, and it brings her joy. She has a selfless spirit like her mama, and it's a beautiful thing.

Her hugs are amazing. You get a hug from Jaela, it lights up your life.

Lisa: When I think back to Isaiah, pulling into the orphanage and picking him out of the crowd by his smile and the sparkle in his eye … I just remember Isaiah with boundless energy, bouncing and jumping around everywhere with his giggle and his easy laugh. There was never any hesitancy with him. He was easy and felt so comfortable with us, like he had known us his whole life.

Marc was so excited to find out Isaiah was a lefty, like him. We brought a little basketball with us to Ethiopia, and when we threw it to him, he caught and threw with his left hand. He was barely 2 when we went there on the first trip, and he's playing catch just like one of our other boys when they were 2.

Marc: I remember the last night on our first trip there, and me and him were just playing catch. We're just having a blast, and the next day when we had to leave, that was horrible. I'll never forget him grabbing onto my leg and not wanting us to leave. He was sobbing. We were all sobbing.

Lisa: Marc and I left the orphanage and stood outside the door and cried. That's the most we've cried together, just sobbing in each other's arms. It broke our hearts to leave them, and it kept us praying fervently for the day we got to bring them both home.

It's pretty amazing to think that Isaiah and Jaela have always had each other. They have such a sweet relationship. If they are given the choice, they prefer to do things together and they choose each other. Isaiah will ask Jaela what she wants to do, and he'll say he wants to do that, too, and vice versa. They play together at recess, and they like to be on the same team. You can tell they are always looking out for each other. They have been at Blackhawk since they were 4 years old and with almost all of their classmates since preschool, so they have very deep friendships with them.

The twins were blessed to have had Marc as their PE teacher in kindergarten and first grade so that their classmates could know and love him in a special way. Marc was in the elementary school building every morning, so he got to peek in on them a lot. Marc is known for giving his students nicknames, and so it was in PE class apparently that Marc gave Isaiah the nickname "Bomber." They were playing kickball, and a kid who could kick the ball a long way was referred to as a "bomber." So when Isaiah was up to kick, Marc would yell out, "Everybody look out! This one's a bomber!" Eventually, he started referring to Isaiah as "The Bomber" at home, and at some point, it stuck.

Isaiah is a quiet leader. The fifth-grade classes voted him to be mayor when they went to BizTown. Jaela was assigned the job title of assistant to the mayor that day. Isaiah, like Jaela, also has a great memory. He and Jaela have been in the same class since preschool, so they are able to review for tests and quizzes together and help each other with homework. The sweetest thing ever is hearing them say their Bible verses together.

Isaiah is so athletic. He loves to play ball whether it's kickball or foursquare at recess or playing basketball with his school team. He loves to tag along with his brothers and go shoot at the gym with them. Isaiah is sweet, patient and helpful with younger kids. You can tell he's always looking out for Jaela.

He's been Marc's junior manager on the team, helping with water bottles, videotaping games and running the scoreboard for practice. Marc has even had Isaiah jump in and play with the JV team when they've needed a player for open gym. He's learning those fun perks and responsibilities of being a coach's kid, and he's been able to be back in the locker room with Marc and the sacred post-game moments, witnessing Marc's response after an exhilarating win and also after a heartbreaking loss. He's heard the put-ups in the locker room after games. I am so grateful Isaiah has been able to experience these special years with Marc and his brothers.

His illness prompted Marc to have even deeper discussions with his children. There was no reason to leave anything unsaid, even with a family that has been incredibly open to feelings. The things he wanted to say needed to last.

Marc: It's been good because I've just been really honest with them. Sometimes people in my situation just kind of sugarcoat stuff and say everything is going to be fine and this and that. I've just been very honest about where my health is at but also really open about what God is doing through that. All of those disappointments point us back to Jesus. I don't mind sharing the disappointments because we've gotten tons of reports and scans and X-rays and blood labs, and it's virtually all been bad news from a human perspective. All those disappointments remind us of our hope in Christ. It's been good to be honest and remind them why we have hope.

The intentional one-on-one time I've gotten with them has been incredible. We've gone out and done different things. It's just being together in some precious time. We've had some great talks, and I've been able to pray over my kids and talk about anything and everything. We've always prayed together, but we've done it more in the past month than we ever have. That's really welding us together.

There's no question it has made our relationship stronger. One thing I have shared with all of my boys and with a lot of different people, the idea of the pyramid. The marriage pyramid: On the top, Christ is at the head, and that's what the Scripture teaches. And the husband is at the base over here and the wife at the base over here. I tell young people, as you get closer to God, what happens to your relationship with your spouse is it becomes closer. We are living that right now. Both of us, our strength in Christ and our faith has grown exponentially as we have pursued Him together, and it has brought us closer together. It really welds that relationship in a way that without suffering, I don't think you can get to where Lisa and I have arrived.

God has given me peace that my children will be there for the twins and for their mother. They will step up.

Marc and the twins • May 2013

CHAPTER 36

Narrator: *Phil Chapman and Marc were lucky enough to have a lifelong relationship. When Marc played Little League baseball, Phil played for nearby Newark, and then they played high school baseball against each other. When Phil became a Christian, he started attending Marc's home church, Helmar Lutheran, and he and Marc attended the same Family Bible Camp. They also exchanged many letters when the Davidsons were living in France.*

"Chappy, one of the greatest decisions that Lisa and I made was to adopt the twins." That was an exclamation that Marc made to me 19 days before walking into the presence of the Lord about Lisa and his decision to adopt Jaela and Isaiah in 2012.

Adoption was near and dear to his heart, as he would frequently quote Scripture regarding his adoption to the family of God. Paul says in Romans 8:15, "For you did not receive the Spirit of slavery to fall back into fear, but you have received the Spirit of adoption as sons, by whom we cry, 'Abba! Father!'" As you listened to Marc make the circuit over the past couple of years, you would catch him proclaiming his adoption to God the Father as he (Marc) became a fellow heir with Christ (John 3:3).

As a follower of Jesus and a phenomenal student of His Word, Marc knew that he and Lisa were being called to follow the example given by his eternal Father to adopt. James 1:27 says, "Religion that is pure and undefiled before God the Father is this: to visit orphans and widows in their affliction, and to keep oneself unstained from the world." So as Marc and Lisa prayed about the decision and leaned into the Word, Isaiah came to the forefront. It says, "But they who wait for the Lord shall renew their strength; they shall mount up with wings like eagles; they shall run and not be weary; they shall walk and not faint."

Adoption was not something random that Marc and Lisa just decided to do in 2012. As an only child growing up, Lisa had begged her parents to adopt. So when she married Marc, that was a desire she had for them. However, adoption did not seem like a reality. Marc and Lisa had five boys early in their marriage, and they moved frequently. In 2007, Marc and Lisa received an invite to a Steven Curtis Chapman concert with their friends in Troy, Michigan. When Steven Curtis shared his adoption story, God sparked Marc's heart and unified his and Lisa's desire to adopt and trust the Lord. However, that desire did not become a reality until another five years.

In the summer of 2010, I was called to serve at Lakewood Park Christian School, first as the elementary principal and then, ten days after arrival, as the superintendent. One of the responsibilities of the superintendent was to mingle around during the Open House. It was there that my wife and I met Matt and Amy Swartz. They were walking around with their four children, including their two newest additions, Bo and Zhana, who were recently adopted from Ethiopia. At that moment, our lives were changed, and so were several other kiddos'.

Shari and I began our process of adoption in October 2010. Shortly after, we were matched up with our two future sons, Jacob and Reggie. We finalized the Ethiopian adoption of our two boys in May 2011.

A month after this, when the athletic director, head boys basketball coach and PE teacher positions opened up at Lakewood Park, I invited Marc to come up for an interview. Marc, Lisa and the five boys drove up to Auburn, Indiana, from Georgia, and the entire interview team knew he would be the perfect fit.

After accepting the position, the Davidsons had the opportunity to spend time with Jacob, Reggie, Bo and Zhana. They fell in love with each of them. Since adoption had been in their hearts for many years, this was the final push they needed. Eventually, Marc and Lisa started talking to each of our families about our process and figuring out their next steps.

Very similar to our journey, they got their home study, filled out the application and waited to be matched up with a kiddo—in this case, a set of twins. So, as friends to the Davidson family, the Swartzes and Chapmans had fundraisers to help bring the twins home.

Matt and Amy Swartz held a fantastic fundraiser at East of Chicago for some good pizza, a lot of fellowship and some sizable generosity.

In August of 2012, Marc and Lisa were able to fly to Ethiopia for the first time and meet their new family members. Lisa's childhood dream of adoption was coming to fruition.

In the early morning of November 28, 2012, Marc opened his email and saw one with the subject "Davidson Family, Cases Cleared." Marc and Lisa weren't able to get back to sleep. They quickly purchased tickets to Ethiopia, flying out to pick up their kiddos! On the morning of December 6, Shari and I had the opportunity to drive from our new location in Newark, Illinois, to Fort Wayne, Indiana, to pick up the five Davidson boys. We took Jacob with us as he was excited about hanging out with the boys. At that time, we had a 12-passenger van that was affectionately called "Betty." The boys had a blast on our way to Chicago's O'Hare International Airport. I introduced them to a game we call "Pass the Buck." On our way, feeding these gentlemen was top on the list, so we stopped at Texas Roadhouse for some good grub. Eventually, after stopping at Grandpa D's house, we made it to the airport and waited with other family members. It seemed like forever, but Marc and Lisa, carrying the twins, finally walked through the doors to grandparents and kids cheering and holding "Welcome Home" signs. It was a fantastic moment in the lives of all of the Davidsons.

When I asked the boys if they could remember our trip, they had these great memories.

Wes said, "I will never forget the day I met Isaiah and Jaela at the O'Hare airport, and my life changed forever. It was our first time meeting them, and up to that point, all that we knew were the pictures we saw and the stories we heard. Jaela was very reserved, and Isaiah clung to my dad. I can still picture him smiling ear to ear as a 2-year-old playing catch with my dad in the house. One of the first phrases the twins learned was, "I love you." On that brisk December day when we were riding three hours home back to Indiana from the O'Hare airport, they were crying profusely being placed in their first car seat. My brothers and I didn't know anything about the twins that first day (except the fact that they were world-class criers), but we all loved them as our blood brother and sister from that very first day. My father spoke often about how adoption is a beautiful picture of Christ's love. Our lives changed forever that day, and the twins clung to my parents like they were all that they had in the world. My father and mother showed me what selfless, unconditional love was through the gift of adoption."

Marcus said, "It felt like we had waited for them for an eternity, but it was so surreal seeing Mom and Dad walking toward us with my new brother and sister. The first time I saw Isaiah cry was walking out of the airport, and dad said we had to get rid of the balloons. Both Isaiah and Jaela (but especially Jaela) were screaming when we put them into their car seats, and we couldn't get them to stop; it moved Frank to tears. Once we got home, I remember holding Jaela inside for the first time after she fell asleep from the car ride home."

Jimmy said, "I can recall all of us anxiously waiting at the airport with big signs for them. I remember finally seeing them and running up to greet them. It was truly a life-changing moment that 8-year-old me didn't fully grasp."

A few days later, on December 9, 2012, we welcomed the Davidson family back to Illinois for a huge spaghetti fundraiser. Because this fundraiser was basically in the backyard of where Marc grew up, tons of people showed up and were able to bless the family. In fact, with matching funds from Lifesong for Orphans Ministry, we were able to raise just shy of $6,000!

God was part of everything. Before the world began, He knew that Jaela and Isaiah would need a forever family, and He knew that Marc and Lisa would answer the call. Adoption is complicated, and a lot happens before, during and after. However, 10 years into their adoption of the twins, I repeat their father's words: "One of the greatest decisions that Lisa and I made was to adopt the twins."

CHAPTER 37

Narrator: *As much as Marc had an impact on every kid he came in contact with, he had an everlasting influence on his sons and daughter. Following are reflections provided mostly before Marc's passing by five of his sons, his now three daughters-in-law and his daughter. Marcus's memories are presented in a later chapter.*

---- WES ----

My best memories with Dad are probably from when we were in France. We would ride the roller coasters even though he hated them. (He was afraid of heights.) I would do anything I could, standing on my tippy toes, to be tall enough to ride. He began to like them with me.

I have a lot of good food memories with Dad. In France, he would make his homemade pizza called "The D Dish," not deep dish. I couldn't tell you many facts about the actual pizza, but it was the fact that he made it. He liked to refer to his "World's Famous" popcorn. Another favorite memory I have is going to those random cities as a family when we were in France. One time, we drove three hours into Germany just to get some Burger King.

I felt often like I was the only kid missing out on all the fun, but looking back, I can be very appreciative that my parents had my best interests in mind. They wanted me to be a man of character and a man of God, and the temporary worldly pleasures won't satisfy. I remember a time at Blackhawk after one of our first practices in the summertime. I was shooting in the gym with Will, and I was coming off my meniscus injury, and Dad was actually kind of upset with me because I was trying to dunk. Then later he made a point of coming up to me and saying, "Hey, son, I'm really proud of you, and I wanted to let you know how great it's been to watch you transition from school to school and how you've made it work."

I went to nine schools, never spending more than two years at one, and I think because of that, I'm always willing to embrace a new situation. There was nothing more exciting than when we moved,

BRAVE AT HEART

and we'd walk into this new house, and I'd find my room and think about how I was going to decorate it.

It was really special when he coached me. I had him in Upward Basketball and at Dominion Christian in Georgia for two years, two years at Lakewood Park and two at Blackhawk. But before that, as a little kid, I remember going to all the games that my dad coached, and those guys were basically NBA players to me. Whenever they would lose, my dad would come up to me after the game and say, "We could have used you out there tonight." I would get so upset every single year when they would lose and the season was over. I even remember when Trinity got eliminated from the national tournament in 2006, and that was the hardest I've ever cried.

At Dominion in Georgia, I played junior varsity even though I was in the eighth grade, and I always sat on the bench for the varsity games. There was no chance I could get into the game, but I always got really excited hoping one of those times he might tap me on the shoulder and put me in.

I just loved watching him coach, too. That was so great. I am a big Chicago Bears fan, but I was never more into games at any level, watching and playing or whatever, than when I was watching my dad coaching.

Some of my other favorite memories were riding in the passenger seat of his truck, listening to the Cubs together. Or we would watch the Cubs games in the house, and we would mute the TV and be the announcers. That was fun.

I'm thankful all those conversations happened. He taught me the value of stepping up and being a leader. I can still hear my dad in whatever I'm doing in life. I can just hear him sometimes.

One year after Marc's death
Not a day goes by where I don't think of my father. I still hear him affectionately calling my mom his "Queenie." I can picture him outside on the grill, I can see him smacking the dashboard above the steering wheel listening to the Cubs on the radio, and I can picture him reading his Bible every time I look at the head of my

parents' dining room table. It's hard to believe he was just one person, because the void he left almost makes him feel like he was larger than life.

Most nights, I will have dreams of my dad. I'm always sure to tell him the Cubs score of the night before, and I've seen him play with my son a few times. (Jack Doyle Davidson, Marc and Lisa's first grandchild, was born July 2, 2022, to Wes and Ashton.) My dad loved kids more than anyone I've ever known. I saw him a million times lead a group of kids through drills in summer basketball camps and then before closing, sit down with them in a circle and share with them his testimony.

My father's legacy lived on through the 2022-23 Blackhawk Christian Braves basketball team. Over the years, going back to when they were in middle school, he would always say how special that group was. He told us, "I've never known a high school group as dedicated to getting better as that class." Jimmy led the charge along with Gage Sefton and Josh Furst; they would go to the school and work out in the weight room together on Saturday nights, when other high schoolers were playing video games or at the mall. They would get to the gym at 6:30 before school started to get shots up. Everyone would stay late after practice to the point where they would get kicked out of the gym.

They fought through adversity, and how they won the state championship was pure toughness. Dad talked a lot about toughness and persevering through adversity. Down 11 points at halftime and facing a red-hot future University of Kentucky commit Joey Hart (whose 18 points at halftime were as much as the entire Braves' team), that's where the Braves tapped into that toughness. Those boys had been playing together their whole lives, and I knew they wouldn't go out without a fight. My whole life, my dad always said it bothered him that people assumed Christians would be soft, timid or weak basketball players. He said a hundred times that if Jesus played basketball, he would be the hardest worker on the floor, and he often challenged his players to "play as hard Jesus would."

In the second half, the Braves came out of the locker room and were diving on loose balls, crashing the glass and playing team defense that would've made the 2004 Detroit Pistons blush. When the final buzzer sounded, it was the Braves on top 52-45. As I saw Jimmy and Coach Roth hug, I was overcome with emotion thinking about all of those early mornings with Dad and him telling me how much he was praying for Coach Roth to succeed him. A week before the Lord called him home, the decision was made to hire Coach Roth, and my father was at peace with the man who would lead the Braves on the court and as young men in Christ off the court. The way the game went couldn't have been more fitting for a team who worked hard and persevered through adversity.

On opening night of the 2022-23 season, the home court of the small but homey gymnasium on Blackhawk's campus was named "Marc Davidson Court" with Colossians 3:23 transcribed below, a testament for Braves in years to come to play hard because they play for the Lord.

Wes's wife, Ashton, remembers what it was like to meet Marc early on in their relationship.

Ashton: To say I wasn't intimidated by my father-in-law the first few months of being around him would be a lie. Not because of anything he did, but simply from looking at him. He was a giant of a man, had a booming voice and stood about 15 inches taller than me. But the more time I spent around him, the more I saw how gentle and kind he was. He led by example. He loved his wife and his kids with all of his heart. And when I became his daughter-in-law, that unconditional love applied to me, as well. We spent so many nights together laughing over movies, playing board games and talking about life. I will cherish those memories for a lifetime.

Every single Father's Day since Wes and I have been together, I texted Dad and simply told him thank you. I thanked him for who he was and for who he raised my husband to be. As Wes and I prepare to become parents, I am constantly thinking of what my in-laws would do. Wes has had the importance of leading a household and family instilled in him from a young age. He's watched his dad discipline in nothing but love. He's seen the impact a sold-out life for Christ can have on others and eternity. He constantly fights to keep Jesus at the center of our marriage.

Dad told Wes so many times the greatest way he could love his kids would be to love his wife, and I certainly feel that. Dad prioritized his children and their faith over so many less important things. He knew the weight of the burden he carried and did so with as much grace and love as I've ever seen.

I do not worry about our future as we enter into parenthood because I know my husband has seen one of the greatest examples of fatherhood. He will play, laugh, discipline and lead with the same faith-filled love as his dad before him. So to my second dad one more time: Dad, thanks for raising my husband to be more than I could ever ask for. All we could ever ask for is that our son grows up to be a man of God like you.

---- WILL ----

I distinctly remember Dad memorizing and quoting passages of Scripture throughout my upbringing. I remember watching him read and recite chapters from the Bible on his phone while cleaning the basketball floor as an athletic director. I can certainly tell you Dad's favorite Bible verses and passages because I've heard him reference them dozens and dozens of times! All of that really made an impression on me and inspired me to treasure God's Word like he does. Dad has always been a man with a deep knowledge of, passion for and commitment to the Word of God.

Growing up, Dad always loved playing sports with us as that was his way of spending quality time with us. When I was a 6- or 7-year-old living in France, baseball was my favorite sport. On Dad's off days when he had no practice, he would frequently drive my brothers and me to the gym. We would each take turns stepping up to the plate, and he would pitch us rubber baseballs. He would simulate a real baseball game by imaginatively broadcasting our hits like a play-by-play and color commentator would. Also, when I had a lunch break in the school day in France, Dad and I would often go to the backyard, and I would pitch to him as he would play the catcher/umpire and simulate a real game. All of that was a ton of fun for me and meant a lot to me. When I started getting more into basketball in middle school, I don't remember him ever saying no to taking me to the gym. He rebounded countless shots for me and played me in 1-on-1 all the time (and just about accidentally broke my nose with his elbow on one occasion when he pulled down a rebound!). Dad is the definition of a family man.

I have seen Dad teach and coach kids from pre-kindergarten to college and make a profound impact on their lives. I have seen the glimmer in countless kids' eyes when Dad calls them by their nicknames and high-fives them in summer basketball camps and PE classes. I have heard many, many of Dad's former high school and college players express how much they appreciate Dad and the way he mentored them. Dad loves people, especially kids.
We moved around a lot when I was growing up, and those decisions to uproot and change locations were not always easy. There were even some people close to us who loved us but didn't agree with every major decision my parents made. I know that my parents' decisions were always guided by what Mom and Dad really felt the Lord was calling them to do. As the head of the household, Dad didn't care what other people would think or say—he just wanted to be obedient to go where God wanted him. I have clearly seen God honor Mom and Dad's steps of obedience and provide for our family in incredible ways. Dad is a truly God-fearing man who walks by faith.

It would be hard for me to overestimate how much Dad taught me about what it means to be a godly husband. Mom and Dad have a very strong marriage, and I was blessed every day growing up to have a prime example of a loving, faithful husband in my father. Dad is a large and intimidating man, but he is a romantic through and through. He loves making Mom feel special. Every day, Dad would express affection to Mom in many different ways. He would frequently tell her how beautiful she is; he would hug her and kiss her in front of us kids, as well. He loves to publicly praise Mom's cooking and has repeatedly told her that she is simply the best in every way.

Dad not only modeled how to be a loving husband, but he taught me the importance of finding the right woman to marry. He taught me that besides choosing to follow Jesus, the most important decision I would ever make would be picking a wife. One thing he would love to tell us boys is that when looking for a wife, "She's got to love the Lord ... but she can't be hard to look at!" I applied Dad's principle to my search for a spouse, and God blessed me with a wife who certainly checks off both of those boxes! Dad exhorted me and my brothers to always remember that marriage works best when the husband and wife are both pursuing the Lord first and foremost.

Dad helped me and inspired me as a husband in many ways, and he continues to do so. He taught me how to look for the right kind of woman and never let her go. He taught me to love God first, my wife second and my children third. He showed me how to cherish my wife and be tender-hearted toward her through my words and actions.

One year after Marc's death
Dad went to be with the Lord just over a year ago now. I think about him and miss him all the time. Many nights, he shows up in my dreams. With every passing day, I realize more and more just how much of an imprint he left on me, on our family and on this world.

It's impossible for me to imagine myself apart from being raised by Marc Davidson. So much of who I am today is because of God's grace through him. Any good in me is largely because of the example he set for me and the values he instilled in me. There's a big part of me that wishes I could be with him right now—to talk to him about life, about following the Lord, about being a husband, about clinging to Christ throughout the hills and valleys of life. At the same time, I thank God as He continues to awe me at all He has done (and is still doing) through Dad's life and death, and I greatly look forward to the day when we'll be together again. It's immeasurably comforting to know that because of the cross of Christ, our best memories together are ahead of us. I can't wait to be reunited with him—with cancer gone forever, with death defeated, with pain as only a memory, with sin destroyed.

Will's wife, Sarah, wanted to offer insight into her relationship with Marc.

Sarah: Will and I started dating, became engaged and got married in about 10 months! With his large build and years of coaching, Dad can easily be intimidating. However, I could tell very quickly that this is not his intention. Dad probably doesn't care much what people think about him, but he does care deeply about people. He usually has a twinkle in his eye, is cracking jokes and is looking forward to life far beyond this one. When he first told me after our wedding, "Just call me Dad," I squeaked out, "OK ... Dad." But he has truly become a second father to me.

He is the No. 1 person I have to thank for why Will is such an incredible husband to me. The way Will looks, speaks and loves me reminds me of how I see Dad love Mom. Will raves about my cooking—probably not because of how good it is but because he's watched his dad do the same thing to his mom (whose food truly does deserve it!). When Mom says something funny, Dad will laugh and look at her in a way that you know she's his favorite person in the world. There's not a chance that anyone else gets that same laugh and doting look from him.

Sometimes when we are celebrating a birthday or special occasion, Dad will eulogize someone. He says that he wonders why people wait until someone has passed to honor them. We would go around the circle and encourage and exhort someone else, explaining what we saw in them that we admire. This was implemented before the cancer diagnosis, and it's ironic because Dad is constantly being "eulogized" now. He has honored those around him, and he is now being honored by so many for the godly legacy that he leaves.

We always talk about Dad and how we miss him. When we visit the house, it's filled with love and laughter, but his absence is also so tangible. It feels emptier, yet my heart is so full in those moments because I'm reminded of what an incredible man of God he was and that I have the honor of being his daughter-in-law. His fingerprints are all over the family, and that will never change. I think more and more recently of how Dad and Mom created such a strong, Christlike, fun family culture. I don't know how, but they make it seem effortless! Dad pointed us to Jesus and eternity; though it may not feel like it many days, we all know that we'll see him again before we know it.

---- FRANKIE ----

Over the years living hours away from family in Illinois, we had many car trips to travel and see them for the holidays or gatherings. On these rides, my father would always need ways to keep his mind occupied. Sometimes, it was '80s rock music. Sometimes, it was snacking on beef jerky, mixed nuts and a gallon of milk for hours on end.

However, something I remember my father constantly doing was passing his Bible back to one of us kids and promptly telling us something like, "Let's go to Romans." He then continued to recite usually at least an entire chapter to us in the car out of sheer memory. Whenever he would do this, I would be amazed at his knowledge and passion for God's Word.

There is no doubt that he frequently visited and committed to memory Romans 8. Reading through verses 18 through 30, I cannot help but think of my father's life in retrospect.

"For I consider that the sufferings of this present time are not worth comparing with the glory that is to be revealed to us. For the creation waits with eager longing for the revealing of the sons of God. For the creation was subjected to futility, not willingly, but because of him who subjected it, in hope that the creation itself will be set free from its bondage to corruption and obtain the freedom of the glory of the children of God. For we know that the whole creation has been groaning together in the pains of childbirth until now. And not only the creation, but we ourselves, who have the first fruits of the Spirit, groan inwardly as we wait eagerly for adoption as sons, the redemption of our bodies. For in this hope we were saved. Now hope that is seen is not hope. For who hopes for what he sees? But if we hope for what we do not see, we wait for it with patience.

"Likewise the Spirit helps us in our weakness. For we do not know what to pray for as we ought, but the Spirit himself intercedes for us with groanings too deep for words. And he who searches hearts knows what is the mind of the Spirit, because the Spirit intercedes for the saints according to the will of God. And we know that for those who love God, all things work together for good, for those who are called according to his purpose. For those whom he foreknew he also predestined to be conformed to the image of his Son, in order that he might be the firstborn among many brothers. And those whom he predestined he also called, and those whom he called he also justified, and those whom he justified he also glorified."

I can hear my dad's voice reciting many of these verses as I read through the passage. Especially in his last year of life, my father would always talk about the depravity of our earthly bodies. He would refer to his body the same way 2 Corinthians 5:1 does as an "earthly tent," describing how we are merely passing through this world before we enter into eternity. In this passage in Romans 8, the word "groan" is used in two different ways. First, to describe our groaning because of the sin within our world and our sinful bodies. But this same word is used positively to describe our eager desire for redemption through the Holy Spirit. In every way possible, my father's body and soul groaned for redemption. He fully experienced the awful suffering of our lowly bodies in ways that many of us cannot begin to imagine. Yet, he understood that the pain he endured on this earth was nothing compared to the glory that awaited him in heaven. Amen!

One of my dad's favorite topics was the idea of hope. He would explain that there are two different kinds of hope: hope in earthly things and hope in eternal things. Hope in earthly things is momentary, transient, fleeting and, ultimately, worthless. My dad would always use the example of Chicago Cubs fans and how we also say something like, "Man, I really hope that this is the year for our team." Through many, many years of heartache as a Cubs fan, my father found out that this kind of hope always lets us down. However, he would always explain that Biblical hope is completely different from this. Biblical hope is a sure thing, something that we can fully depend on. This passage in Romans 8 says that this groaning within our bodies can only be satisfied by one thing, which is the hope that we have in Jesus Christ. If my father made one thing clear in his testimony, it is that everything else in this world will let us down. However, our souls can find rest in redemption through Jesus Christ.

When I look back on my dad's life, I am incredibly grateful when I see how faithful he was to his Lord and Savior. I could not have asked for a better father to be alongside me through the first 21 years of my life. And I will cherish my memories of him forever.

My father's journey through cancer taught me many things. His example of faith through hardship will always stick with me. One of his favorite songs by Matthew West includes these lyrics:

Maybe the reason for the pain
Is so we would pray for strength.
And maybe the reason for the strength
Is so that we would not lose hope.
And maybe the reason for all hope
Is so that we could face the world.
And the reason for the world
Is to make us long for home.

There is no doubt that Marc Davidson's hope in eternity with Jesus Christ has been fulfilled and that he is home, in eternal glory praising his Savior.

On April 23, 2023, two weeks before he graduated from Grace College, Frankie married Anna Frey. These are her observations of her father-in-law.

Anna: Frank and I started dating in December 2021. Very quickly after Frank and I met, he invited me to come to his home and meet his family. Now Frank had informed me of his dad's journey with cancer, and that he was currently doing and feeling very well. That first time meeting Marc was memorable. As I walked into the Davidson home for the first time that cold day, I was greeted with at least seven gigantic hugs, one being from Marc. His big embrace was welcoming, warm and kind.

We sat around the dinner table that evening and shared a big pan of lasagna and lots of milk. Dad laughed hard, asked engaging questions, and made me feel known and seen. Little did I know that every time after this visit, I would see and experience Dad change firsthand. From that December 2021 until Dad met Jesus face-to-face in May 2022, I saw his body physically decline but his spirit refine. Dad repeated this verse often and it comes to mind now: "Therefore, we do not lose heart. Though outwardly we are wasting away, yet inwardly we are being renewed day-by-day," 2 Corinthians 4:16.

BRAVE AT HEART

We saw Dad's body waste away, but his spirit rebuilt in a way that caused everyone to see Jesus specifically through Dad's last six months. It was what sustained him, gave him energy for the day and gave him the motivation to continue bringing heaven to earth until his last breath.

I remember a night at the Davidson home when Frank, a few siblings, Dad and I were all cuddled up together on the couch. Dad at this point wasn't feeling well; however, all the sudden, he started praying in a way I've never heard before. One by one, he went down the members who were lying on the couch and prayed blessings over us. Talking to God gave Dad comfort, peace and joy. I remember streams flowing from my face because of how overjoyed I was by the presence of the Lord that I felt that night. Dad prayed over my life, thanked God that Frank had found "the one" (even though we weren't even engaged yet) and prayed for us a spirit of love, power and boldness.

It wasn't unusual to hear Marc and Lisa praying together upstairs while I would be at the Davidson home late at night. Powerfully together, unified as a couple, they loudly proclaimed God's truths and pleaded for God's will to be done in their lives. I would go home at night and cry to the Lord, thanking him for this godly example of marriage and begging him to do his good will in the lives of the Davidson members.

Almost a year after Marc was in glory, Frank and I got married. A piece was missing on our big day, as we missed Dad more than ever. Our hearts ached, but we rejoiced knowing that we will see Dad again very soon and that Dad is currently dancing on the streets of gold with Jesus.

Through the last six months of Dad's life on earth, my faith grew, just like everyone else who knew Dad and walked through this journey with him. His urgency to proclaim the good news of Jesus, tenderness towards his family in this time, and care to see how I was doing even when he was suffering moves me to think that Dad had the kind of faith Jesus desires in us—a faith that puts others first, clings to the cross and goes out of this life running the race Christ calls us all to. The last thing that Dad told me, when I left his house that day in May, was "Goodbye, sweetie." Even in his last days on earth, he lived a life of love and certainly made me feel like the most cherished person.

---- JIMMY ----

When I was asked to tell Dad's story through one experience with him, I immediately thought of working with kids alongside him. I had the pleasure of watching him teach some of his younger PE classes, being a student in some of his PE classes and spending lots of time with him in basketball camps. His attitude toward children ultimately reflected his attitude in life. He was always encouraging, laughing and sharing Scripture with them.

He would go out of his way to make sure that everybody felt included. His go-to way doing this was by giving everybody a nickname. Just as Jesus did in Matthew 19, Dad always loved and valued children. I feel obligated to share one of my favorites of Dad's quotes. Dad (who loved basketball as much as anybody) said that he could tolerate coaching basketball if that meant that he could share the Gospel with young men. That quote always stuck out to me, and it really encapsulates a lot of the man Dad was.

I think he'll impact how I'm going to be a father because by first and foremost loving God, he always made a big point about the best way you can love your kids is to love your wife. I think he had a perfect balance of being disciplined with us but being tender, too. I can do myself well by modeling my family after how he built this one.

As one of his players, I don't think he changed a bunch on his philosophy between being dad and coach. I always felt he held me to a higher standard than the rest of the kids, but at the same time, I truly believe that if a stranger walked into practice, he would say, "Which one is his son?" I don't think it would have been obvious. Dad always said once we were in the car after practice, "Coach" is off and "Dad" is on. He'd love to talk about practice, but we could talk about other stuff.

This year as a player was definitely different than even last year, because last year, he received the diagnosis, but he was still feeling

BRAVE AT HEART

100 percent. This year, he was gone the whole fall, and he wasn't at anything in the preseason (because he was in Arizona receiving treatment). But he was there for the first practice, and honestly, I still thought he was feeling 100 percent even through December. Then around Christmas break and our Christmas tournament, I started to notice the lack of energy and him hitting the wall. It was amazing how he could always turn it on for practices and games and pregame speeches.

The last five to ten games of the season when the JV was playing, the varsity would be going in and out of the locker room, and he would just be lying in there listening to some Christian music. And then he'd pop up and give the pregame speech. On the court, I didn't notice much difference.

My uncle was telling me a few months ago how he was so proud of how this team handled everything with my dad's situation, how we always displayed Christ well and reflected His glory. I think my dad was the same way. He said this was the most cohesive group he ever coached. We had a lot of senior leadership. It was really special to see how the team was there for me through that whole situation. It was great this year for me because the rest of my family was walking through it, but so were my teammates, and it was great to have them as my community. They were obviously hurting, too. They felt a good portion of that hurt, and they saw more than almost everybody else.

This year as a coach, I think he did the best he could have done, for sure. I think it was great for him to continue coaching.

One year after Marc's death
The last couple years have been a challenging, yet amazing, whirlwind of events. Obviously, going into my senior year, things were a lot different. My dad was no longer here to be both my father and my coach. I knew this would be an adjustment and that I would need to lean on the Lord for strength. At the start of the school year, our new coach and PE teacher, Matt Roth, came and asked me if I wanted to help intern during his eighth-grade gym class period. I gladly accepted.

Looking back on being his student aide, I see how important it was for that time in my life. I already had a really good relationship with Coach Roth from years prior, but this took it to a different level. Every day, we'd stand and talk for the entire period while watching the kids play various sports. These talks ranged from anything as simple as his kids' Little League games to deeper conversations about hardships in each of our lives. Getting an extended period of time to just get to know Coach Roth at a deeper level was huge for me.

On November 29, the day of our first game, my mind was everywhere. I wondered how good a team we were going to be. Furthermore, we had a tough North Side team coming in to play us. It was also my first game without my dad as the coach. They were doing the court dedication before the game, and I had been getting interviewed all throughout the day. So I was all over the place in what I was thinking.

In one of my classes that day, we were doing an activity in which we had to read something out of any book from our bag. I grabbed my Bible and flipped to a random page. I "just so happened" to flip to Jeremiah 31, whose heading is, "The Lord Will Turn Mourning to Joy." Immediately, I felt a peace about the night and, really, the whole season. From that point on, I would read that chapter before every single game.

In the end, our team finished 27-3 and with another 2A state championship. That season truly was one of the biggest blessings in my life so far. I could not have asked for a better coaching replacement for my dad than Coach Roth. He has a very similar focus for the program, developing champions for Christ. The team was a brotherhood that makes me smile right now as I think about it. And to cap it off by winning the state championship was incredible, especially after the devastation of the previous year's loss. I continually praise God for all He did during my senior year!

---- **JAELA** ----

When I think back to my favorite memories with my dad, I think of vacations and road trips. We went to Williamsburg and Branson for a lot of our vacations. We would drive there during the night, and I would wake up and hear him singing to songs. He loved a lot of different music and loved singing along, loud and proud. He loved Pearl Jam and Zac Brown Band and Michael Jackson and Michael W. Smith. We both love the song "Meant to Be" by Florida Georgia Line, and we called it "our song." I remember one vacation to Branson after driving through the night, we woke up to Dad telling us that we were taking an old-time photo. We hadn't even checked into our hotel yet, and it wasn't what anybody felt like doing, but we knew it meant a lot to Dad, so we did it. The picture makes us smile today.

We didn't have a lot of money with seven kids. We always shared things like ice cream and drinks and ordered off the dollar menu. But Dad was always happy to spend money on vacations, so we could make special memories like going to Busch Gardens and Colonial Williamsburg and shows in Branson. He never really liked roller coasters unless he was with his kids, and then he would go on because he knew we enjoyed them. He loved a show called "Celtic Fire" at Busch Gardens with Irish singing and dancing, so we would go every year. Dad would clap and cheer and yell "Bravo!"

Hanging out with our family was my dad's favorite thing to do. He loved us so much, and he loved spending time with us. He loved old movies from the '80s, like The Great Outdoors and What About Bob? They made him laugh so hard he would cough. He always had the loudest laugh in the room. He could laugh at something nobody else thought was funny and something he had already seen a bunch of times before. He loved those movies, and he loved sharing those with us.

Dad wanted to spend a special night with each of his kids. My special night with him was going to see Sing 2. We had the whole theater to ourselves. When Dad heard the song "Sky Full of Stars" by Coldplay, he pulled out his phone and started recording a video to send to Mom. It was the song he played when he surprised my mom for their twentieth anniversary. After that, we went to PF Chang's to eat. I had never been there, but Dad knew me so well, he knew I'd love their orange chicken.

I miss my dad. I am so thankful for the ten wonderful years I had with him. I will never forget his visitation and how many hours people stood in line to see us to give us their love and support. My Dad was someone who wanted to tell as many people as he could about Jesus, even when he didn't feel good. I am very thankful to be a Davidson.

---- ISAIAH ----

My favorite memories of my dad are being in the gym with him. I would go with him when my brothers went to work out. Dad would shoot around with me before going upstairs to lift. Sometimes we'd play one-on-one, and he would usually win best-out-of-three. Sometimes I beat him, and that was fun, but he wasn't really trying hard. He wouldn't run back on defense a lot, so I would get the rebound and just run. He could shoot threes really well. Sometimes he would back me down and push me back. Those times were fun.

I have good memories of playing baseball in our backyard with my dad and brothers. He would hit grounders to me with a bat in one hand. I remember watching him in chapel at school do some of the things he does for Strongman. He could break a wooden bat in half, and we would all cheer so loud. He would ask for kids to come up and stand on this thing he called the yoke, and he could lift like ten kids. He did a tug of war contest between the boys and the girls. He would stand in the middle with his hands gripped together and then have like seven boys on each arm trying to pull his hands apart. The boys could never get his hands apart. Then he would have the girls come up and do the same thing. The girls would start pulling, and he would make it look like he was really trying hard, but then his hands would come apart and he would fall down on the ground, really dramatic. And the girls would be cheering so loud. But we all got really quiet when he talked about Jesus.

I had Dad for a teacher in PE, and that was fun, too. We'd play dodgeball, and sometimes he was on the other team. We all loved it when he said we were playing Dr. Dodgeball for gym that day. That was my class's favorite thing to play.

I got to be with Dad for summer basketball camp and for Future Braves. We would do a bunch of drills, and the winners would get

Gatorade or popsicles at the end. He would have us memorize a Bible verse each week, and he would end each day talking to us about God. He told us to do everything like we were doing it for God.

My Dad asked me to be the assistant manager for his team the last three years, and I guess a lot of kids would like to do that. Mostly, I'd get water bottles and get everything set up before practices, and then I'd get all the balls in the racks after. I remember when Dad would let me do the scoreboard during practices, and sometimes he'd rebound for me after practice. Sometimes, when they watched film at the end of practice, I'd get to play one-on-one with manager Ty Nigg. This last year, I filmed Blackhawk's games instead. I got to see and hear my dad coach.

I remember during the state championship game when Marcus was a senior, I got to go into the locker room and spray water around after they won.

We had a special night when just me and my dad got to go to a Pacers game against the Bulls, and when we were in Arizona, we got to go see the Suns versus the Lakers. Those games were pretty special with my dad.

Basically, everybody at Blackhawk loves him and looks up to him. He is a good man and a good gym teacher and the best dad. It really hasn't been the same without my dad. I mean, I can remember going home after school during the basketball offseason and either watching Different Strokes or Andy Griffith with him. I really enjoyed spending time with him. On Wednesdays, my mom was a youth group leader, so she would go to Blackhawk. And during that time, me and Jaela would spend special time with my dad at home. He made it a really big deal and called it "Wednesday night with Dad." At my house, I wasn't really allowed to eat sweets unless there was something special going on, but my dad would say, "It's a special night with dad," and he would let me and my sister have anything we asked for to eat.

I know my dad loves me and am thankful I am his son. I can't wait to see him again.

Marc gave Isaiah the nickname "Bomber." Coincidentally, about a month after Marc's passing, Isaiah made a huge half-court, game-winning bomb of a shot in the championship game of the 2022 Grace Basketball Lancer Camp. He was mobbed by everyone on the court and buried under all the celebrating bodies.

Marc with Wes and Will at baseball • 2008

Christmas 2019

Marc and Jaela on Marc's birthday • March 1, 2021

CHAPTER 38

Narrator: *The week after Matt Roth returned from his honeymoon with the former Lindsay Enterline in the summer of 2013, he received a breakfast invitation from recently named Blackhawk Christian coach Marc Davidson. A former Indiana University basketball player, Roth was trying to feel his way through finding an assistant coaching position but lacked the teaching components most schools were looking for.*

Matt: Marc and I met at Bob Evans on (State Road) 37 and talked for a couple hours. It became very obvious to me, being extremely young in my faith compared to him at that time, that he had been through a lot of things similar to what I had been through. We had a lot of things we could relate on, as simple as that we both grew up in Illinois, and we were pretty dominant in our respective areas. Early on in that process for me, God was using basketball in different ways, and it wasn't necessarily wins and losses, but highs and lows and growth areas, and that was the first time I had gotten my mind wrapped around coaching basketball. Marc and I connected right away at that the first meeting, and it led to a great three years as he established his culture with Blackhawk basketball.

The Braves went 16-10, 20-7 and 16-12 in those three seasons, winning three sectional titles. Matt taught individual skill development on the side and eventually took a position at Optimum Performance Sports, which limited his participation with the basketball team, so he stepped away. Ironically, at about the same time, Lindsay became coach of the Blackhawk Christian girls volleyball team, and she led the Braves to the 2017 Class A state championship. That was also her last season as coach, as the Roths were growing their family. They now have three children: Hudson, Baylon and Karsyn. Lindsay is the intermediate assistant principal for Blackhawk Christian.

Matt: I still found myself going to Blackhawk games when I could, and Marc and I would stay in touch. Any time we did have a conversation or a phone call or a chat after a game, it was like we had never missed a beat. We still had a unique friendship even when we were not working together.

Matt came back to coaching as a Heritage High School assistant in 2021-22. He was shocked when Blackhawk Christian announced on March 13, 2022, that Marc was stepping down.

Matt: I had been texting Marc back and forth over spring break. I still had the intent of us just getting together and talking, with my goal of coming back on staff with him. I wanted to be around him more, to learn more from him and be around the program and the boys, and I didn't care if it was to be a volunteer or JV assistant. We never got that opportunity.

The announcement that he was stepping away just hit me like a ton of bricks. Then the job posted, and I wasn't mentally ready for that process or the emotion of going through it. It took me a while before I got my head together and felt I was as prepared as I was going to be and sent my stuff in.

Matt was named Marc's replacement on May 4, and Marc came to open gym after school that day to introduce him to the players.

Matt: It was the first time I could see he was fading. You could tell he didn't sound like himself, but you could still feel that excitement and joy in his voice. It was just so unique to have him introduce me, but also to pray with the boys and I. It was a memory of Marc I'll never forget. It was him sharing that testimony of "this is God's will and what He has planned for us." There was never any hesitation or doubt, and he had such a confirmed stance that this is good.

He and I sat for about 15 minutes during open gym, and he gave me a scouting report on every kid right down the list. That's something I cherished and shared with them at the end of the season banquet, the one or two lines that Marc shared with me of what to expect of them and what they meant to the program. That was one of those days I'll never forget, the strength he felt that day and the ability to feel confidence in the transition. The players and I, we didn't have to do anything other than get used to each other because he instilled that faith in us that this was the right thing. It was a powerful day for our program and one I will hold close to my heart forever. All I needed to do was step in and lead them with the confidence and the poise and trust them in the same way Marc trusted them to go out there and compete and play.

It's just funny how things develop because here I am, in my first year of teaching, and they give me Jimmy as my senior assistant. The whole time, it's almost like that first breakfast with Marc because Jimmy and I are talking about anything under the sun. It was just a clean slate, no pressure, no basketball, and we were able to build that relationship and talk. It was such an amazing opportunity looking back at it now, and it provided me with a unique opportunity to see him as a leader, too. It gave me a firsthand look at the type of young man I was getting in Jimmy, but it also was a way for us to get everything out of the way. The hardest thing for me was I just couldn't even imagine ... you lose your coach, but then to lose your dad through that process.

Having Jimmy there, in a lot of ways, was a rock to me because I could go to him and give him one or two lines of what needed to happen, and he could relay it. He was the cliché of a coach's kid on the floor, because he learned from Marc, and he learned from his grandpa. The message just had to loop through me because God had a different plan than maybe everybody else did.

Jimmy was just so incredible. I still get chills thinking of the semistate and his leadership there by being able to calm us down in what was a physical and emotional final game. And then in the state finals game, he was just such a rock and led us well and had one of his better floor games. As we're making that frantic rally in the second half, every time I called a timeout, he was getting to the huddle before I could get in there, and he was all about touching his head and saying it's all about staying true to who we are and staying grounded. Something I learned during those times with Marc, we could be having a great game, but he made sure we were always grounded. The opponent changes every night, but the standard of play we hold ourselves to never changes. Jimmy just took it and ran. We played through a lot, and so many times throughout the year, Jimmy would be relaying a message before I could even get it out.

Besides replacing Marc as coach, there were questions how Matt would do sharing his testimony because the coach's faith had become an integral part of the Blackhawk program.

Matt: It was something I shared with them in the interview because they talked about what a huge platform there was, and they wanted to know, "What does that look like to you?" Part of the answer was, "I don't know yet." It's something I struggled with over the past several years in my previous job, where you are able to get a very good relationship built with players, and at times, I felt like I missed the boat in sharing my faith with them. It's such a tricky line of, "What can I say, and what can't I say?" That drove me nuts internally.

Coming to Blackhawk and knowing Marc, there's no way I can fill those shoes. His testimony, his story is so much different than mine, and he can recite Scripture at will in any situation; I can be in the middle of it and paraphrasing it, and I can know where to go in my Bible and flip through to find the exact Scripture, but to have it just absolutely flowing is just not me, and that's OK. I was able to take and learn and, at the same time, just be open to learning from others who had also learned from Marc.

I felt like the Lord had been working on me to become more outgoing, but Marc was always unapologetic, and "This is faith, this is the Word of God, this is truth, so we don't need to have any shame in sharing that, or worry that it's going to offend somebody. You just need to share the truth and the joy of having a relationship with the Lord." I got to experience that a lot by seeing those young men step up and share that postgame prayer, and the Word is so powerful, and there is great joy in that. It's special.

The Braves maintained the traditions Marc had started, all of which built to another state title run. Matt and Lindsay are the first husband and wife couple to lead individual teams to state titles in Indiana high school history.

One of Matt's favorite memories relates directly to Marc's influence on the entire Roth family.

BRAVE AT HEART

Matt: Baylon was in kindergarten last year, and they had been learning about heaven. They passed the microphone down the line and asked about who they were excited to see in heaven. It gets to Baylon, and I'm thinking he's going to say his teacher or one of his grandparents, and he says Coach Davidson. There I am, sitting in the back, bawling my eyes out. He never had Marc as a teacher, but he was always interacting with him because Marc knew he was my kid and Lindsay's kid and gave him high-fives in the hallway or the lunchroom. Just to see how Marc is still influencing my boys is really something.

Jimmy with Matt Roth

Collage made by one of Marc's former Blackhawk players, Jacob Lindsey; photos by Judd Johnson, Leverage Photography

CHAPTER 39

Narrator: *Asked for a story that typifies the kind of man his father is, Marc responded with a story about a graduation party. As an athletic director and coach, every spring means attending graduation parties, he said. One time, the dad of the graduate came up to Don Davidson, maybe because he was the biggest man there, and pointed out a strange man who nobody seemed to know. "I'm just kind of watching, and Dad goes over, and within a minute, he's praying with the guy," Marc said. "My dad did that kind of stuff all the time. My dad was unashamed and said, 'This is who I am, and this is what I believe.'" Marc was amazed at the example Don always set.*

Marc: I would love to share so many of these little lessons I learned from my mom and my dad, things that stick with you. For a coach, it's not so much what you teach as what you emphasize, and there were certain things that my parents emphasized that were non-negotiables.

First thing my dad taught me was a work ethic. He was a worker, and he's still teaching. He just stopped coaching two years ago. He coached 53 years and is in the Illinois Basketball Coaches Association Hall of Fame with 723 wins. They named the gym at Aurora Christian after him. He grew up on a dairy farm, and you learn how to work on a farm. He just instilled that value of hard work into us. It's not something he just talked about; he lived it.

What was really neat, back in 1993, Dad started a seal coating business for parking lots, driveways and such. He kind of stumbled into it, and he's still doing it. He had a connection who was getting out of the business, and he gave my dad a very basic idea of what to do, and so Dad seal coated the Aurora Christian parking lot with us in 1992. Now, 30 years later, he's still going, and it's been a really good summer job. On and off, I helped out for years. Matt helped for years, and my brother-in-law, Marshall, helped for years. Now he's getting to the next generation. My two nephews, Luke and Joey, did it for several years, and Marcus did it last summer.

That is training on the spot. The memories that we all have had with our dad and grandfather on a parking lot are just so much fun. It's hard work because if it's a 95-degree day, being out on the

BRAVE AT HEART

asphalt feels a lot hotter than that. My dad calls himself a crack master because he's been filling cracks with hot tar for so long. You crank that stuff up to 400 degrees, and it's hot work. I was the pail guy—5-gallon buckets, dump them out there, and you move the stuff around with nylon brushes.

Unbelievable memories being out there with my dad and being able to be with my brother and brother-in-law. You get to know one another for sure. I've even related that to my coaching because some people view it as either we're going to have fun or we're going to work hard. I tell my kids that's a "both-and" thing, and a lot of them have never been exposed to it.

My dad was one of four boys, big boys. My dad most of his life was 6 feet 4 and 280 pounds, and he was the third-biggest of the four. My Uncle Billy was the youngest, and he was mentally challenged. They started him in kindergarten, but the local public school was unable to educate him, so he was basically sent home, and he never went back to school. My grandparents just took care of him. I learned so much from my Uncle Billy. His speech was difficult to understand, but if you had been around him for a while, you could understand what he was trying to say. His attitude was this: As long as he had people to be around and work to do, he was as happy as could be. He would seal coat with us, too, and we had so much fun working with him. My dad grew up defending his brother. I talked about things that you emphasize, and making fun of other people was absolutely not tolerated. You just did not do that. Period. And that stemmed from my dad defending his brother.

Retard—that word is as bad as any profanity to me. It ticks me off. Dad just didn't tolerate it, and neither did my mom. I learned from my Uncle Billy because all he wanted was to be around people and have something to do. When we started seal coating, it was fun for him. My grandma would say the worst thing was when you'd have a rainy day and he couldn't go seal coating. He would be waiting out on the driveway.

I think about the summers for teachers, for a lot of people, it's just time to take a deep breath, but what we really found is you get rejuvenated by being outside and working with family. Those were just really special times.

There was a stretch where Dad was the principal and athletic director at the same time, along with being the basketball coach. My dad loves to work, and I'm glad he taught me the lesson that work is fun. There's a joy in it. It's really a Biblical idea. God built us to work. Colossians 3:23 says, "Whatever you do, work at it with all your heart, as working for the Lord, not for human masters." When you can take that attitude into the simple and the mundane ... As a teacher, you do mundane and simple tasks every day, and when you can infuse Colossians 3:23 into that, there's always purpose. That is something my dad taught me. Whatever he was doing, he was giving it his all.

Lisa: We all had so much respect for your dad. We didn't want to disappoint him, and he raised the bar for how we should be different, always representing the Lord. Your teammates at ACS have brought up how Coach ingrained in them, "Leave it better than you found it." They never forgot that small but powerful way we can be different than the world.

Marc: Both Mom and Dad seemed to have an eye out for the underdog, and I think as a teacher, that's a great trait to have on your radar. Invariably, you'll have that one kid who is not getting it or struggling or whatever. My mother honestly reminds me a lot of Lisa. She has this uncanny gift ... I can't even venture to guess how many people out there would say my mom was their best friend. She was like that with everyone, and she just connected with everybody. She was super inclusive. She never wanted to leave anybody out. She always included people in things and was a real peacemaker. She was a very compassionate person. And she always wrote letters.

Lisa: She was famous for her Christmas letter every year that went out to probably 500 people. She'd send notes of encouragement all the time and was the most generous person. She was the home economics teacher and often used her paycheck to buy all the supplies she needed for her class. After she retired, she made the most incredible scrapbooks of the basketball season. Not just for Matt, Marc, Mindy and Don, but for every player on the team and cheerleader. She would make photocopies of all the articles and grab programs from every school and pass out completed scrapbooks to each of the players and cheerleaders. She also loved to take pictures at people's weddings. She wasn't a wedding photographer; she was just the friend invited to the wedding that wanted to capture as many pictures as she could of the day for the family. She would go to Walgreens first thing in the morning and develop all of the pictures and put them in an album and deliver the album to the parents of the bride or groom the very next morning after the wedding.

Marc: Mom was big on manners and being courteous and being friendly. I remember one time—I forget how old I was—we went to our pastor's house. We had developed a good relationship with our pastor's family. Pastor Harold Masted was a huge influence on my dad, and they developed a great friendship. We'd go to their house for meals, and they came to ours. At their house once, and I took a bite, and I don't know if I grimaced or made a noise, but Mom gave me the stare down, and I got a lecture on the way home. If you are at somebody's house, you are going to eat it, love it and thank them for it. That was another lesson that they just ingrained in us.

It was neat to see how my mom and dad complimented each other so well. It's going to be eerily similar to my and Lisa's story. My dad was an extreme introvert, and my mother was super outgoing.

Lisa: His mom had the best laugh and told the best stories. She was so accepting, never intimidating, never condescending, never unapproachable. She and Dad quickly embraced Julie and I and invited us to all of their family things. She set such an example for me on how to be the best mother-in-law. She somehow made me feel like I was as much her daughter as Marc was her son. I had no doubt that she loved me as much as one of her own. When she told me on their visit to us in France in 2003 that if the melanoma ever came back, it would come back with a vengeance, I remember thinking, "What would we do without her?"

She was the organ player at Helmar, and she and Dad were involved in everything at both church and school. Their lives impacted so many people in the community. She loved family reunions and staying connected to distant family. I never knew anybody who called so many people their cousin. She was the ringleader, the glue of the family, that made everybody feel important and cherished.

Family time was so important to Steph. She was the one to plan family vacations and parties and nights out to eat. She made our collective family time together one of her top priorities.

Marc's dad was the athletic director, the basketball coach and, some years, even our principal, too. Marc was a gym rat, so if his dad was at school, he wanted to be in the gym, so they were always at school together.

Marc: We lived 25 minutes from school, so when you went in, you were there for the day. The other thing about being a coach's kid, you can get into the equipment closet. I would put a jersey on under my clothes and, after school, would shoot around in the gym. Those days were unbelievably fun for me. I was with my dad only part of the time, but all the time, I was just watching him. I think life as a coach's kid, you have to put up with some stuff, but it's fun.

Dad would have "Christian" on the front of every jersey for every sport instead of "Aurora Christian." It was just Christian. There was responsibility in that and a reminder of who you are representing.

Dad also used to teach the high school Bible class.

Lisa: There were probably 175 people in our high school, and we'd all be in the auditorium for Bible class. After my childhood pastor, I would say that his dad has been the biggest spiritual influence on my life. He was a powerful teacher that taught with such conviction, and like Marc, he has so many Bible verses memorized that he can rattle off at any time. Even as a history teacher, he tied the Word of God into every lesson.

Marc: My dad to this day loves to teach the Bible. He leads Sunday School, and he preaches, though he never had formal training. He'll fill in at his church and, over the years, at a couple of nearby churches. He speaks at camps for a week. He's a really gifted Bible teacher.

The memories I have of my dad ... I remember little things like doing stats with him after the games. He was tabulating his stats, and he had a cadence to it. I can still hear him. Amazing memories.

Abraham Lincoln was described as velvet steel, and that's a great description of my dad. He can be hard and strong when the situation calls for it, but he was so tender with my mom. I never heard him raise his voice with her.

Mom was diagnosed with melanoma in 1983. She was fair-skinned and blond. She had this mole on her back, and my cousin David had just been in for a test, and so my Aunt Geri said, "Steph, you need to get that looked at." They looked at it, and it was a level 3 (level 1 being the least dangerous and level 5 being the most). They took it out, a big aggressive chunk, but it metastasized in her liver and lungs 23 years later.

When the cancer was found on a CT scan in December 2006, we were told that it wouldn't respond to chemo or radiation. She had surgery to remove the lower lobe of one of her lungs in January 2007.

Lisa: There was only one treatment the doctors could offer called IL2, and it only had a 4% chance of stopping the melanoma. They decided it was worth a shot.

Marc: She had to be admitted into Loyola to get the intensive IV treatment. After a week of treatments, Dad was on his way to go see her on a Saturday, and he was informed that she had suffered a stroke overnight. She was never the same after that. From that standpoint, Dad had some time to brace himself.

Lisa: We were so thankful we were not in France still. We were living about one and a half hours away in Gurnee, Illinois.

Marc: That was part of the reason why God nudged me to go to Trinity International. I really felt like the Lord led me there.

She passed away October 30, 2007, and Dad was still coaching at Aurora Christian. He coached that entire season, but he was not in a good place. I'd never seen my dad like that. My dad is one who is not good at a poker face and pretending he's okay, and he wasn't okay, and we all knew it. He was struggling majorly. All of us kids were where we just wanted to see him happy.

After Steph's death, Don Davidson approached Marc about taking over the varsity basketball program as head coach at Aurora Christian.

Marc: He had wanted me to take over for him for years, and we had talked about it for a while, but the Lord had to prepare me. It wasn't just a spur-of-the-moment decision.

Then he approached all three of us kids separately and said, "What do you guys think about me dating again?" It was a little bit of an awkward conversation, but we were all three at a point where we hated seeing him like this.

Lisa: Dad loved Mom so very much. I honestly have never known a man to so publicly adore his wife. He would talk about her when he was teaching, and it was so evident that he was madly in love with her and thought she was the most beautiful woman in the world and that he was the most blessed man in the world to be married to her. It was so evident that he was desperately missing Mom so much.

Marc: There was a lady from church, Sig Ostby, who had been a widow for 20 years, and she was a teacher at Parkview Christian, which was 20 minutes away. Sig's dad was a pastor, and he preached for a stretch at Plattville Lutheran, where my mom grew up going to church. My dad's family did not go to church. My dad used to call it a cheap date because he'd go to church with my mom and then they'd go back to her parents' house for hamburgers. Sig, given that her dad was preaching, would have been at those services. Dad is nine years older than her.

Lisa: Sig and her husband Mike Ostby had married and moved to Newark, Illinois, just down the road from Helmar. They had three children: Melissa, Erin and Justin. Mike died in a trucking accident when their kids were young, so she raised them by herself. She was diagnosed with esophageal cancer back in 2001 when she was 46 years old. Thankfully, Sig is in total remission. Sig and Steph had been in choir and a women's small group together. Steph always had a heart for Sig's kids.

Marc: First thing right after Dad and Sig got engaged, Dad flew all of us out to Arizona to visit Matt and Julie—Mindy's family of four and our family of seven had all that family time together. That was something that Mom was huge about.

After they got engaged, he told Aurora Christian he was retiring from coaching varsity.

Lisa: It was Dad's dream to pass on the basketball program that he started back in 1977 to Marc. Marc interviewed for the job and was hired to both replace his dad as the head varsity basketball coach and teach high school PE classes. Dad stayed at Aurora Christian as the athletic director, and Mindy was hired as his athletic secretary. Marshall had already been working there for four years as a sixth-grade Bible and math teacher and assistant football coach. Our five boys and their two boys went to school there together for that year. Dad decided to coach Will's fifth-grade basketball team, which is one of Will's best childhood memories.

Marc: We just loved seeing Dad and Sig happy. They've been married now for 14 years, and she still makes him happy.

Lisa: If we are pointing out blessings over this last year and a half, Dad and Sig, Mindy and Marshall, and Matt and Julie have just been incredible, and my mom, too. They have been in the trenches with us, fighting for us, fervently praying for us. Their schools and churches have been praying for Marc. We've been blown away by the way their communities have cared for us, too.

How do you say thank you to people who love and care so deeply for you? How do you say thank you to strangers who do so much for you? Until our dying breath, we will be grateful for all that God has provided for us through these people.

Davidson family vacation • 1988

CHAPTER 40

Narrator: *Dr. Kevin Rivers was Marc Davidson's pastor for several years at Blackhawk Ministries. He made an impression on Marc's life in many ways besides simply faith, and a relationship with Marc made a similar impression on Kevin's life as well.*

Some people in life do more than leave a mark, they become a catalyst in your life that changes you permanently. Marc Davidson is that kind of person. With a legacy far beyond the scope of those who had the pleasure of having a personal relationship with him before he went home to be with the Lord, Marc became a catalyst for change in countless people's lives, including mine.

Serving Marc and his family as their pastor, parenting kids at the same age, being fellow adoptive parents and being friends often provided a front-row seat to see the eternal impact he consistently made on all who knew or knew of him. Whatever Marc did, he did it with all his heart for the Lord. His life was lived with intentionality to exalt Jesus Christ above all, whether on the basketball court, in the weight room, at school, at church, as a parent or as a person.

Marc made everyone who knew him quickly feel like a friend. He possessed an unmatched natural ability to make you feel at home, no matter what level of prior connection you had. You could not help but feel safe, loved and valued when you were in Marc's presence. There is so much to learn from the way he lived with such intentionality, but three specific adjectives highlight the way he did everything with all his heart, as working for the Lord.

Relational

Marc's ability to relate to all people is a transcendent quality that affected every area of his life. His intimidating physical presence quickly got swallowed up by his capacity to make people feel loved and valued. I remember when I first met Coach. I had already heard about this highly respected, highly successful, physical specimen of a man. With his unforgettable voice, he made connections to our past in Georgia, quickly making me feel like I had a new friend on whom I would always be able to rely.

BRAVE AT HEART

Marc is the reason I have a deep appreciation for Popeyes chicken sandwiches to this day. While sitting at one of our sons' basketball games together, Marc said, "Pastor, you ever had a Popeyes chicken 'sammich' before?" I told him I had not, to which he simply said, "Well, you gotta have one. Want to go get one now?" Every time I see a Popeyes now or eat one of their chicken "sammiches," I thank God for the impact of Marc Davidson.

Deeper than chicken sandwiches is the way Marc cared for the children in our church and school. Coach had a profound impact on the lives of all the athletes in his circle, but so unique is the fact that his relational approach to life equally touched all the non-athletes around him, too. Marc remembered kids' names in an unparalleled fashion. Not only did he remember and call them by name in the hallways at church on Sundays and at school throughout the week, but he would also create nicknames for many of them. To this day, my son, Caleb, has a favorite nickname, "C-Riv." That was a Marc Davidson special. Many parents can relate to the impact of Marc knowing their kids by name and nicknaming them.

That relational ability did not just apply to little kids, either. Marc touched the lives of all the big kids, aka adults, just the same. On Sundays, he served our church as a deacon and greeter at the main front door. This was our church putting our best foot forward to connect with anyone and everyone that came in. His hugs, fist bumps, handshakes and booming voice greeting people made sure that all who came on Sundays felt the presence of Jesus before they even stepped inside the church buildings. Marc's intentional, relational love for people is a target to strive for in all we do.

Sacrificial

Marc's sacrificial approach to life also touched all that he did. He knew the power of making sacrifices and putting in the work, whether in the gym, on the court, in relationships or in life. I marveled at his ability to sacrifice and work hard. Many recall the results of Marc's sacrifice and discipline in Strongman competitions or basketball, but I remember it most off the court and out of the gym.

Marc sacrificed himself and his selfish desires daily to ensure that his authentic faith in Jesus was visible. One simple example stands out. Even after very late Saturday night basketball games, Marc would lead his family to be in church every Sunday. As his health deteriorated, he continued to show up on Sundays. As he was less and less able to stand during our worship times, but he continued to sit and lift his hands in worship. Even though you know he did not feel like it, his sacrificial discipline continues to make me feel motivated to be better for Jesus each day.

As Marc battled cancer and saw his physical strength wain, when asked how he was doing, he would constantly quote 2 Corinthians 4:16 and say something like, "I'm physically wasting away, but spiritually I am renewed every day, stronger than ever." That sacrificial mindset reminds me of the example of Jesus.

Eternal

I am not sure anyone I ever met has taught me more about what it means to live each day in our earthly life with an eternal focus than Marc Davidson. His impact on people was rooted in an eternal focus that caused him to do everything he did to exalt Jesus.

After winning the Indiana state basketball championships, Marc would remind the boys that there is way more to life than basketball. He would often quote Matthew 7, reminding his players to build their lives on a solid foundation, that basketball trophies would fade away, but their relationship with Jesus would not. Marc did not just build basketball players; he built young men with an eternal focus on Jesus.

Marc would creatively do anything to share Jesus in his life and at the school. He did everything in chapel services, from lifting children as weights to sharing his goals in battling cancer. I will never forget one of the chapels where Marc and Lisa spoke to students. He shared that his prayer began and remained that God would heal him but that it had shifted even more to a prayer he summed up in three words: "Jesus be exalted."

That prayer sums up the eternal focus of the life of Marc Davidson. What may have started as a prayer is now indeed a reality. Jesus has been and will always continue to be exalted through the example of Marc Davidson's legacy. His prayer for healing, though it wasn't made a reality in this temporary, earthly life, is also a certain reality as Marc is healed and in the presence of Jesus today. His eternal perspective has now become sight; one day, ours can too.

Jesus is the ultimate champion, and Marc has modeled Jesus so well. May we remember the relational, sacrificial, eternally focused champion who is Marc Davidson. May we not only remember but also emulate his example in all that we do, from sharing chicken "sammiches" to serving at church to parenting to loving the people God has given us to influence each day, in every way.

Marc with Pastor Kevin, Marcus and Frankie

CHAPTER 41

Narrator: *Marc's brother, Matt, is older by two years, and his sister, Mindy, is younger by two years. As we age, that difference means less and less as sometimes the relationships become closer. Marc and Lisa have been blessed to develop a closeness of unbreakable bonds with Matt and his wife, Julie, and Mindy and her husband, Marshall.*

Marc: Matt and I have had an awesome dynamic all the way through. He's the superintendent at Timothy Christian School in Elmhurst, Illinois. He is very outgoing, the life of the party, and I think in some ways, that made me almost a little more content in my introverted nature. If there was a social event of any kind, Matt was all about it, and I was perfectly content not to talk to people. I was not much of a conversationalist anyway.

Matt has always been a very good leader, and it's been fun to watch him professionally kind of climb the ranks from school teacher to principal and now to superintendent.

I learned a lot from him. He tackles things head-on, and we got to see that example, too. I was the team captain my junior and senior years after Matt had graduated, but he was always more vocal than I was. I became more vocal as my career went along, but in high school, I didn't say a lot and just worked my butt off.

Julie is such a sweetheart. In high school, she was really quiet. Matt dated probably almost every girl in the school. He has a little bit of Wes in him—the life of the party.

Lisa: They were the on-again-off-again couple in high school, but they got together once more their senior year and never looked back. Marc's dad always said how he and Steph would pray for their kids' spouses, and the Lord gave each kid the perfect spouse and helpmate.

I tell his dad now just how grateful I am to be grafted into their Davidson family tree.

I would describe Matt as our biggest defender through Marc's cancer journey. He has connections to people who have been able to do crazy things for us. Mindy, too, has reached out to people and researched and looked for every possible way we can fight this cancer. They have been incredible.

Marc: Matt's had to deal with unruly parents, so I'll go to him for advice all the time. He's just been through a lot of those battles, and he's really good at finding solutions. Whenever I have to make any decision that is in the realm of being big, I'm going to talk to him and my dad. Dad is more old-school, this is how it's going to be, and Matt finds the solution that somehow makes peace in tough situations. Walking away, maybe not everything is perfect, but he'll find a solution that both sides can live with.

Lisa: I would say Marc and Mindy have that, too. They can say hard things, but they are respected and loved by people in their circles. All three of them have the gift of being a competitor and problem-solver. The Lord has blessed Matt with a great circle of people who love us because they love Matt. You can tell he's looking out for me and the kids. He just wants to help take care of everyone.

Julie was my matron of honor, and Mindy was my maid of honor. We didn't really get to know each other until Marc and I started dating. Julie and I are pretty different, just like Matt and Marc, but I've come to value her opinion and how she sees things. She had the first grandkid in the family, so she was a mom a year and a half before we had Wes, and I valued her help in how to be a mom and raise kids. I tell her I wouldn't be the wife and mother that I am without her help and advice.

Marc: It's kind of neat when your brother and your sister are basically your two best friends outside of your spouse and your children. Mindy can be a firecracker, and she and Lisa just hit it off. I think what's neat is how well our spouses have gotten along. Sometimes those in-law relationships can be a little surfacy, but those deep connections have always been there for us. When the six of us get together, we just have a great time.

Matt and Julie were the first couple, and they got married in 1993, Lisa and I in 1995 and Marshall and Mindy in 1997.

Marshall went to U of I, also. We had a mutual friend, so I actually met Marshall before Mindy did. Along with my roommate Corey, we all had 8 a.m. classes near the Pennsylvania dining hall, so we'd get together at about 9 a.m. for breakfast. I liked him right out of the chute, and we got along great. I brought up my sister's name; I'm not going to say I was the matchmaker, but I did bring her up to him.

Lisa: Marshall was in our lives before Mindy came to U of I. He was a strong believer, so we hung out and all went to Friday night InterVarsity group. Marc and Marshall were in the same small group Bible study together, and he was in one of the six dorms that shared the same cafeteria, so we ate together a lot. Mindy met Marshall while she was still in high school and thought he was so cute, though he didn't see Mindy as anything more than just Marc's little sister. Mindy came to U of I in 1993 right after Marc transferred to Trinity, so we didn't see him a lot. Everything changed when he came to our wedding and saw Mindy in a different light. So our wedding day is when they became more than friends, and the rest is history. They love and respect each other so very much. Marshall jokes and teases me like a real brother would.

Marc: Marshall is a no-nonsense guy. First of all, he loves the Lord, and that struck me immediately. And he has a knowledge of God's Word. I was blown away. He is seriously impressive. That made an impact. He was involved with the InterVarsity group that we were in, and he was serious about growing in his faith. He has just an awesome sense of humor, and we spent a lot of time laughing together. When the six of us get together now, we do so much reminiscing, thinking back on old times, and you can retell the same story for the 100th time and still just die laughing. It's just a neat dynamic.

Marshall grew up on a farm and knows how to work, too. My dad was not a farmer, per se, but he grew up on a farm, and I grew up working on a dairy farm in the summers. What we find, and I try to tell kids this in basketball, sometimes they try to make work and fun mutually exclusive, but it's both things. There's something to be said for getting outside and manual labor and sweating. Unfortunately, many kids today don't appreciate that. Rake some leaves, push some snow, help a neighbor—there's joy in that and a joy in serving. We just found joy working together, teasing each other. The running joke was who forgot their wallet that day. "Bro, can you spot me?" Great memories, man.

Marshall teaches Sunday School at their church and is one of their elders. He has coached their boys, Wyatt and Hauk, in football because that's really his first love. I couldn't be more thrilled that Mindy ended up with Marshall.

They have four kids, two boys and two adopted daughters. They adopted Maggie from Korea in 2009, and then they adopted Joely from China in 2014.

Mindy handled the time when Lisa and I broke up so well. The Scripture tells us to speak the truth in love, and that's what she did with me. She was able to speak the truth to me about the fact that Lisa and I were not together, but she didn't press so hard that it would have driven me away. She supported me at the same time, and it was a tight spot for her, but she handled it so well, for both me and for Lisa. She was key through that whole thing. My sister and I have always gotten along so well. She's a strong woman with a heart of gold. She and Marshall are both as loyal as can be.

Lisa: The Davidsons are fiercely loyal, and as much as Mindy was loyal to Marc and loved him and thought the world of him, she also somehow had this amazing way of being fiercely loyal to me. I knew, when Marc was going through that, she and her family still deeply loved me, but they supported Marc. I knew I had their love and support, and that meant so much to me because I had gotten so close to them in the three years that we had dated. Mindy and I are kindred spirits, and we see life through the same lens. She gets me, and we get each other. We have the same heart. I love her so much.

Our two years living together at U of I were so much fun. As much as she loves Marc is just as much as she loves me and is there for me. Though I don't have siblings, I see how close our seven kids are, and I see the way Matt and Mindy and Marc love and care for each other, and I see how precious that sibling relationship is. They would do anything for each other.

Julie has three brothers, Mindy has her two brothers and I'm an only child. So all three of us girls grew up without a sister, and we have the sweetest sisterhood. We couldn't love each other more.

Marc: It's so neat to see, and Matt, Marshall and I are the same way.

Lisa: Marc and I are so blessed to call Matt and Julie and Mindy and Marshall not only our siblings but our closest and dearest friends in the world.

Marc, Mindy, Dad and Matt on Father's Day 2021

Davidson Thanksgiving · 2021

CHAPTER 42

Narrator: Marcus may be Marc and Lisa's fourth son, but in many ways, he is similar to a first-born in his closeness with his father in terms of spirituality. He has some of the same gifts as Marc, as he shows in his writing.

My dad typically left for school around 6:15 a.m. to work out and/or set up cones in the parking lot before class. Starting my junior year, I began going with him so I could have time to work out. My motivation was to improve as a basketball player, but the greatest blessing was the conversations with my dad. They could've been about faith, basketball, family stuff, advice about girls, the Chicago Cubs, politics, Seinfeld, classes, weightlifting ... anything. It was truly such an enjoyable experience for a father and a son to share every day.

These mornings were where I learned the value of uncomfortable conversations. Dad always said the biggest hindrance to his spiritual growth was his personal comfort, and that God did the most work in his life when he was out of his comfort zone. So without entirely knowing what I was doing, I pursued these uncomfortable conversations with Dad, and so much growth took place in my spiritual life because of it. When I knew the Holy Spirit was prompting me to have a particular conversation, I knew Dad was always someone I could trust to support me and give me sound, godly advice, encouragement and correction. I never regretted having the conversation after it was over. While I feel like my dad was perhaps my closest friend in this world, I didn't always feel this comfortable around him.

The first memories I have of my dad are fearful ones, and these are my very first memories of life in general. I remember one time while we were living in France—I couldn't have been more than 4—we were hanging out as a family watching TV when he asked me to do something, to which I responded by rolling my eyes or grumbling, or some other whiny gesture. I would soon find out that was the wrong answer. Dad gave me a look, and I must've closed my eyes because the next thing I knew, his hand had a firm grasp on my shoulder and he was speaking strongly and clearly to me, making sure I knew that what I did was unacceptable and wouldn't happen again. I don't remember what he said, but whatever it was, he certainly didn't stutter.

Instances like that led me to have a holy fear of my dad growing up—something I'm incredibly thankful for now because he was training me to someday fear the Lord the same way I feared him as a kid. I never once thought he was in the wrong but feared him because he always wanted the best for me and made sure I stayed on the straight and narrow.

It was a surreal moment on April 3, 2021, when we wept in each other's arms after my last high school game. Dad had his face buried into my shoulder, embracing me after the last game he'd ever coach me. He'd been battling cancer for months, but he said "I ain't crying because I'm sick. I'm crying because this is the last time I get to do this." He said it was extremely hard on him when he had to hug one of his boys after the last time he'd coach them. There was a lot of raw emotion that went into that year, which built up and sort of let itself out in that moment.

Another of those surreal moments came March 5, 2022, as he coached Blackhawk to a sectional victory, but something so much greater than basketball was taking place. He ministered to essentially the entire gym after the sectional win, when a massive group of parents, fans, students, friends, reporters and others circled him as he shared his situation and gave his testimony, as was his ritual after every game. I rode the bus home with him to keep him company since there was no one else with him but the assistant coach, who was driving. By that point, he was getting consistent fevers with chills and a pounding headache about every night, and those kicked in on the ride back to Blackhawk. I had to lay his suit coat over him and rub his arms and back to keep him warm as he lay, body shivering and teeth chattering, in the back row. Once he was able to get relatively comfortable—or once things got calm, as he would often put it—it felt sort of like an ordinary day riding to school just a couple of years prior.

So much had transpired during the two years between March 2020 and March 2022. It felt like we were living completely different lives. But there we were, despite all the twists and turns life had put us through, a father and a son enjoying each other's company. He brought up a passage in Romans 10 that says, "How can they believe in him if they have never heard about him? And how can they hear about him unless someone tells them?" (Romans 10:14). He was moved to tears by the verse and repeated it over and over. "How can they believe?! How can they hear unless someone tells them?"

This snapshot sums up Marc Davidson for those who don't know him. With tumors all over his body and in all sorts of pain, the most genuine cry of his heart was for those who don't know Jesus. He knew God had given him a platform, and he had no choice but to be that voice that tells others about the Gospel. And he was going to continue to do exactly that, no matter what got in the way. I wish I could remember more details about our conversation that night, but we've had so many just like it over the past months.

Since my parents got back from Arizona in the fall of 2021, Dad started sleeping on the couch in the living room because he couldn't lie flat in his bed without wheezing and coughing. So I decided to sleep out there on the couch next to him and Mom when I would come home on weekends from college. There were sweet memories made during those late nights as we'd lie there watching TV. The tumors in his stomach pressed against his bladder, so he had to get up to use the bathroom at least once every hour, meaning he was getting lousy sleep. It hurt to see him struggle, but these circumstances allowed us to squeeze so much more time together out of his last few months. We talked, reminisced, laughed, sang, prayed and cried a lot, too.

There also were lots of extremely painful nights in which we cried and prayed as we begged the Lord to heal him of this disease. These nights were often flat-out brutal, yet the Lord was doing so much work as we struggled together; the Holy Spirit's presence was so palpable. Over a couple short months, we told each other "I love you" and spent more time praying with each other than most people do in a lifetime with their father. Though I would've been a lot more comfortable—emotionally and physically—upstairs in my bed, I don't regret spending these nights with him. They were uncomfortable but productive, a concept I learned from none other than Dad.

The hardest night was the night Blackhawk lost in the regional final to end their season. I could tell his heart was really heavy because the season was over. While we were trying to hope for the best, we all knew that was probably the last time he would ever coach a basketball game. I'll never forget the feeling of being next to him as he was weeping at 3:30 in the morning, thinking about all the years he had invested into coaching and how badly he still wanted to continue to impact lives. He kept saying, "I don't want to think about it. ... I just don't want to think about it. It hurts too bad." And it hurt for us to see how the Lord had made him so gifted and passionate about something and how it hurt him when he realized he couldn't do it anymore.

Ecclesiastes 7:2-4 was the only thing keeping me on the couch that night: "It is better to go to the house of mourning than to go to the house of feasting, for this is the end of all mankind, and the living will lay it to heart. Sorrow is better than laughter, for by sadness of face the heart is made glad. The heart of the wise is in the house of mourning" (Ecclesiastes 7:2-4).

Despite how painful they were, these nights will be so special to look back on.

I rarely saw a very "tender" side of Dad early on in my life. (Please do not misread that—he's always loved with such a passion, and everyone who knows him will testify to that; he just expressed his emotions differently then.) I remember talking with some of my brothers a few years back about how Dad was starting to cry more in his "old age" and how we rarely saw him cry when we were younger. I can recall only a few times in my first decade of life where I witnessed it.

Once was when we saw Matthew West perform his song, "The Reason for the World," at his concert circa 2010; another was while we were watching the movie "Fireproof" as a family; and one more I can recall was when southern evangelist Bill Stafford preached at our church in Georgia. There were some others, but they were few. This isn't to say he was ever hardhearted or tried to be someone he wasn't—he was simply different then than he is now.

He's always just been so strong. Dad was easily the hardest working and the most competitive, intense and determined person I've known—and second place is not close. I was recently asked my opinion on the most competitive Davidson, and without hesitation I said, "My dad," without realizing the question pertained to my siblings and me. The man absolutely loves to compete. That was typically the first thing he would say when asked why he got into the sport of Strongman at age 40: "I love to compete." He would jokingly say, "Yeah, that weight room is probably gonna be where the Lord takes me home," and my mom hated when he said that because she knew how hard he pushed himself and because a wise man once said that behind every joke there's some truth. Something as trivial as a game of checkers, Dad would take so seriously that eventually, it was something I just considered normal. That is, until I noticed when people outside my family marveled at his competitive nature.

And his work ethic was unparalleled. Every day, he would display his commitment to excellence in everything he did. That work ethic was another thing I just figured was normal when I was younger since I was around it every day. The older I've gotten, the more I've seen how one-of-a-kind he really is.

Now that I'm looking on how strong my dad used to be from a worldly point of view, I can see that he's been displaying more strength than ever all through his worldly weakness. When giving his testimony, he often shares a passage from the 12th chapter of 2 Corinthians, a passage in which the Apostle Paul shares about a time in which God gave him a "thorn in the flesh," something meant to torment and harass him to keep him from becoming arrogant. Verses 8 through 10 read, "Three times I pleaded with the Lord about this, that it should leave me. But he said to me, 'My grace is sufficient for you, for my power is made perfect in weakness.' Therefore I will boast all the more gladly of my weaknesses, so that the power of Christ may rest upon me. For the sake of Christ, then, I am content with weaknesses, insults, hardships, persecutions, and calamities. For when I am weak, then I am strong" (2 Corinthians 12:8-10).

Dad's thorn in his flesh is cancer. I'm a witness that it has tormented him day and night. I'm also a witness that not only he, but so many other Christians around the world, pleaded with the Lord, that it would leave him so he could be fully healed. But the Lord has been telling him and the rest of us exactly what He told Paul so many years ago: "My grace is sufficient for you, for my power is made perfect in weakness." So Dad is content with these weaknesses, insults, hardships, persecutions and calamities, all so that Christ's power may rest upon him.

And I'm so thankful for the fact that His grace is sufficient for all of us in this situation. The Lord was very intentional when He said that; he didn't say, "My grace was sufficient for you," or "My grace will be sufficient for you." His grace meets us right where we are and is sufficient for us. Without Jesus, we would all be hopeless.

You might be thinking that it's awesome and inspiring that Christ's grace is sufficient for Coach Davidson. And while I might be stepping on toes, I'm fine with it because Jesus is very personal, so I will be, too. It's not enough to just appreciate how Christ's grace is sufficient for my dad, or even enough to think Christ's grace is simply sufficient in general. The question that you have to answer for yourself is whether Christ's grace is sufficient for you. And to quote my dad, there is no greater decision you could ever make:

"The devil will try to make you question—and it's okay to have questions—but don't ever question God's love for you. He loves you so much. He can't help but love us."

"I can only imagine what it will be like when I walk by your side. Just not for about 30 years, God."

"This old tent is falling apart, man. I'm getting a building from God."

One year after Marc's death
Grief is a process.

As lazy and cliché as that sounds ... it's true. At least, for me it is. C.S. Lewis wrote a book following the tragic loss of his wife to cancer called "A Grief Observed," filled with the most raw emotions and deep thoughts. He described grief as being "like a long valley, a winding valley, where any bend may reveal a totally new landscape," and I'd attest to that sentiment—you just never know what you may encounter on any given day or moment. Contrast these short excerpts from my personal journal as some perspective from me to you:

June 29, 2022: While I've felt tempted to question the Lord at times and ask Him, "Why him? Why us?", I've chosen not to because of Dad's example. Jesus, thank You that You're still using my dad's story to touch lives and that You're so far from finished with me. Give my dad a big hug for me today. I love You.

September 1, 2022: Last night, Dad showed up at home. He was strong and healthy and was so excited to see me. I ran into his arms, and we embraced and cried together—then my alarm went off.

It's been a long four months.

I miss him like crazy. Sometimes I kind of feel like I'm drifting, like there's just a discontentment somewhere deep down. I pray and beg God to help me to just make the most of my situation and be fully content, but it's hard. I want to feel completely content all the time, but I don't. I'm such a work in progress.

The June entry was while I was probably riding one of those spiritual highs that only come every so often, while the September one came straight from the trenches. It initially felt like something perhaps too personal to share. But when I chewed on it and prayed about it, I realized that if I'm not willing to be vulnerable and express what I've truly been through, then what's the point of this? I'm not one to play games, and I never cared for gimmicks; what you see is what you get with me, so that's what I'll do my best to lead you through. There have been twists and turns, ups and downs, tears and laughs, and victories and losses that I never would have predicted on my own. I'd love to say that I've felt nothing but joy and peace since Dad passed away, but it wouldn't be honest. I'd love to say that I haven't questioned God once during that time, but that wouldn't be truthful, either. I'd rather share my most genuine thoughts and what my actual experience has been like.

Waiting on God ...

I'm a few degrees shy of being a psychologist, so I won't assume this to be true for just anyone, but I tend to believe my most true and genuine thoughts come either early in the morning or late at night when I'm not entirely lucid and there's nothing to drown out the soul's yearnings. Sometimes when I'm in that in-between phase of sleep and consciousness, I fall down rabbit holes I didn't even know my brain had the intellectual capacity for until something reminds me of it later on the next day. That then leads to me inevitably try to revisit what was going on only to conclude I can't quite remember everything, but it sure was something. That's a rabbit hole in and of itself, with the purpose of setting the stage for a morning early this past June. I was floating in and out of consciousness as a simple thought that my subconscious had been repressing for months finally wiggled free:

Maybe I'm not waiting on God; maybe He's waiting on me.

It dawned on me how entitled my heart posture had been thus far throughout this grief process, how since Dad's passing, I'd simply been waiting on God to bless me and reward me as divine recompense for the sufferings of my family and I, and for how "good" I had been. While this never would've been something I'd have verbally admitted to, I was essentially living like God owed me. I would read verses like Psalm 27:14 ("Wait for the Lord; be strong, and let your heart take courage; wait for the Lord!"), and I'd pump my fist and pat myself on the back as I reminded God how patiently I was waiting for Him, hoping it would start the blessing process in which God would cure all my wounds and fill every void.

But early that June morning, the still, small voice of God whispered into my heart and reminded me that He is God and He doesn't owe me anything. For so long, I was expecting God to rain blessings down from heaven and into my hands, waiting for Him to bear fruit in the vineyard of my heart—only those hands were clenched fists and that heart was hardened and bitter, soil not ready to receive anything from its Creator. And it took over a year of frustrations and unanswered prayers for God to plow the soil of my heart and open my eyes to the fact that He's already given me everything, so why would I ever live as if He owes me? It took a really long time to realize that perhaps God was waiting on me to commit to Him with a deeper sense of trust and intimacy.

Wrestling with prayer ...

Ironically, so many blessings came about as a result of the simple realization that God doesn't owe me any. I was finally living truly free and chasing after God with a genuine heart, rid of any personal agenda. Yet the consequence of that realization is that I've grown wary and pessimistic about praying for things that I deeply desire, material things that my heart genuinely longs for (e.g., personal success and breakthrough in basketball; finding a girlfriend; building deep, meaningful friendships; feeling peace about what I want to do for the rest of my life; etc.). And this pessimism hid deep inside me until recently, when a slew of prayers that I'd been praying for seemed to all go unanswered one after the next. It felt like God was constantly dangling carrots in front of me, which I'd chase until He closed a door in my face and reminded me how futile my desires and strivings are. My patience dwindled to nothing. I was finally bold enough—or simply dumb enough—to give full vent to the frustration that had been buried under layers of scabs. I figured God already knows these thoughts, so why hide them from Him any longer?

When have You ever answered a prayer of mine?

You already took Dad from us, so I don't know why I'd expect You to answer my prayers now. I love that you're jealous for me, God, but isn't this a little extreme? Why do you keep on depriving me of the things I want so badly?

It feels like You want me to enjoy nothing in this life besides You, Lord.

But in that moment of unadulterated anger, God reminded me how much of a process this thing we call grief really is. This skepticism in my heart about my prayers going unanswered truly took root on May 9, 2022, when my best friend in the world died of cancer. Now that I think of it, those roots of doubt were forming well before my dad died. I can think back to early in 2022 when Dad's health was deteriorating, the late-night drives by myself where thoughts led to doubts, which led to questions, which led to fears, which led to tears, which eventually led to me screaming at the top of my lungs at my loving Father and demanding answers for why it felt like He was answering none of my prayers and why He was taking my dad from us.

In "A Grief Observed," C.S. Lewis talked of a similar kind of skepticism:

"What chokes every prayer and every hope is the memory of all the prayers [we] offered and all the false hopes we had. Not hopes raised merely by our own wishful thinking, hopes encouraged, even forced upon us, by false diagnoses, by X-ray photographs, by strange remissions, by one temporary recovery that might have ranked as a miracle. Step by step, we were 'led up the garden path.' Time after time, when He seemed most gracious, He was really preparing the next torture."

I'm not oblivious to the fact that maybe God isn't answering these prayers because deep down, that skepticism still remains ... and then comes the guilt associated with thinking that God would've saved Dad from cancer had I truly believed in my heart He would do what I was asking Him to do. A prayer I prayed seemingly a million times was, "God, I know that you can heal my dad, I just pray that you will heal him." Then I say I'm being too harsh on myself until another fresh wave of emotion kicks in and the guilt cuts a fresh wound right over what was already scabbed and trying to heal.

See what do I mean by saying that grief is a process? It's just a balance that I'm not too proud to admit I don't have figured out; how do I genuinely believe in my heart that God will answer my prayers yet keep my heart from becoming entitled and living as if God owes me? How do I look forward to heaven with "eager longing," yet also wait for it with patience as Romans 8 says? How do I fix my eyes on eternity yet stay effective in the here and now? These are just a few of the many questions filling my head that I do not have the answer to right now and I just have to live with. It brings me right back to 2 Corinthians 12, where God had to set Paul straight during all of his begging and bartering with the Almighty: "My grace is sufficient for you, for my power is made perfect in weakness." Help me to just be content with these weaknesses, Lord.

Choosing to trust...

I don't know why God made life this way, but I've become more convinced through every season that going through uncomfortable and even painful things is what makes life truly worthwhile. This is something I knew in my head two years ago but have really come to know in my heart in the time between then and now. In "Hope in Times of Fear," Timothy Keller wrote, "There are the good things in this world, the hard things of this world, and the best things of this world—God's love, glory, holiness, beauty. The Bible's teaching is that the road to the best things is not through the good things, but usually through the hard things, as Jesus himself shows us in Philippians 2:5-11." I've found that to be so very true in my life. So even though I wouldn't have set up the route to the best things like this, I can rest assured that God is in control and I'm not. He's painting a picture too glorious for me to behold, so He simply reveals small sections at a time to me, giving me enough incentive to take the next step of faith and trust Him with it. I can recall an instance in the weeks before Dad passed when I was wondering: Is this the hardest time I'll ever see in my life, or will it still get worse from here? And I found the answer to be both yes and no. While that was, indeed, the hardest time in my life up to this point, it was also the most blessed and meaningful time of my life by a wide margin.

I'm inspired by the examples of people throughout the Bible and history who went through unspeakable hardships they never deserved, and yet instead of giving in, they simply made the most of their situation. I wrote a paper about Job's view of God for my "Understanding the Old Testament" course last fall, which was transformational for my view of God's goodness through hardships, and I recently read "Unbroken," a truly unbelievable story. The Lord has been showing me that everyone is fighting a battle of some sort and is therefore faced with a decision between victimhood and victory. We will all reach a point in which the pain of life will either make or break us. So as far as I'm concerned, I can choose to either be broken into a victim so distracted by self-pity that I'm rendered useless for God's kingdom, or I can allow God to pick up the broken pieces and make me into a champion for Christ, whose character has been tested and proven under the fire of life's hardships. I'd much rather be the latter.

And trust me, there are instances where I pause and think about what my life would look like if Dad was still around and how desperately I wish I could go home and give him a hug and tell him I love him; moments like family gatherings, when I'm between Grandpa D and my baby nephew, thinking about how special it would be if Dad was here; moments when I'm conflicted and don't know which way to turn and would give anything for just one conversation because he'd know exactly what to say to encourage and direct me; moments when I think about someday when I'm a father and how much I wish my kids could know the man who raised me. Those are the moments where I feel like throwing my hands in disgust or diving into despair. They don't come around all the time, but my soul feels it when they do.

However, my soul finds greater joy in the little places, sights and sounds that bring Dad back to me all over again. Like the times I drive by Yorkville Square on Illinois Route 47 and see the hot dog stand I used to go to with Dad when I was in kindergarten. Some days, I'll see a father and a son out there sitting on a park bench, enjoying lunch on a beautiful summer day and enjoying each other's company; it's in that moment that I get to re-live the memories we made there and thank God for them as I wonder what we would've been talking about on any given trip to that hot dog stand. Or when I turn my radio to AM 670 and listen to the fuzzy static of a Cubs game, and I can see Dad pumping his fist or pounding the dashboard, depending on what announcer Pat Hughes is saying. Then there are all the times when I'm in the Blackhawk Christian weight room, and I can still see Dad there with a look of channeled ferocity, chalking his hands, taking deep, quick breaths before hoisting ridiculous weight into the air and praising the Lord all the while. Every time I hear "Better Man" by Pearl Jam, I hear his voice singing along, and every time I watch Seinfeld, I can still hear his laugh filling the room with the most genuine, unadulterated joy. Every time I'm in our basement sauna, I see him sitting next to me, and I can hear the Tommy Nelson sermons playing from his phone as he talks me through life and tells me he's proud of the man of God I'm becoming and that he can't wait to see what God will do in my life. These are the moments that keep me going. These are the moments that make those moments of despair feel few and far between no matter how often they happen.

These are the moments that ultimately allow me to see God's hand at work in my life, writing my story one chapter at a time in ways I'd never choose in the moment but never trade in hindsight.

Marc and Lisa at Marcus' senior night • February 2021

Marc and the boys at the Hall of Fame Classic • December 2020

CHAPTER 43

Narrator: *Since his initial diagnosis, Marc has made an effort to send regular emails to his family. Much like his family members do, the topics are things that touch his heart, but the messages are also opportunities to make sure he says everything he wants to say and for them to remember. There's no doubt his children, especially, will treasure those messages and pull them out in later years and still be able to hear his voice. One of the early topics was about prayer.*

Marc: To be honest, God continues to teach me about prayer. One of the things I say in email is that I've tended to think of prayer as a means to an end. Something is wrong, you have a need, you are sick, so you pray. But God has shown me it is an end unto itself, not nearly a means to an end. We are connecting with our Creator. Prayer is not about getting what we want from God, it is about becoming someone He desperately wants to make us. This process has helped me understand that.

Initially, the cry in my heart was, "Heal me," and I was pleading with God. I still pray for healing, but it's not the main cry of my heart any longer. Now it's, "Jesus be exalted in me throughout whatever circumstance you want to walk me through." That has been really healthy, and you just learn to stay more connected. There are times for all of us when we can fall into that self-sufficiency mode. We are going through life until we feel like we need God, and then it's kind of a Hail Mary, where we are crying out to Him. He wants us to walk with Him intimately every day. This experience has definitely helped me to do that.

I think it was A.W. Tozer who said, "He waits to be wanted." God just makes himself so vulnerable at that point. Sometimes circumstances come into our lives that push us closer to Him.

In his book Shattered Dreams, author Larry Crabb wrote, "As long as we view our purpose on this earth being to have a good time, to have soul-pleasure exceed soul-pain, God becomes merely a means to an end—an object to be used, never a subject rightfully demanding a response, never a lover longing to be enjoyed. Prayer and worship then become utilitarian, part of a cunning strategy to get what we want rather than a passionate abandonment to someone more worthy than me. Happy people, though they're right to be happy, face a subtle danger. They tend to spiritually gloat, to publicly express gratitude and praise for the good things they enjoy while privately thinking that blessings are their due.

"It comes down to this: God's best is available only to those who sacrifice, or are willing to sacrifice, the merely good. If we are satisfied with good health, responsible children, enjoyable marriages, close friendships, interesting jobs and successful ministries, we will never hunger for God's best. We will never truly worship. Unbroken people—happy folks who enjoy their blessings more than the Blesser—say thanks to God the way a shopper thanks a clerk. It's harder to discover our desire for God when things go well. We may think we have, but more often, all we've found is our desire to use God, not to enjoy Him."

Wow, that convicts me! We cannot go through life with the expectation that God will simply "fix" whatever it is that ails us. We cannot expect Him to arrange what happens in our lives in ways that will always make us feel good. Read through Hebrews chapter 11 to see how God "fixed" things for the heroes of our faith; verse 39 says that they "were all commended for their faith, yet none of them received what had been promised (in this life)." If God did not "fix" things on this earth for the men and women of Hebrews 11, why do we expect Him to do this for us?

What we can expect from God is to patiently remove any obstacle to our enjoyment of HIM! Romans 8:20-21 says that He allows us to experience frustration in all our endeavors apart from Him. He does this not to torture us, but in order for us to experience freedom! He has done this in my life many times, and though painful at the time, I am so thankful that He continues to remove those obstacles in my life.

The Scripture commands us to pray without ceasing. That just tells me it's more of a posture of our heart. Take every thought captive. It's walking in step with our Creator, and prayer is obviously the best way to do that. You get this attitude of, "Okay, God, we are doing this together. You are in control, and I'm just along for the ride. Wherever you want to take me and do with me, I'm willing."

This process has been good ... not that I'm praying without ceasing, but the attitude and posture of my heart is bent that way more than it used to be.

We've had really special prayer times with our kids. We've always prayed with them and for them. It's been neat just to see God kind of take that to another level. We just pray that our kids will continue to see the Spirit working in us. My dad used to say, "More is caught than is ever taught. They are going to see your example, and that will be more impactful than anything you say to them or teach them." When you get both of those things reinforcing one another, that's powerful. We want to teach them about prayer but also show them the importance of prayer and being vulnerable.

Matthew 6:6 says, "Go find our secret place wherever that is, and your Father who hears what is said in secret will reward you openly."

Even while they were dating, Marc and Lisa prayed together. Sometimes it was during meals or just when they were driving somewhere. Lisa said she already knew then he was a keeper, a man after God's heart.

Marc: Philippians 4:6 says, "Do not be anxious about anything, but in every situation, by prayer and petition, with thanksgiving, present your requests to God." Pray about everything. Anything in your life that has the potential to cause anxiety, worry and fear is an opportunity to surrender that to God and to connect with God in a deeper way.

Lisa: Connecting with God in a deeper way as in trusting Him more. This deepens our faith to take Him at His Word and believe in His promises. And we've been experiencing the next verse, Philippians 4:7, "And the peace of God, which passes all understanding, will guard your hearts and your minds in Christ Jesus." We have been amazed at the peace that God is covering our hearts and our minds with as we have trusted Him instead of letting fear and anxiety take over. This peace that God is giving us, it doesn't make sense!

I have come to find that prayer is a way of life—just like breathing. Praying is being in conversation with the Lord and calling out to Him throughout the day, not just before meals or at bedtime. He is always there for me to ask for strength or help or direction. He is always there for me to give Him the things that have me worried or afraid. It's asking Him to open my eyes to see what He wants me to see, and always seeing His hand in my life. I am more convinced than ever that not a single thing happens in our life by accident or coincidence and surely not luck. It's asking Him to interrupt my day with the people He wants me to talk to about Him. It's knowing that prayer is a way to walk through life together in relationship with our God. Knowing God is with us and promises to never leave us is the thing that we are clinging to.

Marc: I love the Psalms because David brought a rawness to his prayers. If you read through there, he prayed an awful lot for himself. It's okay to pray for yourself, but at the same time, you don't want to neglect praying for others in that process. God described him as a man after His own heart. There's something to be said for that raw, honest pouring our hearts out, like David did.

Lisa: During our first ten years of marriage, I had a calendar for every year where I would write down what we did every day, and I would fill in what God did, ways that He would answer our prayers and meet our needs. I love to go back and be reminded of God's faithfulness and see how everything that has happened had a purpose. I wish I had done a better job at doing that throughout our twenty-six years of marriage, writing down for us to see God's hand in all the things and all the people He's brought into our lives. It's such an encouragement to look back and see what He's brought us through and to. We remember the times that felt so out of control or moments that we didn't see how things were going to work out. But looking back, we can see His faithfulness to us over the years, which helps us trust Him for all of the unknown of tomorrow.

CHAPTER 44

Narrator: *Because cancer continued to increase throughout his body, Marc and Lisa decided to try six weeks of extensive treatments in Phoenix, Arizona, during the fall of 2021. Pastor Ron Williams, who had lost his wife to cancer, counseled Marc to go and try some holistic as well as traditional medicines.*

Marc: The school has been unbelievably supportive. I made a call to Blackhawk's CFO and former athletic director Steve Wild, and I told him financially what we were up against. Steve said earlier in the fall that some people had approached him wanting to help us. He said, "Let me make some calls." Within five minutes, he called me back and said my trip to Arizona for six weeks of alternative treatment is covered. It was a significant amount of money. People wanted to give anonymously, but I sent some thank-you notes for Steve to give to those who gave.

Lisa: When the new tumor was discovered August 31, 2021, we had about two and a half weeks where we didn't know what the next step was. We were waiting for Marc's kidney oncologist at the University of Chicago to advise what we should do. In the meantime, people were reaching out to us and giving recommendations for alternative treatment that we were looking into. We were both still going to school and teaching every day, but Marc was feeling worse. He would have to lay down in his office throughout the day when he had breaks between teaching.

Marc called Pastor Ron on September 18, seeking counsel from someone who had walked the cancer journey with his wife, Laura, and their four children. He told Marc, "Take Lisa and the twins and go. Trust God to provide." With every treatment we were looking into, we were thinking that Marc would go by himself and the rest of us would go out and visit. It seemed like too much to ask of Blackhawk with Marc and I being full-time teachers, asking for a six-week leave of absence, but Blackhawk gave us beyond their blessing. They gave us their resounding support and encouragement without any hesitation.

Marc: Our principal, Mark Harmon, is super supportive. I was a little nervous about approaching him with this because you're talking about six weeks. That's a big deal for him trying to find subs, but he said, "You guys go, and don't even think about school."

My brother used to live in Phoenix. Somehow, somebody he knew there heard our story, and they offered to let us use one of their cars. Another friend of Matt and Julie's paid for our first month at an extended stay hotel just down the road from the clinic. God just kept providing for us every step along the way.

Lisa: There are so many other things that people have done for us and examples of people's generosity that have completely blown us away. I want to tell everyone how God has moved in people's hearts to above and beyond meet our needs. When we checked Marc into the clinic that first day, we were handed the statement stamped "Paid in Full." Six weeks of alternative treatment, not covered by insurance, but instead paid for by families at Blackhawk who know and love us and wanted to help. It's just been amazing. And to see how He's moved in strangers' hearts, people that we don't even know, has completely blown us away.

Marc: I am naturally super independent, as Lisa can testify. I mean ridiculously independent. God has used cancer to break that in me. I still have that fighting spirit but also this understanding that I'm so much stronger in community with people around me than I am by myself. My spirit has always been, "If you want to do it right, do it yourself." The Lord gradually has been breaking me of that.

It's really been freeing as I've let people in and let them help me. Even when we went to Phoenix and people were giving us money. Ron Williams said somebody told him this when Laura had cancer: You have to learn to let people bless you. I've learned what a blessing it is to receive, and people want to bless us. We can see the joy it brings them. I'm learning to invite others in to help and bless me when they want to, and it has been huge. In a way, it can still be hard to receive. We'll both be in tears, and I don't know what to say. And they say they are just happy to help.

The Davidsons returned from Phoenix on November 3, five days before basketball practice started. Because of the treatments and the anticipation of the season, Marc was feeling energized.

Lisa: When we left Fort Wayne in September, Marc was feeling horrible, so bad that he was lying on the floor at O'Hare because our flight out of Fort Wayne was delayed, causing us to miss our connecting flight. He was lying underneath a huge dinosaur skeleton display while I was at the United Airlines counter getting our flight to Phoenix figured out. He felt so horrible that he didn't even care. When we arrived the next day at Brio Medical Cancer Clinic in Scottsdale, he was feeling so badly, but thank God, within two weeks, he started feeling pretty good.

Marc: I know just from a functional standpoint I felt a whole lot better. There was a tornado of inflammation inside. The easy fix is a prednisone regimen, an anti-inflammatory steroid that shuts down the immune system. In the immediate, it definitely helped me feel better,

Lisa: He received a lot of alternative treatments while we were in Arizona, and they definitely brought relief. He drastically changed his diet to no gluten, no sugar, no dairy, and even tried to go vegan most days. I would drop him off at the clinic Monday through Friday, and he would spend from about 8 a.m. to around 2 or 3 p.m. The twins had the morning to get their schoolwork done so that when we picked Marc up in the afternoon, it was 100 percent family time. The four of us had the best six weeks together. It was extra special since Marc and I never got to focus all of our attention on just the twins. We were blessed with our other kids and family coming out to visit, too.

Marc's days at the clinic were so good for him physically as well as emotionally and spiritually, sitting alongside others who were receiving treatment. He had a lot of time to have some great, spiritual conversations and form sweet friendships. I know God used Marc those weeks at the clinic to encourage other clients and also the staff.

Scans before we left Arizona told us the tumors hadn't shrunk, but they hadn't grown, either. We left Arizona on November 3 and returned to school the next day.

Marc looked great and was back for the start of basketball season. He felt good enough to teach full-time and had enough energy to get through practice and games. Those are long days, and we thanked God that we were back home and life felt "normal" again.

Marc: Coaching is therapy for me, something you can throw your energies into.

After winning the title in 2021, the expectations for us were really low from the outside. My dad has coached forever, and he always told me, if you have a good hand, you slow-play that bad boy and let people think you aren't going to be any good. We really thought we had a chance to be pretty good because we had some kids who had been waiting in the wings, and this year was their chance. They ended up having a really good year. I loved our team, an extremely cohesive group, no egos, just a bunch of kids who loved to play and worked hard.

But at Christmas, I started feeling worse.

Lisa: It was Christmas Eve, and Marc started feeling the extreme fatigue again. We had the Bobcat of North Daviess County Classic tournament down in southern Indiana. It was Jimmy's junior year and we went into the tournament undefeated, so it wasn't a question whether Marc felt well enough to go. He did like he's done this whole season and kept on trusting that the Lord would give him the strength to coach when it was game time, and He always did. We won each of the three games to win the tournament.

The next day, Marc had a PET scan that showed the tumor in his abdomen had grown since the scan in early November. We had a quiet New Years Eve, thanking the Lord for 2021 and trusting Him with 2022.

Marc: School started January 3. I started teaching, but I told Kim Brown, the primary principal, I didn't think I could continue doing the primary PE. I hated that I was stepping away from my primary classes, but I knew physically, there was no way I could do this. I was trying to do just afternoons, but it quickly became evident there's no way I could. I think they knew. They were super supportive. They said, "All right, you're going to coach and be the community relations guy, and we'll find a teacher."

Lisa: We're so grateful for the school's support that allowed him to give up his teaching responsibilities and continue coaching.

Marc: For me, the biggest thing is my level of energy. There were times during the junior varsity game where I'd lay face down on the floor in the locker room, just dead tired. I did that a whole bunch. On the bus, I was letting assistants drive, when before that, I always had to be the one who drove. We started taking two buses so I could lay down on the back row of seats or on the floor.

It's been an ongoing battle. My faith in Christ has sustained me. His strength is made perfect in our weakness. I'll freely tell people I have weakness to go around, but that's when the power of God comes in, and the Lord has continued to fill me with His strength in ways I can't even explain. He's done that time after time after time.

Lisa: I saw how the Lord gave him the strength to coach every single time. It was the same for the times he was asked to speak at different chapels and events. Beforehand, it seemed impossible, like there was no way he would be able to get up there and coach or speak, but each time, God gave him the strength to do what he could not have done on his own. I witnessed his energy return, and it was like a glimpse into the old Marc. As soon as it was over, he was back to feeling pretty miserable. He started riding home with me and not on the bus with the team in February.

Marc: I didn't have a lot of clothes that fit because I got even skinnier post-surgery. I was losing weight steadily through October and then had the surgery. I got back up to 280 pounds early on, so I could still wear a lot of those clothes. Then I slid back down to 230, and I was swimming in my usual clothes. The coaches all had to do a swap of gray sweats.

Basketball was Marc's refuge. The Braves started 11-0 before losing in overtime against Homestead, another area team with state championship hopes. Blackhawk Christian entered state tournament play with a 19-5 record after playing one of the state's toughest schedules.

BRAVE AT HEART

Marc: That kind of drove me for a while, throwing myself into the team and the season. I think I had a different perspective on coaching this year. Last year, it had changed, but this year, to an even greater degree. Pastor Williams talked about the gift of today, and I understood that it's easy to let your mind wander to events that may or may not happen in the future. I just tried to stay in the moment. Your mind is right here, and you can really zero in on what's going on with the team.

The Braves' season ended in the regional championship game with an overtime loss to Central Noble. The game was immediately followed by the mid-court huddle, with Marc testifying and leading in prayer. The postgame locker room was the same as always after a season-ending game.

Marc: That was powerful. For me, I wanted it to be about the players, specifically our seniors. I was going to keep the train on the tracks, and I wasn't going to make it about me. We just started doing tributes to the seniors. The seniors all shared, all the underclassmen shared, all the coaches shared. Those last games are always pretty raw emotionally because you are not expecting it.

You're not expecting it to be your last game, and all of a sudden, it hits you like a freight train. I like to talk to them at that time about what matters most. Basketball is going to be full of ups and downs; that's how it goes. Our faith in Christ is that solid foundation we can build upon.

Marc, Frankie, Marcus, Will and the twins in Arizona • October 2021

CHAPTER 45

Narrator: *Almost as soon as Marc was diagnosed with cancer, word began to spread among former players and friends. Part of that was because he had to ask for time off from Blackhawk Christian to go for surgery and medical treatments, and at the same time, he was continuing to coach. Social media took care of letting most everyone else know. In many ways, this allowed Marc to see the impact he had on the lives of others.*

Marc: We never hid it, and former players started to reach out immediately. "What can we do for you? We are praying for you." Just to see that was amazing.

Before I got sick, I communicated with former players all the time. I was only at Trinity coaching for two years, but we have built this bond with those players that still lasts. We get together every year for Homecoming, and then in the summer, we'd get together for open gyms. We built some really deep bonds there with that group. They'd come in from all over.

Chris Schmidt came to Georgia when we were there, and he's still down there. Eddie Pascual also ended up there, and he's still there. They were starting a new junior high and had openings, and the principal down there, Chuck Lawson, used to be the principal at Aurora Christian. When I accepted the job at Georgia, he said, "Hey, we have a couple of other positions to fill." Chris was in education, and he came down, and Eddie came down the year after.

Lisa: They came up for a visit right before our 2021 state title.

Marc: In 2021, some of my players at Trinity came to visit the weekend between semistate and state finals. There were probably eight or nine of them that came. We had an open gym, we came back here to our house for pizza, and we were just sitting around talking. It turned into this sweet time of fellowship, just talking about what God has been doing in our lives and how He's been teaching us. Just an unbelievable time. We read Scriptures together.

All of those guys and some other Trinity guys came back this year in January 2022, including a kid from Texas, Adam Cora, who is the guy who got me into Strongman. He moved to Texas a few years ago, but he wanted to be at the game that the Trinity guys had arranged to go to. He made a 17-hour trip, and he didn't get to the game until after halftime. He came in with his cowboy hat, and I gave him a big hug. After the game, we got pizza. My dad was here, and we were just sitting around telling stories. My dad was just soaking it in. Adam Cora shared Scriptures over me and prayed over me. They don't know what it means. I tried to express it to them, but it's hard. You can't put it into words.

Adam Cora left after midnight and drove straight back.

Those relationships with former players are the victories in coaching. When you maintain those relationships and see those kids follow the Lord, it is so rewarding.

Lisa: One of the players that we were really blown away by was Kurt Vahle. He came both in April 2021 and again in January 2022. We met his wife, Courtney, and this is what she said to me in person and resent in a message on Facebook:

Courtney Vahle: I can't put into words how much of an impact Marc has had on Kurt's life. I know that Marc helped change the direction of my husband's life. If it wasn't for his godly influence, I know I wouldn't be married to him. Kurt has spoken so highly of Marc, and his influence has continued to shine through in the way he coaches and leads our family. I am brought to tears every time I think about the man Kurt has become and how much of a role Marc continues to have on him. I am eternally grateful. I know Marc gives all glory to God, but it was Marc as the hands and feet of Jesus that got my husband and our family where we are today.

Lisa: It's so humbling. We had absolutely no idea that God used Marc in such a powerful way in Kurt's life.

Marc: You try to connect with players, but you don't know if you are, and a lot of times, you never find out.

All of this has prompted me to say thank you to them all for coming back and reaching out. That has been huge for me.

Chris Schmidt and his wife, Courtney, came back to Trinity on the night the school retired Marc's jersey in April 2022, just weeks before Marc would pass away.

Lisa: Our last words when they left, she hugged me and said, "It's never been lost on me the huge influence (Marc's had) on who my husband has become."

One of Marc's quirks is that he has a nickname for almost every one of his students, basketball player or not. One of those non-basketball players was Jared Weber, a student at Blackhawk whom Marc called "J-dub." He sent the following letter to Marc:

Hi Mr. Davidson,

I just wanted to reach out, update you on my life journey, and thank you personally for the impact you had on me.

Even though at the time I may not have seen it, over the past four years, I've grown to strongly appreciate your support throughout my high school career. Whether it was asking how the bowling season was going, or even just the occasional 'J-Dub!' from across the hall. In the moment, I may have shied away, but looking back, that last part is one of the things I remember the most from those 4 years.

Right now I'm getting ready to enter my last semester at Huntington University, and I'll be graduating this May with a degree in Film Production, with a focus in Screenwriting. This fall I was able to be the Director of a film I helped write, and soon we'll see if it wins any big competitions! I'm definitely a different person from who I was at Blackhawk. Whatever walls I had up, and avoidance I had with social interaction, is all but gone. I'm currently unsure where I will end up after college, but I am equal parts nervous and excited to be done!

Spiritually, I've spent the past four years strongly thinking, and have grown from having an agnostic viewpoint to becoming a believer, though I'm not super vocal about it. The college experience and relationships I've found, along with past experiences at Blackhawk, have pushed me in this direction.

I can honestly say I would not be the person I am today without your impact. The motivation you gave, the random greetings, and the kindness you showed me in a class that was not at all in my wheelhouse (Phys. Ed.) was insurmountable. I can only hope to one day impact others the way you did me.

Thank you so much for everything.

Yours truly,
J-Dub (aka Jared Weber)

While he was playing in France, Marc and Lisa became very good friends with teammate Fred Macquet and his wife, Arlette. Fast-forward to 2018, and Fred asked Marc and Lisa if his 15-year-old son, Celeste, could come and stay with the Davidsons for a summer visit.

Celeste: I really didn't want to go, but that was the best summer of my life. I was welcomed with open arms and generosity, kindness, tolerance and love. That's all I could feel everywhere Marc took me, with every member of his family. I feel so grateful to have lived all these simple things alongside Marc and have those memories forever: sharing a good meal with everyone while Marc was grilling steaks on the barbecue, listening to his instructions to repaint the fence, watching him get grumpy when I would play a trick on him during a board game, wishing that I could have him as a coach when I watched Blackhawk Christian play, bursting out laughing with him when telling some random memory from his time in France ... I could genuinely feel through Marc's laughter the complicity he had with my dad twenty years before. It was still there.

That summer of 2018, I felt what it was like to have several siblings. I learned how to play basketball properly. I learned to believe. I learned the most important thing in life, "Love your neighbor as yourself." These memories with Marc will last forever. I went to Fort Wayne again the next summer, but this time, I was the one that asked to go. It was even better that time—countless other unforgettable memories. When I think about a period of serenity and happiness in my life, this is the period I think of first. It had such a profound influence on the person I have become today and has turned me into a more caring and tolerant person. For that, I am forever grateful. It has been one of my greatest blessings to have been part of Marc Davidson's life, even if it was only for two summers.

Some players from Marc's 2006-2008 Trinity International teams • March 2021

Marc and the family with Celeste • 2018

BRAVE AT HEART

CHAPTER 46

Narrator: *When Marc first arrived at Blackhawk Christian, Joey Morlan was one of the cornerstones around which he built the new program. Joey became the Braves' third all-time leading scorer and set a school record for career three-pointers.*

I've told people that I had the unique opportunity to have three kinds of relationships with Marc Davidson.

During my high school days, Marc was my coach and mentor. He was an authority figure I dared not disobey. Seeing Marc at his physical peak would make it easy to understand why he commanded the complete respect and obedience of each and every player. At Blackhawk Christian, the athletic locker rooms are situated directly beneath the weight room. Often, we would be getting ready for practice and would hear loud grunts or screams, followed by what sounded like truckloads of weight crashing to the floor. That's how we knew Coach was getting his workout in. Players would look at each other with wide eyes, the kind of look that communicated complete intimidation.

Coach never leaned into that persona. He really won us over with his genuine love and care for us, his desire to intentionally invest in our lives, his godly leadership example and, of course, his extremely high knowledge of basketball. In my time as a player, it was not uncommon to spend 15 minutes in a team devotional with Scripture readings, devotional videos and prayers. For Coach Davidson, earnestly investing in the young men in his program was more important than a couple of extra reps in defensive slides.

One of my favorite memories from that time was our team mission trip to Panama the summer before my senior year. Our activities included basketball clinics, delivering food to impoverished churches and playing against club teams before giving our testimonies. One day on the trip at a school/after-school care facility, the kids there were allowed outside on the playground to play and interact with us. We spoke very broken Spanish at best. Coach was surrounded by a swarm of Panamanian children, all eagerly waiting as he picked them up and lifted them over his head. Their screams and laughs of total joy still ring out in my mind. No words were needed to communicate because love has no language. He was perfectly reflecting God's love for his children in that moment. I learned so many things on that trip, but one was watching Coach and learning what true and complete service to God looks like.

After graduation, my relationship with Coach changed, although anyone who has ever played knows that coach/player relationships never truly end. I didn't see Coach much anymore, but I would often receive texts along with Facebook messages checking in on me or delivering encouraging messages.

Throughout my entire college career, never much time went by before Coach would reach out and check on me. Every conversation would end with a "Keep trusting Jesus," or "Keep Jesus first." He always emphasized my spiritual growth and poured that aspect into my life. I attribute a large part of my spiritual growth to his guidance and investment in my life. Those phone conversations throughout college were no different.

Going into my senior year, I decided to stop playing basketball. Every athlete reaches that point. The ball inevitably stops bouncing for everyone, and this was that moment for me. I moved out of college at Christmas break and was home in Fort Wayne working at my internship when Coach heard I was back in town and reached out to me about being an assistant at Blackhawk. I had never thought about coaching, but the idea of getting to coach alongside Marc really excited me, so I joined his staff midway through the 2018-19 season.

This is when my relationship with Coach really evolved, when he changed from "Coach Davidson" to "my colleague and friend, Marc Davidson." There was mutual respect, but the dynamic is different between coach and player than it is between coach and coach. I felt like an equal. We would talk strategy, and he would ask for help on scouting reports, showing he valued my input. It was a drastic change.

I always cherished my relationship with Coach, but this blossoming relationship with him was the most special. We were colleagues during practice and games and friends outside of that. I spent time at his house with his family, and he spent time at my house with my family. It wasn't because I felt I had to since he was my coach but because I wanted to and valued our relationship. This shows how important it was to him to continue investing in me and my life, a job he felt was never finished.

Not many people knew, but I was going through an identity crisis that first year of coaching. I wasn't in some deep depression, but I was definitely struggling as playing basketball had been my whole life and I felt empty without it. People always knew me as Joey the basketball player, and now, I didn't even really know who I was. Marc taking me under his wing and letting me be a part of something as special as coaching and influencing young men really helped me, really reignited that sense of purpose and identity.

It was being a part of something bigger than yourself. It wasn't about any individual, game, win or trophy, but about the overall mission God has tasked Marc and his staff with of disciplining young men for Jesus. All the court results were secondary to what was going on in the hearts and minds of the young men. Marc allowed God to work through him to create that atmosphere and culture in his program, and it was a powerful and humbling experience to be part of. During this time, I learned that we aren't defined by our achievements or our titles but by WHO God says we are and by WHAT Jesus did for us. That was always Marc's message to anyone that would listen.

I was lucky to coach four years alongside Marc, including the last year and a half as Marc fiercely battled cancer. People outside of our program saw maybe 25 percent of Marc's struggle. As coaches, we witnessed all the behind-the-scenes and day-to-day struggles. There were days Marc would show up to practice and didn't have the energy to stand. He would sit off to the side as assistants would run practice. There were game days where the team would warm up and Coach would stay in the locker room, resting on the floor, trying to gain enough strength to coach that game.

I always knew Coach was tough, but this past season, I learned what true toughness looks like. He fought his own body and gave everything he had for us coaches and our players. After every game, Marc liked to do what we call put-ups, where we would huddle in a circle, arms wrapped around each other, and players would take turns calling guys out for things they did well in the game or just things that they appreciated about them. In one of our put-up huddles, one of our players called out Coach Davidson in a special way, telling Coach he knew he spoke on behalf of the team when he said how much they appreciated him. Everyone on the team saw what Marc was going through, and it would have been easy to resign his position and focus on himself and his treatments, but that's not who Marc was. Despite all the challenges, Marc still fought to be there every day and invest in his players, showing all of us what true selflessness looked like. Those words from a 17-year-old kid perfectly encapsulated the way everyone in that locker room felt about Marc and how much we all appreciated him.

His response to this put-up is one I'll never forget. He looked around our huddle, smiled and said, "Fellas, being here with you guys fills me. Throughout the day, I feel tired and weak, and then I come here with all of you, and I'm refilled with energy. Being here is better than any medicine or treatment a doctor could prescribe me, so thanks for the therapy session, fellas."

Recently, a Facebook memory popped up: a picture from my high school graduation 7 years ago of myself, Coach and six other basketball seniors huddled with our arms around each other in our caps and gowns. We were all looking directly at Coach as he addressed us one last time. I don't remember exactly what was said, but his caption read, "Proud moment with my 7 graduating seniors—I love each of you—looking forward to see all that God is going to do in and through you guys. Reminded again that I have the best job on earth!"

Marc was always my coach, and I will always remember him that way. I think about when I will see him again in heaven. More importantly, I will always remember him even more fondly as one of my dearest friends and truly one of my heroes. I think to some extent, he became a hero to many who heard his story. They say not to meet your heroes because you'll be disappointed, but I can tell you, I had the privilege of intimately knowing my hero, Marc Davidson, and it was one of the most cherished blessings in my life.

CHAPTER 47

Narrator: *Early on during his challenges with cancer, Marc realized he could not fight it on his own, and frankly, he wasn't convinced he was supposed to. He'd always shared every part of his life with God, but this was something different. He had to give up total control to the Lord. He hoped for a full recovery so he could spend more time with his family, but he truly had to learn to let go and allow the Lord to work His plan.*

Marc: What I've learned is there is freedom in surrender. We feel like the opposite is true. We feel like this is my stuff and I'm in control of it, and I'm going to do what I want. But that is not freedom because you are a slave to your stuff when that's how you live.

Early on, I was living in bondage to basketball, and I never realized it because I never had any adversity. The game was easy, and I never really dealt with anything hard, and I thought this is how it is. What I didn't realize is it was feeding this monster inside of me, and it became this hill of pride. I got possessive with basketball. Basketball defined me. It was still so hard to let go. God had to just break me down to nothing. It was a process of prying my fingers off so I would hold it with open hands.

The other thing I've learned about surrender is that it is ongoing. There will be times when I surrender something in the morning, and in the afternoon, I'm picking it up again. We have to continually surrender to be in tune with the Spirit and what the Spirit is doing. I've found there is freedom in that when we can truly learn to surrender. That is the work of the Spirit, it's not something we can look at and think, "I have to muster up the strength to do this."

It's a work that God does in His grace. He allows us to let go. Romans 8:20-21: "For the creation was subjected to frustration, not by its own choice, but by the will of the One who subjected it, in hope that the creation itself will be liberated from its bondage to decay and brought into the freedom and glory of the children of God."

None of us would choose the way of frustration. But it was the will of the One who subjected it so we could be brought into the glorious freedom. He allowed me to experience frustration that I never had before, but it brought me to a place of freedom.

Larry Crabb said, "Despair is God's unexpected pathway to joy." I was in a place of despair, but eventually that led me to a joy and understanding that is only through my relationship with Christ. None of this other stuff will ever fulfill me.

That's been a process of the Holy Spirit molding my heart. Early on, my prayer was, "Heal me." The book of James says that's what we're supposed to do. I'm still praying there, but my primary prayer right now is I want Jesus to be exalted in me through whatever. I want Jesus to be exalted, even more than I want to be healed. I wasn't always there, that's the work God did in me, and I'm thankful for it.

The family piece is the hardest part—and that's hard. I've wrestled with God in prayer, and I've done a lot of it about my family, specifically. The Lord has spoken to my heart that He's going to take care of my wife and take care of my family. But that piece is super hard. That reminds me of our hope of eternity. My wife and children have all accepted Christ in their lives, and we have eternity together.

I honestly am not afraid, and that is the power of God. I'm not afraid, and I don't fret about tomorrow. I live in the moment and I'm here right now, and I want to make the most of every opportunity God gives me today. I'm not going to fret about what may or may not happen weeks and months down the road. I know that's the work of the Spirit.

I can't explain it other than it's the Holy Spirit at work. My wife has been unbelievably supportive. We've had some hard conversations, but it has brought us so much closer. We know we have eternity together.

Sometimes we can even fall into "hoping" for good things. Things like meaningful relationships, responsible children, good health,

BRAVE AT HEART

finding fulfillment in our work—these are all good things, right? We ought to desire these things, we ought to pray for these things, but we ought NOT to place our hope in these things.

Our hope is in one thing: the finished work of Jesus Christ on a hill called Calvary some 2,000 years ago. And the fact that three days later, He came back to life, He conquered death and the grave, and He offers to each one of us the free gift of salvation. That is the Good News of the Gospel! It's called substitutionary atonement, which simply means that He took my place! God made Him who knew no sin to become sin for us so that we might become the righteousness of God; that's how 2 Corinthians 5 puts it.
THAT is the Gospel. And THAT ALONE is our hope!

Do we truly dwell in the presence of God? I confess to you all that oftentimes, I do not dwell there. I may "stop by" or "pay Him a visit," but not often enough do I truly dwell in His presence. God is teaching me how to dwell—it is a wonderful place to be!

Marc and Lisa at Homecoming • January 2022

Marc and Lisa at Marcus' senior night • February 2021

CHAPTER 48

Narrator: *Imagine the duty and stress involved in being present at the death of a brother, a best friend even—both a blessing and an incredible burden. Marc's brother, Matt, is two years older, and he has been present for all the milestones and accomplishments in Marc's life, even the most difficult times, including his passing. They shared a bond in this life second only to Marc and Lisa.*

This is what Matt texted to Marc the night after he passed, knowing that Marc would not see it in this life:

Marc, this is my last communication until we meet again in heaven. I'll miss our daily interactions. Hardly a day has gone by over the last two and a half years where we didn't have some form of communication.

I miss you so much already. We've been best friends, teammates and brothers. I love you so much, Marc.

At this moment, I can't imagine life without you. But I know God is faithful. Your legacy lives on! I'll do my best to honor you ... and as I promised, I'll help watch over your kids and grandkids. Your children are so amazing. You and Lisa built something special and lasting.

You are a warrior, Marc. You finished strong!!

We will dwell in the house of the Lord forever.

I love you, Marc.

See you soon.

Matt: At the time of Marc's passing, there were very few people on planet earth who knew him longer than I did. I have 49 years of memories that I could share. Believe me, I could go on and on and on. But instead, I've chosen to focus on the final days I had with Marc on this side of eternity: May 6, 7, 8 ... and the 9th.

As my dad and I were leaving Marc's house late in the afternoon on Friday, Lisa called us back in just before we got in the car. Marc wanted to say goodbye ... a final goodbye. I'd been dreading this moment but also selfishly longing for it. I had been intentionally avoiding it because I didn't want Marc to think that his big brother had given up on him. What a blessing that Marc initiated this moment.

My dad walked in first. Marc stood up out of the hospital bed stationed in his living room (it was a struggle for him to stand), hugged my dad, told my dad what he meant to him and said "I love you" over and over. Then Marc prayed over my dad. It was so powerful. Lisa, her two college-age sons, a dear family friend and the two hospice nurses were all witnesses to this. Then Marc pulled me over and did the same with me. We embraced each other for such a long time ... and then he told me what I meant to him, and we said "I love you" over and over. I could barely speak, but I promised him I'd watch over his children, that they would serve the Lord and that we would spend eternity together in heaven. Then he prayed over me as well. He was so filled with the Spirit. Before we let go of each other, while still standing, he recited the 23rd Psalm, and I joined him in unison while whispering the final verse in his ear: "And I will dwell in the house of the Lord forever."

I thought that would be the last time I would see Marc, but he lived another three days before the Lord took him home on Monday, May 9, at 4 p.m. So I spent most of those four days in Fort Wayne or in my car. I only went home to sleep. I had so many other powerful moments with Marc. Here are a few more.

On Saturday, Marc decided to get up and go to the bathroom instead of using the medical "urinal" provided by hospice care. He was a little confused because of the morphine in his body, and he was absolutely determined to get out of bed. There was no stopping him (he's a Davidson). A couple of his boys and I helped him into the bathroom to make sure he didn't stumble. Then it was just the two of us in the bathroom ... brothers. The physical exertion made him nauseous, so I helped him to his knees at the toilet. I sat next to him on the floor, just the two of us in the bathroom. His knees and elbows were so sore, so I put towels or pillows under them. His arms were resting on the toilet seat and his head was pressed against the lid. He was so tired.

He said, "Matt, I think I'm gonna go," meaning that he thought he was going to die and go to heaven right then and there. I said, "Marc, not here in the bathroom. Let's try to get back to the bed." Entirely exhausted, Marc said, "I don't have any strength left." He was stuck there ... on his knees at the toilet. He couldn't move a muscle. This was my brother, Marc Davidson, the professional basketball player and the Strongman. At his peak, he was bench-pressing nearly 500 pounds, and now he couldn't even push himself up from the toilet. Then I heard Marc say the following words: "What are we going to do, Matt?" It was one of the most powerful and memorable moments I had with my brother during those final days. Why? Because he said, "What are WE going to do?" He didn't say, "What am I going to do?" He said "WE." Because he knew that his big brother was not going anywhere and that I was going to stay with him. This was OUR problem, not just his.

I long for a worldwide community of believers like that ... a community that says, "What are WE going to do?" when someone in our circle needs help. Long story short, we actually carried Marc back to his bed. Marc has seven children, and six of them are boys, and five of those are 17 years old or older, so I had help for this. It was a combination of carrying and sliding on the floor, but we were successful. Once Marc got back to his bed, he could see that I was panting for air. Marc had lost over 100 pounds, but his frame was still big. Combine that with the adrenaline built up in my body—and me being out of shape—and I thought I might have a heart attack and beat him to heaven. Lying in his bed, Marc could see that I was laboring to catch my breath and said, "You OK, Matt?" I said, "I think so." Then Marc extended his hand to me for a handshake and said, "We got it done, brother." Marc and I were not only brothers, we were best friends, and we had been teammates during much of our life. We had plenty of athletic achievements together over the years. We were successful in almost every challenge. This was our final challenge together ... and just like countless times before, we were victorious.

Marc spent most of the day on Monday struggling. His family read the Bible to him throughout the day. I'm so proud of his kids. Marc kept opening his eyes to see Lisa, his wife of nearly 27 years. He was entirely unafraid of death, and he knew that heaven was awaiting him, but you could tell he didn't want to leave Lisa. Later in the afternoon, he became restless again, and he was trying to get out of bed. I joined others at his side and told him to stay in bed. His family was praying aloud for Jesus to take him Home ... he was struggling so much. It was hard to watch. His breathing rhythm changed, and he went several seconds without taking a breath. And then he would wake up again and become restless. I put my hand on Marc's chest and whispered, "Marc, it's time to go." He did not take a breath after that; he entered into Glory surrounded by his family and with precious Lisa holding his hand. I kissed his forehead and said, "I love you. We will dwell in the house of the Lord forever. I'll see you soon."

I'm sharing all of this for a few reasons. Yes, I suppose it's somewhat therapeutic for me. We all process things in our own way, and this is helpful for me. I also want to document these memories. But more importantly, it's a reminder for me. People all around us experience various levels of hardship, adversity and suffering. People need Jesus and will only find strength and hope in Him. It's up to us—WE—to share the life and love of Jesus with those God places in our lives. I intentionally left out a portion about our private moments on Marc's bathroom floor over the weekend. There was another person there with us, also sitting on the floor with His arms around us. We called upon His name, out loud, and He heard us. You know who He is; His name is Jesus. Eternal life— dwelling in the house of the Lord forever—awaits everyone who calls upon the name of Jesus.

Marc and Matt at
2 and 4 years old • 1975

Marc and Matt in Arizona •
October 2021

CHAPTER 49

Narrator: *On December 31, 2019—10 months before he was diagnosed with terminal cancer—Marc Davidson posted a poem from British missionary C.T. Studd on his Facebook page. It's a relatively long poem, but the highlights include the lines, "Give me Father, a purpose deep, In joy or sorrow Thy Word to keep; Faithful and true what e're the strife, Pleasing Thee in my daily life; Only one life, 'twill soon be past, Only what's done for Christ will last."*

Many people find their faith when faced with a horrible challenge, but Marc was already standing on the solid rock of his faith in Christ. For the most part, he faced this challenge calmly, knowing Jesus was in control. Even when the pain got bad and the end neared, Marc had complete peace. He was already an example to everyone who knew him, but now cancer presented him an opportunity to reach out to even more people and explain the reason for his hope and peace.

Throughout this battle, Marc never saw it as a losing effort. He saw it as a submission to God and wondered where the Lord would lead him during this process. He wasn't sure of the direction—many people would be panicking—but he was comfortable letting God lead and use him. And his consistency and lack of hesitancy inspired everyone he came in contact with. With Lisa's strength and continuing encouragement, it was an amazing example of obedience and fulfilling God's purpose.

Marc: The peace I have is because of the eternal life I have in Jesus. That is my hope. The apostle Paul said that. If our hope is only in this life, we should be pitied more than anybody. But our hope is not only in this life but in eternity. If I didn't have that hope of eternal life in Christ, I can't even imagine the level of despair I would be at right now.

Just knowing I'm going to be with Jesus for eternity and that my family has all surrendered their life to Christ ... we have an eternity to celebrate together. That is the game-changer for me right now. I can't imagine not having my hope in Christ for eternal life. That's what Peter calls it, an anchor for our soul. It steadies us because we don't get tossed and turned by everything or every bit of bad news from the doctor because we know we are going to be with Jesus. We are victorious. We are more than conquerors, and that changes everything.

I seriously can't imagine. We've had those moments along the way where it just slugs you in the gut, but then you remember your hope in Christ and in eternal life. Without that, I can't even begin to imagine.

Lisa was Marc's anchor, always supporting him during this and every time. Together, they comforted each other, but they also took comfort in the Lord. They got a preview of the end on April 14, 2022, the day Blackhawk Christian announced Marc was relinquishing his coaching duties. That came two days after receiving the final diagnosis from his oncologist. For all of his reaction, he might as well have been told the stock market dipped. His faith in God never did. Every time someone asked Lisa how she was doing, she always said, "I'm just so amazed at what God's doing." And she totally meant and lived it.

Lisa: Today my tears are because I'm just in awe at how amazing God is. To know what we are going through and yet feel this peace. … It surely is the work of God. It builds my faith to trust Him with whatever the future holds. We have already experienced how He's given us strength and peace beyond anything we could imagine with all that we've already been through. Monday, when we were in the doctor's office, hearing the doctor tell us that there was nothing more they could do to fight the cancer, that any further treatments would just be prolonging the inevitable, my heart didn't drop. Like Marc has said, our hope is not in a doctor's report. Our hope is entirely in Jesus and His finished work on the cross for us that saves us for all eternity. The peace of God that surpasses all understanding is surely covering us and just amazes me.

Recently, my favorite verse has become Romans 15:13, which says, "May the God of hope fill you with all joy and peace as you trust in Him, so you may overflow with hope by the power of the Holy Spirit." We are trusting Him, and that makes all the difference, to trust and be confident that His will for us is good and to know that He's got us and is working all things together for our good and for His glory.

To be honest, I just feel like I'm overflowing with hope and joy and peace, and it's not of myself. I'm the girl that cries at the beginning of "Up." I can't help but cry every time I see that movie. You see Mr. Fredrickson lose Ellie, his wife and best friend, his partner in adventure, the love of his life. That is Marc to me. To know this is reality for me. It's unbelievable how God is holding me together.

God has already done the unimaginable; I never thought it would be possible to have so much peace and strength and even joy while walking through the hardest year of our lives, so we're going to keep on trusting Him. The Lord is carrying us through this. I'm going to trust that God is going to get me through and cover me and help me for whatever He has in the future for us.

Then there's what became Marc's favorite song over his last few months, "Only Jesus" by Casting Crowns:

> *And I, I don't want to leave a legacy*
> *I don't care if they remember me*
> *Only Jesus*
> *And I, I've only got one life to live*
> *I'll let every second point to Him*
> *Only Jesus*
>
> *All the kingdoms built, all the trophies won*
> *Will crumble into dust when it's said and done*
> *'Cause all that really mattered*
> *Did I live the truth to the ones I love?*
> *Was my life the proof that there is only One*
> *Whose name will last forever?*
> *And I, I don't want to leave a legacy*
> *I don't care if they remember me*
> *Only Jesus*
> *And I, I've only got one life to live*
> *I'll let every second point to Him*
> *Only Jesus*

When asked what his legacy might be, Marc said, "It's not about me, but about how great God was in my life. Nothing I did, all what he is doing."

BRAVE AT HEART

While cancer robbed Marc's body of its stature and his Strongman strength, his faith maintained and, if anything, became more disciplined without faltering because he kept his focus on Jesus. Nothing changed for him, and that was an example of true power and stamina. Rip my body from me, he seemed to be saying, but you'll never touch my devotion.

Marc Davidson fulfilled his mission on earth by fulfilling God's will for him and passed into heaven on May 9, 2022. He left a legacy in his seven children and in the thousands of others he coached and taught who will carry on his message for decades. He didn't need cancer to focus his faith and his mission; he lived it from the beginning to the very end. It wasn't something he forced, bluffed or convinced himself of, but the way he lived and loved, a perfect example of God's grace on earth.

Marc knew exactly what would last of this life, and he trusted it into the next life. He proved the strength of his faith would even outlast him. Without hesitation or question, he allowed Jesus to use him fully, leaning into that purpose every day.

"Only one life, 'twill soon be past, Only what's done for Christ will last."

Marc and Lisa in Arizona · October 2021

CHAPTER 50

Narrator: *It was an amazingly busy and blessed 18 months for the Davidson family following Marc's passing. The first grandchild, Jack Doyle Davidson, was born to Wes and Ashton; Blackhawk Christian named its basketball court for Marc; Marc became the first inductee in the Aurora Christian Hall of Fame; during his senior season, Jimmy and the Braves won their third state title; Frankie graduated from Grace and married Anna before signing to play professionally in France; and Lisa adopted a puppy, as well as making two trips to France. Those are just the highlights.*

Lisa: How do I begin to sum up all that the Lord has done since bringing Marc Home? To be honest, it feels impossible, and the weight of it has kept me from writing, not because I don't know what to say, but because I don't know how to even begin. We experienced the lowest days of our lives without a doubt, but at the same time, we experienced the peace that only God could give. I am in awe and have been at a loss for words, other than to say that the Lord is so good. He has answered our prayers exceedingly, abundantly beyond anything we asked or imagined by giving us the two sweetest additions to our family this year, Jack and Anna. I cannot help but think of Psalm 23:6, "Surely goodness and mercy shall follow me all the days of my life."

Jack and Anna are two of the greatest gifts the Lord has ever given Marc and me. We have prayed together for our children's future spouses since before our children were even born, so Anna and Ashton and Sarah are answers to our prayers. And we have prayed for our children's children, the next generation of Davidsons, that they would grow up believing and trusting in Jesus themselves so that they will live lives that honor the Lord in all they do. We knew Wes and Ashton were having a boy, and we even knew his name would be Jack, so although my heart aches that Marc never got to hold him, it brings me great joy to know that Marc had already been praying for and loving our Jack. Marc knew Anna was the one for Frankie; it was clear to us all that Frankie and Anna complimented each other so beautifully and spurred each other on in their faith. I thank God that He in His grace gave Marc the gift of knowing and loving Frankie's future wife and, before he

BRAVE AT HEART

was even born, loving Jack, too. Surely God's goodness and mercy followed Marc all the days of his life and beyond.

By the grace of God, this year has seemed more like a year of celebrating than grieving. I can't believe I can say that. Surely it is the work of God and His goodness and grace that is covering and carrying us. We miss Marc so much, and it hurts to not be sharing with him the incredible milestones we have experienced as a family this year. Yet somehow, I find myself filled with such peace and gratitude for all the years we were blessed to have together. Only God could do that. We have experienced the joy that David speaks of in Psalm 30:5: "Weeping may last for the night, but joy comes in the morning." This entire year has felt like we have received blessing after blessing, the overflow of Marc's well-lived life that aimed to honor God in everything he did. I feel as if our baskets are bursting, reaping what Marc so faithfully sowed over the course of his lifetime.

Our family has had so many special moments this past year where Marc was remembered and honored. We are humbled and amazed at what God has done through Marc. These are just some of the moments forever impressed upon my heart where we were reminded again of the impact Marc made and the legacy he left behind.

June 5, 2022: The week after Marc's funeral, a good friend of ours reached out to let me know he and his wife wanted to fund a college scholarship, named in Marc's honor. The Marc Davidson scholarship will award $2500 each year to one graduating Blackhawk female athlete and one male athlete whose life has displayed integrity and Christian character along with a high GPA. They have decided to award the scholarship for all four years of college.

August 10, 2022: Blackhawk Principal Mark Harmon challenged students on the first day of the 2022-2023 school year to live out Marc's favorite verse, Colossians 3:23, to "work heartily as to the Lord and not to men." It meant so much that he was remembered as we started the first school year without him. Remembering how he lived still challenges and inspires us today to live with such passion and intentionality and boldness.

November 29, 2022: During Blackhawk's home opener of the 2022-2023 basketball season vs. North Side, Blackhawk's gym was named Marc Davidson Court. Before the game, our family, along with the teams from Blackhawk and North Side, huddled at center court where Marc's dad pointed people to Jesus as he honored Marc.

January 13, 2023: We returned to Aurora Christian, where Marc was honored as the first inductee into their Hall of Fame. It was a special night to be reunited with old high school friends and teammates and to go back to where it all began.

March 2, 2023: The Northeast Indiana chapter of Fellowship of Christian Athletes celebrated their 25th anniversary and posthumously honored Marc with the distinguished Coach of the Year Award for the impact he made on and off the court. They also announced that they were renaming the award FCA's Marc Davidson Coach of the Year Award.

March 25, 2023: Blackhawk won their third state championship with a group of boys that Marc had coached along with his entire coaching staff. They were led by head Coach Matt Roth, who had been one of Marc's assistant coaches from 2013 to 2016. Marc passed the baton to Matt five days before he passed away. It honestly felt like Marc was ready to go Home once he knew Matt would replace him. Words will never be able to express how this entire season and championship win was like a healing balm for our family. It really felt like the closure for this special team that we all had hoped and prayed for. These players and coaches and their families will forever hold a special place in our family's heart.

April 21, 2023: Marcus gave his best-man speech at Frankie and Anna's rehearsal dinner, sharing marriage advice that Marc had given our kids over the years. Anna's dad asked Wes, Will and Jimmy if they had any other marriage advice they thought that Marc would share if he were here. What a blessing to hear them share the ways they were impacted and shaped as they witnessed Marc being such an amazing husband and dad.

May 9, 2023: On the one-year anniversary of Marc's passing, Blackhawk Christian primary school dedicated a tree on their playground in memory of Marc. Next to the red maple tree are Marc's three Atlas stones that he used in Blackhawk's weight room to train for Strongman.

May 13, 2023: Marcus, Frankie, Anna and I returned to France with the Grace College basketball team. We left the team one night to go watch Prissé, one of Marc's old teams, play. Marc's coach, several teammates and the president of the club came for the special night. They honored Marc and our family before the game and hung Marc's #15 jersey in their gym.

May 16, 2023: Perhaps the moment that hit me the hardest was when we stopped by the old gym in France that Marc had played in when he played for Charleville back in 2003 through 2006. I had heard that the team didn't play in that gym anymore, so I didn't expect that we would be able to get in. We were so excited to see that there was a basketball team practicing there that night. The last time we had been in that gym was when Frankie was just 6 and Marcus was 4. I went down to the court to introduce myself to the young man, who appeared to be the coach. I wanted to explain why we were there. I told him that my husband used to play for Charleville twenty years ago. He told me that he knew Marc and me. It was actually Wes and Will's old teammate, Théo Henrot, and he was 10 years old when we saw him last. He then went over to his gym bag and pulled out a #15 jersey with "Davidson" across the back! He explained how he wears Marc's jersey when he plays. Marc never wore a jersey with his name on the back, and there was definitely no team merchandise to buy back in the day for anybody else to have a Davidson jersey, either. We were just blown away to realize Marc had made such an impact on a 10-year-old French boy's life that 17 years later, he still thought of Marc and was inspired to play and be like him!

Isn't it crazy that in these 50 chapters, we aren't even really talking about what Marc achieved on the court as a player and a coach but, rather, the impact he made? We aren't measuring his success in life by the number of wins or trophies or accolades he received but by the way God used him in people's lives along the way. Look at what God has done through a man who lived a life wholeheartedly devoted to God and wanting to be used by Him, whether he was playing basketball or teaching kindergartners in PE class or stressing the beauty of marriage to junior high boys in health class or coaching his teams or reaching out to those quiet kids who didn't know where they belonged. Marc wanted God to use him, and he trusted God completely until his last breath on this side of heaven.

I have read these chapters, and there is still so much more to say! There are so many stories yet to share of the ways people have loved us and gone to such great lengths to show Marc and our family how much they care. We have been so touched. We are so grateful for those who made such an effort to see Marc in his last few months: family and old friends, old teammates and former players, and parents of former students and players. Others who couldn't make the trip to Fort Wayne reached out by email or Facebook. Every day, we had cards and letters in our mailbox at home. So many people took the time to write thoughtful, encouraging notes and many times included money, too. We were so encouraged and blessed to know so many people were faithfully praying for us.

The outpouring of love and care for our family has been such a blessing. We were humbled by the generosity of so many, from people we knew to strangers. Coaches and teams Blackhawk played against extended such thoughtfulness and generosity, too. Marc's players and families, Blackhawk staff and Blackhawk families all blessed us with meals and gift cards. Twice our front porch was loaded with food and necessities from Costco. Anonymous envelopes with cash appeared in my school mailbox. The week Marc passed away, Blackhawk invited families to contribute money to a fund for our family. There was even a small group of Blackhawk families who came together to pay off the mortgage on our home. We have felt loved and so incredibly blessed by the way God moved in people's hearts to show us their love and support. Marc's heart was at peace, knowing the Lord had brought us to a place where our children and I were surrounded by a community that loved us and who would be there for us.

These chapters don't even begin to testify to all that God did in, through and for Marc in 2022. His strength and health were failing, yet we saw God give him the strength to do what he did not have in him to do in his own strength. In Marc's weakness, the power of Christ was so beautifully displayed over and over.

The strength God gave him wasn't to coach another game (although he did that!) but to give Marc another opportunity to point people to Jesus—be it in the hospital with a nurse, in the huddle after a game or on an episode of "The Journey" on Big Ten Network. When the season was over, Marc asked us to pray that the Lord would keep bringing people into his life with whom he could share Jesus. He wasn't wallowing in his pain or stuck in the disappointment of the season not ending how he'd hoped and prayed it would. He still had his eyes fixed on his ultimate goal: to tell others about Jesus.

Over this past year, I've read Marc's texts, emails and speeches, and one thing is so clear: He wanted to use every opportunity and every platform he was given to talk about the Lord. When Trinity retired his jersey on a special evening with former teammates just a month before he passed, he said, "When I started down this cancer journey a year and a half ago, the Lord spoke to my heart that He was going to provide a platform through cancer that I otherwise would never have. And my responsibility, my calling, is to proclaim the Gospel of Jesus every chance I get—to make HIS name great. As long as there is breath in these lungs, that is exactly what I intend to do, by the power of God."

Marc was kingdom-focused. When he was in high school, his favorite Bible verse was Matthew 6:33: "But seek first the kingdom of God, and all these things shall be added unto you." It was deep within Marc's heart at a young age to seek God and honor Him with his life. Soon after his cancer was discovered, Marc was asked what his favorite verse was. Without hesitation, he said, Colossians 3:23: "Whatever you do, work heartily as unto the Lord and not to men." Marc lived for the audience of One.

Marc's kingdom focus guided how he coached, taught, lived and loved. He saw a greater purpose in his life than just winning games and making money to provide for our family. His prayer was that God would use him to impact lives for eternity, for the kingdom. I am so blessed to have shared my life with this man who extraordinarily sought after God. He led us in our marriage to trust God beyond common sense, and look at all the lives God crossed our paths with because of his faith to walk through the doors opened by God!

One thing I had to do last summer was clean out Marc's office at Blackhawk. I didn't want to just quickly put everything in boxes but instead take my time, savoring the last hours in that office that was like a second home to Marc for nine years. Marc wasn't an overly sentimental saver like I am, so the things in his office were meaningful to him.

If you ever peeked into Marc's office, you saw quite the hodgepodge of memorabilia, but he could care less what it all looked like. He just had so many special memories that he wanted to set out and be reminded of: pictures from his days playing for his dad at ACS; another of them kneeling to pray in the locker room; pictures of our family and the teams he played for and coached; some of his favorite quotes, printed in huge font and taped on his desk as daily reminders of how he wanted to live his life; a shelf of books that impacted him greatly as a man, husband, father and coach; awards and accomplishments; state championship and Strongman trophies; handwritten cards from our kids and me over the years, and stacks of handmade cards and pictures from his primary students; letters from friends and from strangers; and even a cover letter Marc sent to a Christian school in North Carolina in 2003.

It ended up being such a sweet, therapeutic time for me.

I love that the French word souvenir means "to remember." I love to look back on these souvenirs to remember God's precious, sovereign hand on our lives and all of the places He led us to and through to bring us where we're at now ... souvenirs of a beautiful life surrendered to God and in trust of His perfect will. We have no doubt in our minds that the Lord has ordered our steps for a reason and an eternal purpose: to intersect our lives with the people we have met along the way. And so these souvenirs become like the stones of remembrance in the Bible that God's people were commanded to set up to remind them of God's provision, protection and the mighty works that only He could have done.

I also randomly found a piece of a cracked clay pot with the date "August 12, 2011" and the words "wherever, whenever" in Marc's handwriting. Only the Lord knew that one year later, we would be in Ethiopia meeting Isaiah and Jaela for the first time on August 12, 2012. Only the Lord knew how He would use Marc's surrendered life, to use Marc "wherever" and "whenever" in ways we never could have imagined.

I can't help but think of 2 Corinthians 4:7: "But we have this treasure in jars of clay to show that this all-surpassing power is from God and not from us." Marc's cancer-ridden, weakened body, a crumbling jar of clay, so beautifully displayed the treasure he had inside of him that was Jesus. The power of God shone through him while he continued to coach and share Jesus in the midst of physically wasting away. We knew that it wasn't the will and determination of a Strongman that got him through those last months but the power of God that gave him strength at his weakest, that did "exceedingly, abundantly beyond anything we asked or imagined according to His power that is at work within us," Ephesians 3:20.

And the beautiful thing is that I have seen that same power of God in my life and our kids' lives. It wasn't anything special or unique about Marc, and he said that himself. It was the power of Christ in Marc that we saw. And the power that rose Jesus from the grave is the same power that lives inside of every believer who has put their faith and trust in Jesus for salvation. That is the Gospel, the good news, the BEST news that Marc couldn't keep to himself and shared at every opportunity he was given.

It surely was the power of God giving us strength, covering us with peace and even filling us with joy when I think about those last days as we were sitting around Marc in his hospice bed at our home. Several times, we said the 23rd Psalm together, clinging to verse 4, "Even though I walk through the valley of the shadow of death, I will fear no evil, for Thou art with me." Oh how comforting to know that Jesus, our Good Shepherd, is with us, and we are never alone.

Marc did not fear death. He couldn't wait to see his Savior face to face. He knew heaven is going to be more amazing than anything we could ever imagine. Yet he loved us and wanted to stay with us as long as he could. We could see the fight and determination and perseverance that he had as an athlete, fighting hard to keep living. It was as if he was pushing himself to get through another rep in a Strongman competition. He asked us to help him get out of bed when Matt came over, but Matt put his hand on Marc's shoulder and told him, "It's time to go." Holding my hand, and surrounded by our family, he let go of this life and took his last breath, and he was welcomed Home.

That moment that we had been praying for, for the Lord to bring ultimate healing to his body, came. And we wept. Our hearts broke that our time on earth with Marc was over yet rejoiced to know that he was no longer suffering. He had been looking forward to the day when God would touch his body with healing that would last for all eternity, never to die or get sick again. We have all been clinging to the promise of 2 Corinthians 4:16-18: "Therefore we do not lose heart. Though outwardly we are wasting away, yet inwardly we are being renewed day by day. For our light and momentary troubles are achieving for us an eternal glory that far outweighs them all. So we fix our eyes not on what is seen, but on what is unseen, since what is seen is temporary, but what is unseen is eternal." More than anything, we rejoiced knowing that Marc was in the presence of his Savior. His faith was made sight.

I remember sitting on the couch in our house two days after he passed away. Everyone was gone. I was finally alone, sitting in the room where Marc passed from this life to Glory. I remember being hit with the realization that I could say, "It is well with my soul." And that amazed me, to know how much I love Marc and how very heartbroken I was that we were not going to grow old together, yet at the same time to experience God's peace that truly surpasses all understanding and to have the eternal perspective to know in the deepest part of me, "We are going to be okay. God's got us. He's in control. Look at what He's already done. He's not finished yet. Keep trusting Him. He is working all things together for good. God isn't finished using Marc and our family to impact lives for eternity."

And so I am filled with such hope! To get a tiny glimpse into what God has been doing has fueled my faith to trust Him with all the unknown of the future. To experience this peace of God and His strength in our weakness makes me trust Him with whatever He has in store for our future. To know I am never alone, that God is by my side, fills me with confidence that He has a plan and purpose for my life until He calls me Home too. To see our children walking with the Lord and inspired to let the Lord use them like He used their dad ... Oh, how I am abounding in HOPE for all that the Lord is yet to do in and through this family. TO GOD BE THE GLORY, GREAT THINGS HE HAS DONE AND IS YET TO DO!

"May the God of hope fill you with all joy and peace in believing so that by the power of the Holy Spirit you may abound in hope."
Romans 15:13

Lisa Davidson • September 2023

Jack Davidson • September 2023

2019 State Championship team

2021 State Championship team

Marc Davidson Court dedication at Blackhawk Christian · November 2022

BRAVE AT HEART

ACS Hall of Fame Induction • January 2023

Jimmy and Lisa with Coach Roth and family after sectional championship win • March 2023

Frankie and Anna's wedding • April 2023

Frankie and Marcus in Prissé, France • May 2023

Frankie playing in France for Marc's former Charleville team • September 2023

WHY MARC HAD SUCH PEACE, AND YOU CAN, TOO

"For all have sinned, and come short of the glory of God." **Romans 3:23**

"For the wages of sin is death, but the gift of God is eternal life through Jesus Christ our Lord." **Romans 6:23**

"But God demonstrates His own love toward us, in that while we were still sinners, Christ died for us." **Romans 5:8**

"That if you confess with your mouth Jesus as Lord, and believe in your heart that God raised Him from the dead, you will be saved." **Romans 10:9**

"Everyone who calls on the name of the Lord will be saved." **Romans 10:13**

"Therefore, since we have been justified through faith, we have peace with God through our Lord Jesus Christ." **Romans 5:1**

ABOUT THE AUTHOR

Blake Sebring has worked in journalism since he was 15 years old—more than 40 years—mostly with The News-Sentinel in Fort Wayne, Indiana (1980-2018), and as a freelancer for The Journal Gazette. "Brave at Heart" is his 17th book, including five novels, all available on Amazon.

He covered the Fort Wayne Komets hockey team for more than 1,500 games over 28 years through 2018 and was inducted into the Indiana Sportswriters and Sportscasters Hall of Fame in 2015.

He is currently the News Center director at Purdue University Fort Wayne, where he is inspired daily by the passion of the students, faculty and staff.

ALSO BY BLAKE SEBRING • *All books available on Amazon.com*

EXCERPT FROM EYES TOWARD HEAVEN

Since she was diagnosed at age 4 with a degenerative neurological disorder, Tonia Graber has been confined to a wheelchair because of limited use of her limbs and has undergone more than 100 surgeries and medical procedures. Though she has full cognitive abilities, constant spasms and tremors mean she can emote only one or sometimes two words at a time.

But for more than three years, Tonia has experienced visions of heaven, regularly visiting with Jesus, talking with angels and receiving keys and gems. Besides telling her she will be healed and walk again, the consistent messages are "Jesus is coming back soon" and "Tell everyone everywhere." Remarkably, Tonia can talk with some normalcy during her visions, of which her parents have docu-mented more than 1,600.

During these interludes with Jesus, Tonia walks, runs and leaps in fields of long grass; rows across a lake to eat fish; and is told to prepare herself to become a worldwide missionary. "I ready! I go!" she always responds. As the episodes have progressed, Tonia has received visions in heaven as well as several places on earth, and she often sees angels throughout her daily life.

"And a woman was there who had been crippled by a spirit for eighteen years. She was bent over and could not straighten up at all. When Jesus saw her, he called her forward and said to her, 'Woman, you are set free from your infirmity.' Then he put his hands on her, and immediately she straightened up and praised God." **Luke 13:11-14**

CHAPTER 1

At 6:45 a.m. on Jan. 23, 2019, as Paul Graber rolls out of bed to walk into the kitchen and start the coffee machine, his wife Nancy snuggles in for a few more minutes. It's a usual Wednesday morning in their home just outside of Fort Wayne, Indiana, during their 55th year of marriage. Paul is a semi-retired residential designer and builder, and Nancy is a former X-ray technician with a degree in radiology who became a housewife to raise their four children. These days, they primarily take care of their daughter, Tonia, who was born with a neurodegenerative disease that restricts all parts of her body and, since age 4, has confined her to a wheelchair.

In her 52 years, Tonia has always dealt with tremendous physical challenges. Because of tremors and spasms, even speaking haltingly—one and sometimes two words at a time—takes extreme effort. Both hip joints have been removed because the spasms would pull them out of their sockets, often leaving her in a full-body cast trying to reestablish cohesion. Sometimes, hospital trips have been necessary because of her jaw locking up and hindering her breathing. She suffers from severe kidney stones and uses a feeding tube because of swallowing and coughing challenges. Her parents estimate she's undergone more than 100 surgeries and substantial medical procedures.

Though she has normal cognitive abilities, her issues come from limited body control, and sometimes it takes up to 20 minutes to say a short series of words. (Some of her spoken sentences portrayed during this book are combined to make them easier for readers to comprehend.)

To this day, doctors do not have a name for her condition.

Life has not been easy for Tonia—or her parents, who were informed when their daughter was very young that she would not live past her teenage years. They were advised it would be better for their other three children if they placed Tonia in a facility or institution.

They never have, and their commitment to their daughter makes what they are experiencing now all the more intriguing.

As Paul heads to the kitchen that morning, he hears Tonia speaking in her room, saying, "Jesus, Jesus, Jesus!" Over the monitor, Nancy hears the same thing.

"My first thought was, 'Oh my word! Is she leaving this earth?'" Nancy said.

When they rush into her room, a sobbing Tonia is saying "presence" and "touched."

After Nancy asks if she saw something, Tonia says, "Bright yellow light." Where? "In my room." Where in your room? "Behind Jesus."

Nancy remembers her knees feeling weak because the presence of the Lord was suddenly so strong.

"I don't know about you," Nancy says, "but I feel like we're standing–"

"On holy ground," Paul finishes, with awe in his voice.

The Lord's presence feels as real in the moment as anything they have ever experienced. They later compare it to being as real as talking face-to-face to a crowd of listeners.

Then Tonia says, "White robe."

The Grabers are stunned in the moment at how Tonia conveys the words without tremors or spasms. They are easily understandable, completely unlike normal, when they often have to guess what she says until she nods.

"Tonia maybe speaks three or four words at a time, but to say something twice in a row, it just isn't there," Nancy says. But this time? "Every word was clear."

Previously, Tonia had told her parents she doesn't dream, so this was something remarkably different. Paul runs to grab a notebook and pencil so they can document her thoughts.

Nancy asks, "How do you know it's Jesus?"

"He LOVE. He kind. He fun. He know me," Tonia responds.

In the following months, Tonia's description of Jesus will get more specific.

When Nancy shows Tonia a painting of Jesus on the artist website akiane.com, completed when the artist was only 8 years old, Tonia squeals and kicks her legs up. "That it. That Jesus!" she says.

After the Grabers watch "The Chosen" during COVID-19, Nancy asks Tonia, "Does that Jesus look like your Jesus?" Tonia says, "My Jesus darker. Skin darker, hair darker. Eyes blue."

And some months later, during the writing of this book, Paul says, "Tonia's description of Jesus is not some worldly definition. Not all the questions can be answered, and our desire is the questions will provoke people to seek Him."

When Paul returns with a notebook, the questioning continues.

Did Jesus speak to you? "Yes, say my name Tonia ... Say coming back ... Jesus said tell everyone everywhere."

To Nancy, it feels like Jesus is standing next to her. Always devout Christians, the Grabers are all crying with emotion.

Is Jesus coming back to take us or for your healing? "Both." Can you give one word that you are experiencing right now? "Hope, love, power."

"Jesus say my name Tonia." Does Jesus have a nice voice? "Oh, yeah ... Love, kind."

Later, Tonia says, "Jesus is powerful."

After the experience passes and Tonia is sitting up in a recliner, she appears weak. She needs a few days to regain strength, during which time she sings, sleeps and cries. She keeps repeating, "Jesus coming back ... Tell everyone everywhere."

Among the first things the Grabers do is call pastor Bill Campbell of Life Bridge Church for guidance. They want to be under spiritual authority and not rely strictly on their own interpretations. They want to respect the moment and understand with humility. After hearing about the situation, Pastor Campbell tells them this was truly a visitation and to expect more.

It takes about two weeks until the second visitation happens, on February 8 at 2:48 a.m. Over the monitor, the Grabers hear Tonia crying, something which usually only happens when she's experiencing pain.

What's going on? "Lamb."

"We just stood there amazed and didn't know what to think," Nancy says.

"Lamb, touched, presence." What color is the lamb? "White." Did the lamb say anything? "Say coming back ... Tell everyone everywhere ... He also said going to walk."

Does the light look like what was behind Jesus last time? "Yes ... Hallelujah ... I hear 'Holy, holy, holy.'" Is the lamb standing? "No, sitting." What is it sitting on? "Big white chair."

Later that afternoon, Tonia is again resting in the living room recliner when she says, "Jesus is the lamb of God." She says it without hesitation, without any spasms or tremors, as clearly as anyone without physical challenges.

"When she says presence, we just feel the presence of the Lord coming over us," Paul says. "Touched means her heart is touched."

The next episode comes sooner, on March 14, and this time Tonia says, "Jesus beside me ... White robe, coming back ... Tell everyone everywhere."

Are you processing in your head what you experienced earlier, or did this just happen? "It happened, tell everyone before it too late."

"When she said, 'before it too late,' I knew it had just happened," Nancy says.

Where is Jesus? "By my bed."

"Tonia's nurse, Lori Baumgartner, came into the room one afternoon after all of this had happened, and she said, 'Just think, Nancy, Jesus was right here by Tonia's bedside.'" Nancy says. "I said, 'Yes, dust and all, Lori.'" Lori responded, "Don't you remember, Nancy? Jesus was born in a barn. He doesn't mind dust."

During the fourth visit, just after 1 a.m. on March 20, Tonia is heard saying, "Jesus, Jesus, Jesus," "He say my name, the Lamb say my name," and "Jesus is hope, love, power."

Did Jesus say anything else, Tonia? "My name ... Going to walk." Now? "Not yet."

Later, sitting in her chair, Tonia says, "I go there. I go everywhere. Tell people." Tell people what? "Good news. About Jesus."

The sequence lasts about 20 minutes.

The fifth visit, in some ways, is the most powerful. After hearing Tonia say "Mom!" over the monitor, the Grabers arrive to find her cheeks wet with tears.

"Lion," she says. "Touched. Presence ... He say my name." What did he look like? "Big, brown." Was the lion standing or sitting? "Standing on big white chair." Did the lion speak? "Say coming back ... Tell everyone everywhere every word."

"He love. And power. Said get up and walk."

Tonia starts singing, praising God and saying, "Hallelujah!" And she continues to say, "Hope, power, love."

ALSO BY BLAKE SEBRING • *All books available on Amazon.com*

Lethal Ghost Book 1: Luke Rennison Chronicles

Law officials catch serial killers by looking for patterns, but what if there's a monster who is unique? There's a serial killer at work across the country who has been effective for so long that no one even suspects he exists. He works with such precision and practiced perfection, how do police officers even hope to catch such a killer? They wait for a mistake.

It's going to cost county sheriff deputy Luke Rennison something precious and test him, his family and his faith unlike anything he's ever dreamed. This killer is about to make his first and biggest mistake possible, but will his anonymity and unique methods provide another escape?

Lethal Justice Book 2: Luke Rennison Chronicles

After the shocking conclusion to Lethal Ghost, everything in county sheriff Officer Luke Rennison's life is disrupted, including his family, his friendships and his career. Lines are drawn in his midsize city, and Rennison is isolated, second-guessing his actions and facing down his own doubts as the trial for his life begins.

Lethal Family Book 3: Luke Rennison Chronicles

Heroes in movies never worry about doubt, hesitation or consequences. They just react and plow ahead with conviction, and somehow everything works out perfectly.

That's just not how things work in the real world. There's always somebody second-guessing, judging and making you think before you act. There are always results and ripples of action that you can't account for.

Somehow, by taking out a serial killer, I have created someone who is now hunting me and my family, someone who has been inspired by a monster into becoming something almost as bad. We don't know who, when or where, but we know they're coming for us. So the real question is will we be prepared when they do?

Made in the USA
Monee, IL
16 November 2023